Hopeful Visions, Practical Actions

Hopeful Visions, Practical Actions

Cultural Humility in Library Work

Edited by
Sarah R. Kostelecky, Lori Townsend, and
David A. Hurley

Published by Facet Publishing
Room 150, British Library, 96 Euston Road, London NW1 2DB
www.facetpublishing.co.uk

Facet Publishing is wholly owned by CILIP: the Library and Information Association.

First published in the USA by the American Library Association, 2023.
This UK edition 2023.

British Library Cataloguing in Publication Data
A catalogue record for this book is available from the British Library.

ISBN 978-1-78330-633-6 (paperback)

CONTENTS

FOREWORD

IN THE LAST NINETEEN MONTHS, WE HAVE SEEN A PROLIFERATION OF articles, op-eds, special editions of journals, podcasts, webinars, and numerous other types of publications and programs on the topics of racism, systemic racism, and antiracism. To *some* communities (emphasis intentional), the discourse on diversity, equity, and inclusion (DEI) has never been so visible or so poignant, especially after the murder of George Floyd in May 2020. To many communities—especially communities of color, and in particular those who identify as Black—the inequities that became more visible from that tragic event are simply a reality of everyday existence. The worldwide racial awakening that followed, perhaps compounded by the global pandemic, launched statements in support of Black lives (and others) from corporations, higher education, not-for-profits, and many other sectors. In the library and archives profession, reading lists on the topic were developed and disseminated at perhaps record pace. Discussion groups were formed. DEI and antiracist trainers and facilitators have been unable to keep up with demand. Philanthropic organizations with immense resources, such as the Ford, MacArthur, Kellogg, and Andrew Mellon foundations, have committed unprecedented amounts of money to racial equity efforts. And a highly contentious presidential election brought the concepts of systemic racism and critical race theory into the living rooms and vocabulary of most US citizens even though there were and there remain, in the opinion of this author, broad misconceptions about what either of those terms mean.

Nevertheless, the quest for understanding and "answers" seems to be the focus of much activity. Individuals and organizations appear to be committed to uncovering the solutions for this seemingly intractable problem that, according to many social scientists, historians, and thought leaders, has existed for centuries. What training can one attend that will provide a convincing argument of the severity of the problem? In what institute can one enroll that will provide the tools for action that might lead to systemic change? What assessment methodologies can be deployed that will provide us with the data we need to advance equity in organizations and in society? Society needs answers and solutions. And these need to be accessible, expedient, tenable, and sustainable.

But is that realistic? Is it just that the magic formula or the most convincing analysis has eluded us to date? To those paying attention, even prior to 2020, the tenor of conversations around diversity, equity, and inclusion were changing dramatically. To that litany of terms, organizations and institutions added *belonging* and *engagement* in addition to *antiracism*. The framing of "multiculturalism" seemed, to many, out of fashion and insufficient at addressing the root causes of inequities based on racial/ethnic identity or other marginalized identities. Did this trajectory, prior to 2020, hold any promise? Or was the tendency to provide framing of our common humanity and the universalism of the human experience too safe an approach? To what extent do we derail efforts by introducing the most challenging of phrases such as *white privilege* or *white supremacy*? What exactly is the approach, what are the exact terms, and which is the exact methodology that will lead to enduring change?

I posit that it is the quest for perfection—for quick and easy solutions—that stalls us in our efforts. Perhaps there is room, if not necessity, for every approach, depending on context and urgency. It is clear that decades of efforts have fallen short. It is evident from data about differential outcomes for communities of color when they (we) engage with any social system that the US is not in a postracial reality. It is equally clear that socioeconomic status alone does not account for those differential outcomes in healthcare, education, access to housing, the accumulation of generational wealth, the criminal justice system, or demographic representation in the library profession, among other measures. It is also clear that no single approach to these issues will resonate with—much less convert—those who doubt if not outright deny the realities of systemic inequities and injustice.

The concept of cultural humility is not new to libraries and information science. Many attribute the development of the framing to the medical profession and concerns about the shortcomings of "multiculturalism" as it relates to patient/healthcare providers and physicians (Tervalon and Murray-García 1998). The concept has been adapted by many other professional sectors, including librarianship, which has seen numerous presentations and articles surface in the literature within the last five years. Among those, perhaps the most impactful has been the *Reference Services Review* article by the editors of this compilation, "Cultural Humility in Libraries" (Hurley, Kostelecky, and Townsend 2019). In their review of the literature and of the concept, they emphasize several key dimensions or hallmarks of cultural humility that are especially cogent in contemporary times. The first is that cultural humility is an ongoing process that involves self-reflection, not a finite set of skills that can be mastered by any individual (Hurley, Kostelecky, and Townsend 2019, 13). The second is that cultural humility, in any interaction, demands deference to the characteristics that are most salient to the object (person) of the transaction—that is, the person who embodies the difference and whose experience and life we are trying to improve (Hurley, Kostelecky, and Townsend 2019). In this way, there are no assumptions that even people from similar cultural backgrounds hold the same values and prefer to be treated or represented in a similar way. Moreover, there are no presumptions that the values and behavioral characteristics (or preferences) of people from majority cultures and identities (e.g., white, straight, cisgender, able-bodied) align with those from different cultural identities or expressions. Finally, and most important, the concept of cultural humility demands that we address the power differentials, either real or perceived, that exist between the parties involved in any transaction. In this way, whether at micro-, macro-, or mezzo-levels, we can begin to redress the long trajectory of disadvantage experienced by communities of color and people from other marginalized and underrepresented identities. Perhaps this framing can lead to systemic change in our profession.

The chapters within this collection are diverse, representing authors from varied personal backgrounds as well as professional contexts—from library administrators in higher-education environments, to library and information science educators, to public and community college librarians. Readers will no doubt be challenged to think about the implications of cultural humility on our professional practice, certainly, but also on the way we live our lives, day to day. We are challenged, through the lens of cultural humility, to embrace paradox—that is, to embrace "both/and" thinking, rejecting the traditional, Western either/or approaches (Gulati-Partee and Potapchuk 2014). In addition, we are encouraged to become comfortable with nonclosure, which is a "direct challenge to the cultural norm of perfectionism that dominates" the work of libraries, archives, and other cultural-heritage and -memory institutions (Gulati-Partee and Potapchuk 2014, 33). Engaging these counter-cultural norms will allow us to reify the core principles of cultural humility, which, in turn, may lead to more meaningful experiences and more equitable outcomes for all those for whom access has been denied for generations.

Mark A. Puente
Associate Dean for Organizational Development, Inclusion, and Diversity
Associate Professor, Purdue University Libraries and School of Information Studies

REFERENCES

Hurley, D. A., S. R. Kostelecky, and L. Townsend. 2019. "Cultural Humility in Libraries." *Reference Services Review* 47, no. 4: 544–55. https://doi.org/10.1108/RSR-06-2019-0042.

Gulati-Partee, G., and M. Potapchuk. 2014. "Paying Attention to White Culture and Privilege: A Missing Link to Advancing Racial Equity." *Foundation Review* 6, no. 1. https://doi.org/10.9707/1944-5660.1189.

Tervalon, M., and J. Murray-García. 1998. "Cultural Humility Versus Cultural Competence: A Critical Distinction in Defining Physician Training Outcomes in Multicultural Education." *Journal of Health Care for the Poor and Underserved* 9, no. 2: 117–25. https://doi.org/10.1353/hpu.2010.0233.

ACKNOWLEDGMENTS

WE THANK ALL THE AUTHORS, WHO GENEROUSLY CONTRIBUTED THEIR stories and experiences to this volume. We appreciate the time and effort you spent to write down your thoughts for readers and for us; you inspired us, made us reflect, and gave us hope that things can change.

Thank you to our editor, Rachel Chance, and the team at ALA Editions for all their work and support to make this volume a reality.

Thank you to the colleagues who have been speaking and writing about cultural humility and those who have attended our presentations about cultural humility. Your questions and conversations helped guide and further our thinking about the concept.

We are grateful to the people who provided support to us during this project, in person and in spirit:

Anthony Coca
Emily Lena Jones
Diana and Steven Kostelecky
Pamela and Ray Kostelecky
Heidi and Chuck Markham
James Markham
Virgil and Myrn Townsend
Rowena and Alfonso Zunie

INTRODUCTION

AS WE ARE WRITING THIS INTRODUCTION, IT HAS BEEN ALMOST EXACTLY A year since we put out a call for the chapters in this volume. We are also two years into a pandemic that has changed every facet of our lives. The year in which these chapters were written was a year filled with despair, hope, despair again, and then a more cautious hope intertwined with frustration, anxiety, and, yes, bouts of despair even still. Perhaps this is an apt metaphor for what we hoped to achieve in bringing together these authors in a book on cultural humility: a cautious hope in the face of so much trouble, but one too grounded in experience to be a naive hope.

You may already be aware of the concept of cultural humility emerging as another approach to equity, diversity, and inclusion efforts within librarianship. Though there are a number of definitions of *cultural humility*, we have defined it for library contexts as "the ability to maintain an interpersonal stance that is other oriented in relation to aspects of cultural identity that are most important to the other person, the ability to recognize the context in which interactions occur, and a commitment to redress power imbalances and other structural issues to benefit all parties" (Hurley, Kostelecky, and Townsend 2019).

Cultural humility's core tenets include an awareness of and commitment to challenging inequitable structures of power. A culturally humble approach to work recognizes the need for partnership and gives individuals concrete tools for undertaking and continuing such work with patience and hope. In this way, cultural humility offers an approach for navigating our work, whether the interpersonal interactions with patrons and/or between staff members, or the behind-the-scenes work of collection development, cataloging, or administration.

Much of practicing cultural humility involves self-reflection and so happens within the mind. This can make it difficult to recognize specific actions as resulting from cultural humility. Instead, we (Hurley, Kostelecky, and Townsend 2022) have identified some key mental practices of cultural humility, including:

- Don't be defensive.
- Recognize other perspectives.
- Practice critical self-reflection.

The contributions in this volume tell stories that illustrate these elements. Our hope is to share the many ways people engage with this approach in libraries with colleagues and patrons, leading to meaningful change and growth—making things a little bit (or a lot) better.

Within the following chapters are visions of cultural humility and the changes, big and small, that it facilitates. The authors represent a diverse set of life, work, and library experiences, which reinforces the relevance and applicability of a cultural humility practice across individuals and environments. Though we have grouped the contributions into distinct sections, they do not exactly fit their labels—a statement that applies to many of the authors as well. Many of the stories shared here start from a place of not fitting in. This is enough of a theme that we think this experience may be an asset in practicing cultural humility. We think it is a strength of this volume too, that the chapters bring different approaches, styles, and purposes, creating a whole that is richer than it is tidy.

Many of the authors in this volume have bravely and generously shared their personal stories and experiences, illustrating the many ways people practice cultural humility. Writing in such an open and honest way can be difficult, and we are grateful for the trust they have placed in us, as editors, and you, as readers, to share and receive their stories.

Origins

The first section of this book focuses on origins, roots, and beginnings. We don't mean the origin of cultural humility itself—that is documented elsewhere (e.g., Foronda et al. 2016; Hurley, Kostelecky, and Townsend 2019; Tangney 2000; Tervalon and Murray-García 1998). Rather, in this section, we hear from authors about *their* origins with cultural humility, starting with its deep roots in Indigenous cultures, then exploring individual journeys to understand and implement the concept, and finally, considering cultural humility at the beginning of a journey into librarianship.

In some ways, this is also the origin of this book project itself. Like many of our colleagues, we were introduced to cultural humility from outside the field of librarianship. Seeing its potential, we immediately looked for examples of cultural humility being used in libraries. While we were sure they existed, we couldn't find any back in 2014. And so we began work on our vision of what we thought cultural humility practice might look like for libraries.

Over the next several years, as we began to write about and present on cultural humility, we started hearing it mentioned in other presentations, saw it referenced on our social media timelines and in books, and, eventually, encountered other visions of cultural humility in webinars, presentations, and writings from people like Twanna Hodge, Xan Goodman, Nicola Andrews, Sunny Kim, and Josie Watanabe. We learned later that Omar Poler had been discussing it in courses in the Tribal Libraries, Archives, and Museums Project at the iSchool at University of Wisconsin–Madison. Clearly, many people in many libraries were thinking about, engaging with, and doing cultural humility in a variety of ways. This book stems from a desire to discover and learn from those colleagues throughout the library world.

As we started looking for and talking about cultural humility, we noticed two things. First, many people who were engaged with the concept had very personal stories of how they relate to or value cultural humility. Second, many of the people we talked to who hadn't heard the term *cultural humility* had a response along the lines of "Oh, there's a name for that?" For us, this second group often (though certainly not exclusively) consisted of Indigenous people. Though this is certainly partly explained by our social networks—two of us are Native, and all of us have worked in libraries in Native institutions—we repeatedly noted the interesting work on cultural humility being done in Native communities, such as by the First Nations Health Authority in Canada.

We are therefore delighted to have Loriene Roy and Leisa Moorhouse's chapter, "'Time Is a Ship That Never Casts Anchor': Indigenous Adages in Promoting Cultural Humility," to open the collection. Loriene and Leisa share a variety of Indigenous adages that can help individuals in their own cultural humility practice. They highlight the importance of adages and how these can give an individual a tool for reflection and guidance to go forward in the world. The lessons imparted in Indigenous adages reflect the tenets of cultural humility and can be useful reminders for engaging with others using the approach. Adages can be referred to when needed in difficult times throughout life, supporting the lifelong learning that is part of a cultural humility practice. This chapter will help readers think about cultural humility in new ways and open a space to think about the values conveyed in familiar adages from their own cultures.

We are equally delighted that Xan Goodman and Twanna Hodge, two pioneers of cultural humility in libraries, collaborated on "Redressing Power Imbalances in Librarianship Using Cultural Humility: A Perspective from Two Black Librarians." Using critical race theory and autoethnography, they share their own counterstories of their individual experiences as Black women working in libraries. Their stories illustrate how race, ethnicity, culture, positionality, kinship ties, and socioeconomic aspects can create and reinforce power imbalances, anti-Blackness, and oppression within the profession. Cultural humility, they argue, can change personal, organizational, and systemic practices that create and perpetuate these problems. They also share practical ways to engage in self-reflection and strategies for addressing power imbalances. This chapter can help readers recognize, articulate, and reflect on the many subtle and unsubtle assumptions, norms, and values that contribute to the problems in the profession.

Liliana Montoya and Sarah Polkinghorne, together as student and instructor, reflect on the benefits of introducing cultural humility to library school students. In "Getting Past 'Approachability': What Cultural Humility Brings to Library and Information Education," they explore the concept of service as taught in library and information science classrooms, typically through the lens of "approachability." They problematize and deconstruct approachability, highlighting that power dynamics are always at play when a person assesses whether or not a librarian seems approachable. Cultural humility, which they point out is "user-centeredness in action," makes these issues salient to students who are considering how to be information providers. This chapter will be useful to both new and experienced librarians who want to incorporate cultural humility into their ethos of librarianship.

Reflective Practice

As we grow from our origins, we seek diverse examples of cultural humility in practice. In the following chapters, individual librarians make change—in their own practice and in the world—through both transformative shifts and bold remakings, as well as smaller but still meaningful remodelings. As we hear their stories, we see how their practice moves all of us toward positive change. Their generous sharing of both professional and personal growth, beginning with self-awareness and continuing with reflective practice, clarifies how we realize cultural humility in everyday library work.

In "Reflections on Culturally Humble Practice in Bibliography, Scholarship, and Readers' Advisory: A Case Study," Michael Mungin contributes a warm and engaging reflection on cultural humility in his work, from teaching information literacy at the University of Washington to creating a queer and trans people of color (QTPOC) film bibliography. He shares his background and his experiences with libraries growing up, and how these have informed his current positionality. Michael discusses the QTPOC Film Canon resource using a cultural humility lens, and the story of its development serves as a reminder of the potential positive impact we as individuals can have through our work in libraries. This chapter will appeal to anyone interested in the practice of cultural humility in public services, and it's a great place to start thinking about what a culturally humble practice looks like and how to think about cultural humility as an individual library worker.

Silvia Lin Hanick and Kelsey Keyes, both academic librarians who were members of the American Library Association's committee Rise: A Feminist Book Project for Ages 0–18, provide practical guidance on incorporating cultural humility into the practice of selecting children's literature in their chapter "Cultural Humility and Evaluating Books for Young Readers." They use vivid examples and relatable personal narratives to reflect on the emotions they experience as professionals, mothers, and readers when selecting children's literature. They show us how cultural humility can be applied not only to our interpersonal interactions but also in the relationships we form with books. In so doing, they expand the boundaries of our (the editors') understanding of cultural humility and have developed an insightful set of principles for applying cultural humility to an important part of librarianship. This chapter provides an example of cultural humility in practice and will be particularly valuable for librarians interested in children's literature.

Meggan Houlihan, Amanda Click, and Dina Meky explore cultural humility in the context of international librarianship in "Learn, Act, Connect: Thriving as an International Librarian and Global Citizen," as American academic librarians who have lived and worked outside the United States. They frame these experiences through the lens of Tangney's dimensions of humility and Goodman's pillars of cultural humility. Using lively and pertinent examples from their own and other international librarians' experiences, they express the appreciative joy of cultural humility as they discuss exploring, learning, making mistakes, and experiencing wonder in new and unfamiliar environments. This chapter will be helpful to anyone thinking of working abroad, but also in reflecting on how we approach the world as "outsiders" and how we might use those approaches in thinking of how we work with our patrons and colleagues.

In "Cultural Humility in Instruction on Health Outreach Projects: Revising a Course on the Grant-Writing Process," Jarrod Irwin describes how he incorporated principles of cultural humility into an online course about grant writing for health outreach and education projects. He highlights the importance of libraries working in partnership with local community members and organizations and how a culturally humble approach must be taken with these partners. He details the changes made to the course in adding cultural humility elements and explains the reasoning for each change. This chapter offers guidance for those readers looking for concrete ways to use cultural humility in their own contexts, even if those contexts don't initially appear directly related to diversity, equity, and inclusion efforts.

Community

The contributions in this section illustrate the impact of community in shaping one's practice of cultural humility, within the library and more broadly. Libraries can cultivate an environment that helps individuals in their cultural humility practice. As we engage with the individuals from the communities around us, we can listen to their needs and experiences to advocate for changes to power structures within libraries. The authors in this section describe the process of examining embedded library practices and policies through the lens of cultural humility and, as a result, implementing changes that center the other person and their needs. They help remind us to reflect on seemingly small aspects of an interaction with someone (saying "have a good day" to a patron) to the larger ones (taking patrons to court for lost books) and how those reflections may help us in our interactions going forward.

In "Embedding Diné Culture in Individual and Institutional Cultural Humility Practices: A View from the Tribal College Library," Rhiannon Sorrell shares her reflections about cultural humility practice as a librarian at Diné College, where she engages with members of her own tribal community. She discusses how humility is embedded within Diné cultural teachings, although there is no specific word for the concept in the Diné language. Rhiannon thoughtfully shares how she realized she had to "unlearn" norms from Western education to help library users at Diné College. Writing about her experience of self-reflection makes the process visible, which can help others in this effort. This chapter provides an example of the value of cultural humility practice in an Indigenous context (where the librarian and patrons are of the same cultural background), and how it can be practiced by and for Indigenous people and communities.

The next two chapters present case studies of making changes in libraries. In "Beyond Late Fees: Eliminating Access Barriers for Everyone," Carrie Valdes, director of the public library in Moab, Utah, shares how a light-bulb moment several years into her tenure as director led her to begin a complete reevaluation of her library's policies, procedures, and services, engaging her staff, the library board, and the local government along the way. Realizing that library policies were creating barriers for the people who most needed its services, she changed how cards are issued, how lost books are handled, even the forms needed to check out equipment, with more changes planned. But beyond the specific changes, Valdes presents a model for how to think about library services and the policies that support, or prevent, the community from using them. Anyone who has ever felt that some things just can't be changed will find inspiration in this chapter.

From the public library in a town of 5,300, we move to a university library serving a population of 38,000. In "Small Changes Make an Impact: How Access and Metadata Services Teams Address Cultural Humility," Melanie Bopp, Tricia Mackenzie, and Kimberley A. Edwards share their experiences working to embody cultural humility as a core value of their departments in the library at George Mason University and the additional challenges that come from operating within a consortium. In Access Services, they were able to be flexible with policies and rethink interactions with patrons as a way to mitigate the hierarchical nature of patron/employee relationships. In Metadata Services, they not only changed the labels for metadata, such as replacing .N for "Negroes" with .B for "Black people" in their Cutter numbers, but also rethought what metadata should be recorded at all for nontraditional collections. The care for both the patrons they directly serve and the creators whose works appear in their collections stand out. This chapter will be especially useful to people working in big systems, where even small changes matter.

In his chapter "Cultural Humility and Servant Leadership," Mark Emmons, associate dean at the University of New Mexico University Libraries, considers the connections between the theory of servant leadership and that of cultural humility through an analysis of the scholarly literature. He also reflects on his own experience growing up as a "third culture kid" and how that has impacted his views on leadership and service. Mark provides a starting place for conversations about cultural humility in leadership, suggesting leaders can benefit their organizations by employing a servant leadership and cultural humility approach to their work, and that these approaches are complementary.

Hopeful Visions

The closing section is formed by contributions that express a vision for cultural humility, whether engaging critically with it and future imaginings of it, or embracing it and making it manifest in the world through generous practice.

In their thoughtful piece "Knowing (un)Knowings: Cultural Humility, the Other(s), and Theories of Change," nicholae cline and Jorge R. López-McKnight share reflections about the potential of humility broadly and engage in critique of the cultural humility concept as an act of love. The promise of humility as a core value is explored, with the authors considering the potential impact if we truly engage in a humble way. Critique is raised through questioning: Can cultural humility truly be a way to make change while it is "haunted" by cultural competence, the model from which it came? Will cultural humility become institutionalized as a concept but do little to change the composition of the library and information science field or its structures? They also share their cautiously hopeful perspective on the use of cultural humility while recognizing the concept may be misappropriated. The vision for a future of cultural humility centers practice, reflection, and engagement with others in order to strengthen the approach while gathering stories and experiences highlighting its usefulness.

We close the book with "Cultural Humility: A Journey to Radical Self-Love" by Naghem Swade and Daniyom "Dani" Bekele. Part of a team tasked with creating a cultural humility workshop at the Denver Public Library, the two authors share a journey of discovery through critical self-reflection—honestly and insightfully exploring how they have unconsciously replicated their own experiences in their interactions with others, and occasionally adopted assumptions about people even though those assumptions would have been incorrectly applied to themselves. Naghem and Dani present their work as a way to help others in their own understanding of cultural humility through sharing their respective paths to engage in the practice themselves.

As we edited this volume, we found the collection as a whole inspired us with the many ways that cultural humility practice manifests across libraries and librarianship, by people bringing a range of experiences and backgrounds. The diversity of this collection reinforces for us the belief in the benefits of a cultural humility approach within the diversity of our libraries, our patrons, and our staff. The contributions in this volume also give hope that each of us may find ways to change and improve our libraries, our services, and our profession through the practice of cultural humility.

REFERENCES

Foronda, C., D.-L. Baptiste, M. M. Reinholdt, and K. Ousman. 2016. "Cultural Humility: A Concept Analysis." *Journal of Transcultural Nursing* 27, no. 3: 210–17.

Hurley, D. A., S. R. Kostelecky, and L. Townsend. 2019. "Cultural Humility in Libraries." *Reference Services Review* 47, no. 4: 544–55. https://doi.org/10.1108/RSR-06-2019-0042.

Hurley, D. A., S. R. Kostelecky, and L. Townsend. 2022. *Cultural Humility*. Chicago: ALA Editions.

Tangney, J. P. 2000. "Humility: Theoretical Perspectives, Empirical Findings and Directions for Future Research." *Journal of Social and Clinical Psychology* 19, no. 1: 70–82.

Tervalon, M., and J. Murray-García. 1998. "Cultural Humility Versus Cultural Competence: A Critical Distinction in Defining Physician Training Outcomes in Multicultural Education." *Journal of Health Care for the Poor and Underserved* 9, no. 2: 117–25. https://doi.org/10.1353/hpu.2010.0233.

PART I

ORIGINS

1

"Time Is a Ship That Never Casts Anchor"

Indigenous Adages in Promoting Cultural Humility

LORIENE ROY AND LEISA MOORHOUSE

INDIGENOUS CULTURES HAVE TEACHING APPROACHES THAT EXTEND across time and generations. One legacy that tribal nations have left to their descendants is their adages. These sayings are more than phrases or promises. According to the Yup'ik people of southwestern Alaska, these proverbs, instructions, warnings, laws, or prohibitions are yuuluaqautekat: "advice that helps one live a proper life" (Fienup-Riordan 2005, 13, 318). In this chapter, we will use the words *proverb*, *adage*, or *saying* to refer to cultural phrases that have gained meaning over time to illustrate prescribed behaviors and predicted outcomes. While we rely on adages to illustrate the points we are making throughout this chapter, we include a special focus on the sayings that are compact lessons on the meaning and value of humility.

Who might you turn to for advice? In cases when no human is available, a voice from the past might be the best teacher. You should "close [one] ear while listening" when reading this chapter, so that the instructions do not simply come out the other side of your head (Fienup-Riordan 2005, 24). Instead, let these phrases, from tribal nations including the Māori, Sámi, and Yup'ik, stay inside your head so that you will absorb their meaning; they will become part of your seeking and understanding. They help us understand, recognize, and gain humility. Indigenous adages remind us that we have the capacity to think things through; Yuum-gguq Umyugaa Tukniuq—"They say that a person's mind is very powerful" (Fienup-Riordan 2005, 65, 46). Others remind us that we also have a role in teaching ("A hand that writes has a wide reach" (Gaski 2010, 45)). Just as we are told, "It's hard to move forward without shoes," we need to prepare to make progress (Gaski 2010, 22). From these sayings emanate a strength gained over time. Meanwhile, we share that strength when we greet each other with the Māori words *kia kaha*, "stay strong," knowing that humility is a form of strength. We invite you to reflect on the following adages as you engage in your own efforts to cultivate cultural humility in your work in libraries, archives, and museums.

What Are Indigenous Adages?

Adages may appear as statements, sound like commands, or appear as questions (Mensah 2013, 97). We grow up hearing and using sayings, not often pausing to consider their source. For example, we might tell someone, "Don't throw the baby out with the bathwater" if we advise them to consider the impact of discarding a friendship. Proverbs are so rich that they have been referred to as "oral performances" (Mensah 2013, 87).

Mutonyi (2016) reminds us that sayings are found in cultural communities around the world. When these proverbs come from Indigenous communities, we might see them as "perceptual frameworks or conceptual grids that highlight fundamental cultural values and mores as well as reinforce and instill acceptable social behavior" (Mensah and Eni 2019, 178).

While adages may be familiar, their use signifies matters of importance. As Mutonyi (2016, 945, 946) explains, "Proverbs provide hard hitting messages in a profound way rather than in a demoralizing manner"; as a result, "proverbs give a greater potency to any message you are trying to convey." Njwe (2014, 118) describes their impact on everyday speech: "The importance of proverbs, especially in spoken language as well as written texts, cannot be overemphasized for the color and flavor they introduce and sustain in language." When Apt (1992, 131) explains that "proverbs fulfill an indispensable function of expressing, enhancing and codifying cultural beliefs and attitudes," we see that sayings provide structure.

Understanding proverbs of specific Indigenous communities helps us grasp their importance. We start by considering such examples used by Māori. It is important to note that, while the term *Māori* is used to refer to the Indigenous peoples of Aotearoa/New Zealand as if they constitute one homogenous group, ngā tangata Māori (Māori people) are a collection of iwi (or tribes) with dialectical and customary differences. It is understood that prior to colonization, ngā tangata Māori referred to themselves by their various tribal affiliations rather than as *Māori*.

In te ao Māori (the Māori world), one of the major forms of oral tradition is whakataukī or whakatauākī (proverbs) (Metge 1967; McRae 2017). Whakataukī refer to proverbs whose author has been forgotten with the passage of time, whereas whakatauākī refer to proverbs where the original orator of the proverb is known (Moorhouse 2020). Whakataukī can be specific to particular tribes or geographical locations or common across tribes. Thus a saying may be shared by multiple tribes with only slight variation of wording (Kawharu 2008).

Whakataukī number in the hundreds (Metge 2010), denoting "guidelines for behaviour, religious and philosophical concepts, historical events, famed ancestors, and the characteristics of individuals, tribes and places" (McRae 2017, 81). Whakataukī are used to reinforce, explain and précis beliefs, practices and privileges or permissions (McRae 2017). They "carry ideals and concepts. . . . They advise about morals and standards of behavior . . . of what is acceptable and unacceptable" (McRae 2017, 89). Thus, they have been said to "epitomize the thinking of a people" (Kohere 1951, 9) and, in so doing, provide powerful "ethical precedents" along with a wealth of information on Māori values (see Patterson 1992, 47).

Indigenous Adages Exist across Time

Te Ao Hurihuri
te ao hurihuri ai ki tōna tauranga
te ao rapu:
ko te huripoki e huri nei
i runga i te taumata o te kaha

Te Ao Hurihuri
Is a world revolving
a world that moves forwards
to the place it came from;
a wheel that turns
on an axle of strength (King 1981, 175)

The relevance of Indigenous adages reaches across time as proverbs are words from the ancestors (Avoseh 2012). We can look to the Māori worldview to help us gain understanding of how time is perceived within Indigenous nations.

For Māori, there is not a clear distinction between the living and the dead, or the past and the present (Marsden and Royal 2003). Metge described a

Māori worldview where Māori "continue to believe in a spiritual reality that transcends limitations of time, space and the human senses, and at the same time pervades and operates in the world of human existence" (1967, 54). Not unlike the saying "The more things change, the more things stay the same," the adage above, "Te Ao Hurihuri," highlights that there is a thread linking all things, irrespective of time. This thread is apparent in tikanga (cultural practices) in both formal and informal settings, and consequently, evident in oral traditions. In examining the two key components of the word *whakataukī*, the phrase *whakatau* (to settle or come to rest) coupled with *kī* (to say or tell) alludes to the fact that proverbs recall previously uttered statements that settle or sink in over time.

Whakataukī traditionally were, and often still are, introduced by way of a statement such as "E ai ki te kōrero' or 'e ai ki ngā tupuna . . ." (according to what is told . . . According to the ancestors) (McRae 2017, 83). The retelling of whakataukī, as with other oral traditions, requires a drawing on the past while relating to the present. Such recounting of traditional whakataukī reflects a key value of both traditional and contemporary Māori society, which is knowing one's place in the whānau (extended family), hapū (subtribe), iwi (tribe), and te ao (world). All living things are believed to have a whakapapa (genealogical line) whether plant, animal, or person, that links each being to creation narratives (Marsden and Royal 2003). By virtue of each person having a whakapapa connection to others—again, whether human, animal, or plant—a bond exists that in turn establishes obligation and reciprocity between the parties, whether kaitaiki (guardian or steward) or teina/tuakana (younger or elder sibling). This relational connection reflects a humility in knowing one's standing, emphasizing belonging while understanding one's place in a wider system.

Indigenous Adages as Instruments of Instruction

"Proverbs are 'wise sayings.' They express a deeper meaning than the observable external meaning" (Njwe 2014, 119). Each of these strings of words tells a story, teaches a lesson, and provides an answer.

Whakataukī were and continue to be considered tools of education (Hemara 2000). In short, these pithy ancestral sayings provide insight into those things the ancestors deemed important (S. Kāretu 1981; Mead and Grove 2003). Like other types of learning, understanding an adage requires practice:

"The Yup'ik view [is] that instructions need to be heard numerous times in different contexts to be fully understood" (Fienup-Riordan 2005, xxxvii). Mensah describes the levels of meaning underlying a proverb: the first way to consider meaning is to be aware that a proverb is both a literal statement and a metaphor. Second, the meaning is enhanced and further developed each time a proverb is stated, as "there is new meaning behind the transfer" (Mensah 2013, 89).

Listening to a saying is just the first step. As the Yup'ik elder John Philip has explained: "The teachings are like something that pushes one to a good life. The one who does not listen will not live a good life. Those who listen and apply the teachings will live good lives" (Fienup-Riordan 2005, 11–12). Meanings attributed to a saying multiply as each listener brings their interpretation. Thus, the listener and speaker have formed a bond or partnership surrounding and remembering the adage. Metge (2010) describes unpacking the concealed layers of meaning in whakataukī as a "duel" between the speaker of the whakataukī and the listener. She notes that a great deal of the meaning in whakataukī relies on knowledge of the "backstory." Because whakataukī rely on the interpretation and application of the listener, they are relevant to a range of contexts. In this sense, their relevance to a given situation relies on the understanding or applicability drawn by each person such that there can be multiple interpretations of one whakataukī (Metge 2010). This notion is shared by many commenters on whakataukī (Department of Māori Affairs 1987; Alsop and Kupenga 2016). The key "messages" or moral standards of behavior that permeate whakataukī broaden their applicability and, therefore, appeal. Whakataukī are open to interpretation by the audience and the application given to specific context, suggesting no "right" or "wrong" interpretation (Alsop and Kupenga 2016; Mead and Grove 2003).

McRae highlighted the significance attributed to whakataukī in knowledge transmission (2017): such oral traditions "were pragmatically and emotionally important; telling their histories, preserving knowledge, and giving explanation, justification and reason for who they were and what they did" (McRae 2017, 12). Whakataukī were traditionally (as they are now) used in whaikōrero (formal speeches) as well as on a day-to-day basis. The use of a supporting proverb was seen as strengthening a speaker's position or argument, whether in decision-making or presenting an argument in either formal oratory or casual conversation (Patterson 1992). Kohere (1951) recalled hearing elders use proverbs on a daily basis.

The following examples of Sámi proverbs illustrate how a saying might accomplish educational goals: "It is better to be on a journey than to stay put at one place" (Gaski 2010, 16) and "where you find the evidence, you also find tracks" (25). Education is needed in order to make progress: "You can't row in a straight line with only one oar" (67). Fear of making a mistake will prevent learning, since "accidents make us wise" (73) and "you'll never catch any fish if you are afraid of getting your feet wet" (80). One should take action to put cultural humility into action: "Nothing comes of a would" (120) and "happiness doesn't come by our waiting for it" (111). If learning is sustained change, then for real learning to take place, one needs to study, practice, and review: "Knowledge that is put on loosely doesn't stay on" (123). Some sayings remind us to be aware that learning comes from all directions: "The silent one will teach you too" (56). Even those who know something could learn more: "No one is so tall that he doesn't need to reach farther" (131). This last adage connects learning with a reminder to be humble.

How Might Adages Help Us Learn More about Cultural Humility?

The path toward cultural humility includes:

> [1] A lifelong commitment to self-evaluation and self-critique . . .
> [2] A desire to fix power imbalances . . .
> [3] Aspiring to develop partnerships with people and groups who advocate for others (Waters and Asbill 2015)

Adages can help with reflection and critique by serving as a continuing thread to advice. Adages draw attention (Avoseh 2012), causing us to pause and take in what is said in a form of active listening (Foronda et al. 2016). Because an adage is stated in third person, it is easier to hear, as its meaning is inferred. Further, while the moral of the adage might relate to an individual, an adage does not single anyone out. Instead, a proverb is a message for all. Adages, therefore, serve to illustrate how power is shared equally—their meanings apply to everyone. These sayings as prefaces to a story can be remembered through life events, eventually accumulating in personal case studies that illustrate the meaning of the adage.

Cultural humility is about interaction with others. With their humble use, sayings can be applied to fix imbalances in power (Foronda et al. 2016).

Proverbs are an especially pertinent entrée to considering humility, as they "symbolize the people's traditionality, preserve their philosophy, and sustain their worldviews by their appropriate use and application in their sociocultural interactions" (Mensah and Eni 2019, 183). Some point to the positive features of human contact: "Similar souls recognize each other" (Gaski 2010, 29). Others remind us that contact with others does not always result in positive outcomes: "The evil ear is always alert" (Gaski 2010, 63).

Māori traditionally lived communally, with shared understandings of common experiences or viewpoints (McRae 2017). Through the sharing of whakataukī, for those repeating the saying and those hearing it, the group had a shared reference and therefore a greater understanding of the allusions contained therein. Having a shared understanding meant one could imply "a great deal in a few words" (S. Kāretu 1981, 41). Proverbs were consequently constructed to be "succinct and pithy" (Kohere 1951, 10)—which, in a society based on oral tradition and oral literature, was beneficial in both the recollection and the retelling of proverbial sayings (McRae 2017).

Seeking Guidance on Humility from Indigenous Adages

How might we learn to be more humble, to walk across the earth in the aura of cultural humility? Adages condense a conversation: "A six-word proverb can carry the weight of a six-chapter book" (Avoseh 2012, 248). Proverbs themselves are humble: they conserve time and energy while still being direct. Thus, this feature is seen in this Sámi adage on humility: "It's better to think more and say less" (Gaski 2010, 41). Adages modestly recognize the authority and wisdom of ancestors over self. This position is captured in whakataukī such as "Kia mau ki te kupu a tōu matua" (Hold to the word of your elder) and "Kia heke iho i ngā tūpuna, kātahi ka tika" (If it comes down from the ancestors, then it is valid) (McRae 2017, 83). Indigenous proverbs are the voices of the elders as they leave lessons, such as in the following examples.

Remember that our reputations reflect our actions.

"It's not good to leave smelly tracks behind you" reminds us that the decisions we make today follow us into the future (Gaski 2010, 27). "A good reputation reaches far, a bad one even farther" (141). "You don't live by your name alone" (142). One's behaviors will be widely known because, according to the Yup'ik, "ears, they say, have eyes" (Fienup-Riordan 2005, 79).

Generosity is a step on the road to humility.
The humble person is seen and remembered for their generosity: "The generous person gives from the little he has, while the greedy one does not share his wealth" (Gaski 2010, 36). Generosity, like humility, is rewarded: to the Yup'ik, "those who are generous are given another day" (Fienup-Riordan 2005, 96).

We benefit from the help of others.
We humble ourselves when we take advice just as easily as we give it: "There are many wise people on the shore when bad things are happening out at sea" (Gaski 2010, 105). "One solitary log does not burn" (133). We need to reach out to others because "with small wings it is hard to fly particularly high" (32).

We should be aware of our limitations.
Arrogance is a detriment: "No one is so short that he doesn't need to bend down" (Gaski 2010, 130). Greed is also an antonym for humility: "It is easy to cut a big slice when you are not cutting from what's your own" (37), and "it's better to leave some of the good food uneaten than to eat until your stomach bursts" (75).

We can look to see how this cultural value of humility is reflected in Māori whakataukī.

> "Kāore te kūmara e kōrero mō tōna māngaro." (The sweet potato does not say how sweet it is.) (T. Kāretu 1996, 90)

Specific whakataukī that convey humility include this proverb well known in Aotearoa/New Zealand. A kūmara is a knobbly, pitted root vegetable, unappealing to the eye. It is only by cooking this unattractive vegetable that its sweetness and goodness are discovered. At first glance, this whakataukī is stating the obvious: that unlike some fruits or vegetables whose appearance invites consumption, the unassuming appearance of the kūmara gives no indication of what lies beneath. Considering the underlying metaphorical message, the whakataukī reinforces that asserting one's own virtues is undesirable or unacceptable. In other words, self-praise cannot be considered a legitimate recommendation (Kāretu 1981). Inherent in this is the need to take time to look beyond the obvious, demonstrating patience and perseverance to benefit from what lies beneath.

> "Ko te koau anake e whakahua ana
> I tāna ingoa : ko au, ko au, ko au!"
> It is only the shag (koau, kawau)
> That cries its own name:
> It is I, it is I, it is I! (Dewes 1981, 46)

The Māori name *kawau*, for a black shag (cormorant), is an example of onomatopoeia—the shag's call is heard as "ko au," which doubles as its name, kawau. The bird seemingly not only calls its own name, but it also shamelessly draws attention to itself, calling, "It is I." In addition, because kawau lack waterproof feathers, they need to dry themselves with their wings outstretched after swimming (Zealandia Te māra a Tāne, n.d.). This whakataukī highlights egotism as inappropriate. Such behavior in birds is seen negatively, as a quality that is frowned upon even more so in humans.

> "Ko te whakaiti te whare o te whakaaro nui." (Humility is the bastion of the generous person.) (Te Ao-Māori News 2019)

The late Professor James Te Wharehuia Milroy coined this saying. Translated more literally, it reads, "It is through the house [person] being diminished (made small) that the expansiveness/superiority/abundance of thoughts are evident." In other words, an individual is but a small part of a broader grouping and strategy. The larger goal is of more importance than that of the individual. Rather than emphasizing that an individual is of no importance, the opposite is being emphasized: each person is vital for the fulfilment of te whakaaro nui. We model our humble stance to that of others.

> "Ehara tāku toa i te toa takitahi, engari he toa takitini." (My success is not that of me alone, but of many.) (Kāretu 1996)

This saying highlights that individual success is the result of the efforts of the collective rather than solely of the individual concerned. Humility is necessary to value both the supporter and their support, knowing that achievement would not have taken place without them. Inherent in this whakataukī also is the concept that contributions made to the success of others benefit both the giver and the receiver of such contributions.

> "Waiho ma te tangata e mihi." (Let someone else acknowledge your virtues). (T. Kāretu 1996, 90)

It is considered more acceptable for others to acknowledge your prowess than to initiate this yourself. This whakataukī repeats themes of avoiding self-praise and self-promotion. The underlying attitude of humility does not suggest a weakness, but instead demonstrates a strength of character. It is likely that this whakataukī alludes to achievements being witnessed and appreciated by others. It celebrates the importance of everyone having a part to play, irrespective of the size or position of their role.

> "Ko tāu hīkoi i runga i ōku whāriki, ko tāu noho i tōku whare, e huakina ai tōku tatau" (Your gentle steps on my doormat, your respect for my home, opens my door.) (Source unknown)

This whakataukī is a perfect platform from which to discuss how those in service professions—even those as diverse as social work or librarianship—might guide their approach to their patrons. The proverb prompts reflection on who might "take the lead" in an interaction and who has the "power" to unlock information and relationships in what ought to be a collaborative working alliance. Consideration of how to approach another's space (whether physical or figurative), and allowing oneself to be led in terms of the customs of welcome and connection, has the potential to significantly shape the course of interaction. Being guided by the "other" requires the ability to put one's own agendas, ego, and familiar patterns of interpersonal conduct aside, demonstrating a vulnerability of sorts, allowing humility to steer the interactional journey.

> "Mahia i runga i te rangimārie, me te ngākau māhaki. With a peaceful mind and a respectful [humble] heart, we will always get the best results." (Attributed to Sir Apirana Ngata, cited in Moorhouse 2020, 7)

Here, the importance of not being arrogant, but being guided by others, is heralded as desirable. Such an approach requires a willingness to listen and to hear, focusing on the issue at hand rather than being distracted by the "noise" of other matters or relationships. Approaching intervention in this way would result in an increased likelihood of success for all involved, and itself epitomizes practice grounded in humility.

Every other year since 1999, Indigenous librarians have assembled at an International Indigenous Librarians' Forum (IILF) (Roy 2000). Delegates have been hosted at venues including Jokkmokk, Sweden; Santa Fe, New Mexico; Regina, Saskatchewan, Canada; and Brisbane, Australia. In April 2011, IILF met in northern Norway, where attendees split their time between the towns of Karasjok and Kautokeino (Roy 2011). In Karasjok, forum events took place in the Sámediggi (Sámi Parliament) building. The interior lights resembled the star patterns of the Milky Way, a homing beacon for those walking toward the building at night (Roy 2013). Within the building was a work of art named *The One Who* that consists of Sámi sayings in the duodji, or handicraft, tradition of using braided metallic threads embedded in a wooden-lath wall to spell out words. The sayings completed the sentences beginning with "The one who," with phrases such as "puts off a coffee break will also put off a marriage" and "gets hiccups will be remembered" (Samediggi Sametinget, n.d.). While the sayings are set in wood, they come alive when someone utters them as a well-remembered phrase or encounters them for the first time. Humorous and serious, these quotes remind us that we have only to reach for a saying that helps us stay afloat in the rough waters of today by being humble with ourselves and others.

Summary

- The title of our chapter introduced the Sámi saying "Time is a ship that never casts anchor" (Gaski 2010, 3). While time does not stop, Indigenous sayings can help direct our thinking and action by connecting us with lessons that have helped people throughout the ages.
- The road to cultural humility is a long one, but cultural sayings can be packed away in reserve and used when needed for sustenance. This is akin to "a long Yup'ik tradition of storing words, like fish, for future use" (Fienup-Riordan 2005, xxxvi).
- Just as learning about one's culture is a lifelong endeavor, it also takes a lifetime to learn cultural humility (Foronda et al. 2016). One needs to be humble to be open to the lessons of a proverb.
- Understanding a proverb involves understanding its layers of meaning, a process that requires awareness of the context of the saying, its many meanings, and its appropriate application today. Once one gets the meaning of a proverb, the rewards are ample. Those who understand become part of the cultural chain of thought that the proverb illustrates, as "proverbs do not exist in a cultural vacuum but draw upon the collective human experience or traditional wisdom" (Mensah 2013, 89).

Questions for Reflection and Discussion

1. What sayings did you grow up hearing that have continued to help you in decision-making?

   ____

   ____

   ____

2. How might libraries incorporate sayings into their architecture and design?

   ____

   ____

   ____

3. What sayings might you use in group work that would promote successful interdependence?

   ____

   ____

   ____

Resources

Gaski, Harald. n.d. "Folk Wisdom and Orally Transmitted Knowledge—Everyday Poetry in Adages, Rhyme, and Riddles." Sami Culture. Retrieved June 29, 2021. https://www.laits.utexas.edu/sami/diehtu/siida/language/folkevisdom.htm.

MāoriLanguage.net. n.d. "Proverbs—Ngā whakataukī, ngā whakatauākī." Retrieved June 29, 2021. https://www.maorilanguage.net/maori-words-phrases/proverbs-nga-whakatauki-nga-whakatauaki/.

Massey University. n.d. "Whakataukī: Māori Proverbs." Retrieved June 29, 2021. https://www.massey.ac.nz/student-life/māori-at-massey/te-reo-māori-and-tikanga-resources/te-reo-māori-pronunciation-and-translations/whakataukī-māori-proverbs/.

Moorfield, J. C. 2021. *Te aka Māori–English, English–Māori Dictionary and Index*. Retrieved June 29, 2021. https://maoridictionary.co.nz/.

Moorhouse, L. 2020. "He kete whakataukī: Using Narratives and Values in Māori Proverbs." He Puna Rauemi. Retrieved June 29, 2021. https://hepunarauemi.co.nz/. [Fifty-page pamphlet and deck of thirty cards.]

REFERENCES

Alsop, P., and T. R. Kupenga. 2016. *Mauri ora: Wisdom from the Maori World*. Nelson, New Zealand: Potton & Burton.

Apt, N. A. 1992. "Trends and Prospects in Africa." *Community Development Journal* 25, no. 2: 130–39.

Avoseh, M. B. M. 2012. "Proverbs as Theoretical Frameworks for Lifelong Learning in Indigenous African Education." *Adult Education Quarterly* 63, no. 3: 236–50.

Department of Māori Affairs. 1987. *He whakataukī*. Whangarei, New Zealand: Department of Māori Affairs.

Dewes, T. K. 1981. "The Case for Oral Arts." In *Te Ao Hurihuri: The World Moves On*, edited by M. King, 46–63. Auckland: Longman Paul.

Fienup-Riordan, A. 2005. *Wise Words of the Yup'ik People: We Talk to You Because We Love You*. Lincoln: University of Nebraska Press.

Foronda, C., D.-L. Baptiste, M. M. Reinholdt, and K. Ousman. 2016. "Cultural Humility: A Concept Analysis." *Journal of Transcultural Nursing* 27, no. 3: 210–17.

Gaski, H., ed. 2010. *Time Is a Ship That Never Casts Anchor*. Karasjok, Norway: ČálliidLágádus.

Hemara, W. 2000. *Māori Pedagogies: A View from the Literature*. Wellington: New Zealand Council for Educational Research Press.

Kāretu, S. 1981. "Language and Protocol of the Marae." In *Te Ao Hurihuri: The World Moves On*, edited by M. King, 31–45. Auckland: Longman Paul.

Kāretu, T. 1996. *The Reed Pocket Māori Proverbs*. Revision of a work by A. E. Brougham and A. W. Reed. Auckland: Reed Consumer Books.

Kawharu, M. 2008. *Tāhuhu kōrero: The Sayings of Taitokerau*. Auckland: Auckland University Press.

King, M. 1981. *Te ao hurihuri: The World Moves On*. Auckland: Longman Paul.

Kohere, R. 1951. *He konae aronui: Māori Proverbs and Sayings*. Wellington: A. H. & A. W. Reed.

Marsden, M., and T. A. Royal. 2003. *The Woven Universe: Selected Writings of Rev. Māori Marsden*. Otaki, New Zealand: Estate of Rev. Māori Marsden.

McRae, J. 2017. *Māori Oral Tradition: He kōrero nō te ao tawhito*. Auckland: Auckland University Press.

Mead, H., and N. Grove. 2003. *Ngā pepeha a ngā tīpuna: The Sayings of the Ancestors*. Wellington: Victoria University Press.

Mead, H. M., and J. T. R. Mead. 2010. *People of the Land: Images and Māori Proverbs of Aotearoa New Zealand*. Wellington: Huia.

Mensah, E. O. 2013. "Proverbs in Nigerian pidgin." *Journal of Anthropological Research* 69: 87–115.

Mensah, E. O., and R. A. Eni. 2019. "What's in the Stomach Is Used to Carry What's on the Head: An Ethnographic Exploration of Food Metaphors in Efik Proverbs." *Journal of Black Studies* 50, no. 2: 178–201.

Metge, J. 1967. *The Māoris of New Zealand*. Rev. ed. London: Routledge & Kegan Paul.

Metge, J. 2010. "Whakataukī: Wisdom in Proverbs." In *Tuamaka: The Challenge of Difference in Aotearoa New Zealand*, edited by J. Metge and E. T. Durie. Auckland: Auckland University Press.

Moorhouse, L. 2020. *He kete whakataukī: Drawing on Māori Narratives and Values to Support Purposeful Conversations*. Auckland: He Puna Rauemi.

Mutonyi, H. 2016. "Stories, Proverbs, and Anecdotes as Scaffolds for Learning Science Concepts." *Journal of Research in Science Teaching* 53, no. 6: 943–71.

Njwe, Eyovi. 2014. "'The palm oil with which words are eaten': Proverbs from Cameroon's Endangered Indigenous Languages." In *Georgetown University Round Table on Languages and Linguistics*, 118–26, 193. Washington, DC: Georgetown University Press.

Patterson, J. 1992. *Exploring Māori Values*. Palmerston North, New Zealand: Dunmore Press.

Roy, L. 2000. "The International Indigenous Librarians' Forum: A Professional Life-Affirming Event." *World Libraries* 10, no. 1/2: 19–30.

Roy, L. 2011. "The International Indigenous Librarians Forum 7 (IILF7): Karasjok and Kautokeino, Norway, April 4–8, 2011." *IFLA Library Services to Multicultural Populations Section Newsletter*, Summer, 6–8.

Roy, L. 2013. "Place." In *Library 2020: Today's Leading Visionaries Describe Tomorrow's Library*, edited by J. Janes, 121–126. Lanham, MD: Scarecrow.

Samediggi Sametinget. n.d. *Proverbs*. Karasjok, Norway: Samediggi.

Te Ao–Māori News. 2019. "Waikato-Tainui Pay Homage to Te Wharehuia," May 8. Retrieved June 29, 2021. www.teaomaori.news/waikato-tainui-pay-homage-te-wharehuia.

Waters, A. J., and L. Asbill. 2015. "Reflections on Cultural Humility." *CYF News*. https://www.apa.org/pi/families/resources/newsletter/2013/08/cultural-humility.

Yankah, K. 1989. "Proverbs: The Aesthetics of Traditional Communication." *Research in African Literatures* 20, no. 3: 325-46.

Zealandia Te māra a Tāne. n.d. "Black Shag." Retrieved June 29, 2021. https://www.visitzealandia.com/About/Wildlife/Birds/Black-Shag.

2

Redressing Power Imbalances in Librarianship Using Cultural Humility

A Perspective from Two Black Librarians

XAN GOODMAN AND TWANNA HODGE

What Is Autoethnography?

In this chapter, we will use the technique of autoethnography as a tool of self-reflection to examine our positionality within librarianship. Autoethnography is a qualitative-research method where the researcher is the subject (Watson 2001). Our essay in this book is not a form of research; however, we use the form of autoethnography to create an entry point for readers to think about cultural humility as a lived practice. We think autoethnography is the best method to reveal how cultural humility is lived by each of us. As such, we share our personal narrative as a way to situate cultural humility within the social context that includes political and social factors. In this chapter, we aim to open up pathways for cultural humility to be adopted as a practice by library workers. We both identify as Black, but with key differences. Xan is a Black, African American who grew up in Detroit, Michigan, and attended public schools and state universities. Twanna is a Black Afro-Caribbean person who grew up in the US Virgin Islands, an unincorporated territory, and attended public schools and universities. She came to the US mainland as an adult for graduate school.

The framework we will use to explore autoethnography is critical race theory. Critical race theory (CRT) is a legal scholarly theoretical framework used to draw connections between race and law (Crenshaw 2011). "The terms 'whiteness' and 'dominant culture,' as applied in CRT, are used interchangeably and can be defined as invisible, visible, and hyper-visible hierarchically privileged positions of Eurocentric cultural standards and values" (Dunbar

2006, 113). Critical race theory has been expanded to other fields, including library and information science and higher education. We are using "counterstories, which are helpful in exposing microaggressions within both interpersonal interactions, as well as marginalizing dynamics within social institutions" (Dunbar 2006, 113). As we use critical race theory, we are adopting a stance of critical cultural humility to incorporate themes of power and of the practices of white supremacy in library science (Sealey-Ruiz 2021; Kendrick and Damasco 2019). Sealey-Ruiz (2021) describes critical cultural humility as having the ability to adopt a stance of awareness regarding worldview and ideological position.

What Cultural Humility Means to Xan's Practice of Librarianship

In 2010, while teaching as an adjunct instructor for Wayne State University, I learned about the concept of cultural humility. However, it was not until years later that I began to think more deeply about cultural humility and its potential as an approach to change librarianship. My experience up to this point as an instructor was to assign readings from sociology and librarianship in the course I taught about multiculturalism in libraries. Teaching as an adjunct instructor with a majority of white-identified students was jarring. Frequently when asking students about their cultural background, many expressed that they felt they had no culture. I was shocked. As I began to read in literature about the education of preservice teachers, this phenomenon of white students who expressed feeling that they lacked culture was a dominant theme in education literature. My teaching experience along with my life experience as a Black person have also encouraged me to reflect further on cultural humility as a way to enact hope.

What Cultural Humility Means to Twanna's Practice of Librarianship

In my practice of librarianship, cultural humility has brought about a metamorphosis in how I work, engage with individuals, and perceive the world. In the fall of 2015, I was introduced to the concept of cultural humility when I was the first diversity resident librarian at the University of Utah. A colleague and I were working on a presentation on implicit biases and how incorporating cultural humility could improve our practice and help us and other library workers be more other oriented.

My stance was that if library workers do not understand their identities, and if they lack cultural awareness and knowledge and do not understand how this affects their work, they cannot provide services or programming; they cannot liaise; they cannot conduct outreach that is culturally validating or tailored to what the patrons need. Cultural humility centers our humanity. It lays out how crucial and influential culture is to our realities. Culture is everything. Cultural humility is the foundation that supports me.

How Do You Engage in Cultural Humility, Xan?

As I have reflected more deeply on cultural humility, I have identified some ways to engage in cultural humility using what I refer to as humble practices. Humble practices are actions or ways of engaging with the world that I can do to put cultural humility into practice. Here are a few of the practices that I consider humble: active listening; empathy; lifelong learning; redressing power imbalances in librarianship; and connecting to the communities I support. Some of these practices are embodied, which means that I intentionally try to connect to my body as a way to monitor how I am showing up in the world.

To actively listen, practice empathy, or redress power imbalances as humble practices, I must ask myself the following questions: Do I feel overwhelmed? Do I feel stressed? Can I create spaciousness for students, faculty, or colleagues? If I am stressed or overwhelmed, I cannot act to remove power imbalances, be empathetic, listen actively, or do any of the other humble practices I have mentioned. I miss the mark on many occasions; however, I am striving to show up rested and able to hold space for the demands of the day.

How Do You Engage in Cultural Humility, Twanna?

Ever since 2015, I have dived into learning about cultural humility from the medical, social work, education, and librarianship fields. I strive to be other oriented and centered in my work and collaborations. I work to understand power dynamics and negate or minimize them as much as possible. I encourage folks to take up space, undertake a reflective practice (Schon 1984) (individually or in a group), critically engage with their understanding of their world, and understand others' realities. Cultural humility is integrated throughout my scholarship, daily work, service, and relationships. I see cultural humility as an inclusivity strategy. It challenges my and others' assumptions, norms, and standardized cultural practices and views the culture as dynamic, constantly changing. It urges us to reflect on our identities and the culture within/about them, along with continuously learning about my culture and others. Who I interact with influences the interaction; we are knowledgeable and bringing something to the situation; no one is inferior or superior to another. As a Black Afro-Caribbean woman, first-generation American, and first-generation college graduate with intersectional visible and invisible identities, cultural humility has been a survival mechanism to help navigate librarianship and living on the mainland. I do not know everything there is to know about mainland American culture. I do not know everything there is to know about US Virgin Islander culture. But there is a freedom in this not knowing, as well as a responsibility to not settle on what my current knowledge is. For each of us, our existence is crafted by cultures from micro to macro.

Xan's Reflective Practices

I see, the key aspects of cultural humility require thoughtful and intentional practice. In the daily rush of teaching and other functions, it is hard to take time to reflect. A surprise gift from the COVID-19 pandemic was an unexpected opportunity to start taking reflective walks in my neighborhood. During these walks, I had the chance to reflect on my interactions—to ponder how successful was I with enacting the humble practices I have identified as important to my practice of cultural humility. The pandemic allowed me time. Freed from my car, I had time to deliberately use walking as a means to contemplate my actions. On these walks, I gained time to create space to think, reflect, and even create.

Twanna's Reflective Practices

Having a reflective practice means you think, on an ongoing basis, about your thoughts, words, actions, and behaviors and their effects (Leftwich 2019; O'Connell and Dyment 2013; Reale 2017; Schon 1984). Reflection is a critical strategy for self-awareness and self-improvement. My reflective practices are solo and group based, using prompts when I journal and engage others. I involve my support networks of trusted people who have and will call me out or call me in as needed. I use scheduled and impromptu breaks during my day to partake in self-evaluation, going for walks, and more. It is intentional. I spend my time thinking about how I acted: what I said; people's responses; my and others' discomfort levels; what I didn't know at the time; what I need to know for future interactions; if I gave adequate support in the moment; what I could do now or later; if I disrupted when necessary; did I speak my truth; was space made for others; were those most affected in the room or not in the room; were those perspectives centered; and so on. Additionally, I try to consider the influence of my interactions and others, including the mediums and formats along with the sociocultural movements, and what is happening locally and globally, acknowledging that geography does impact the context and interactions. I think about the multiple, complex, and nuanced intersectional identities that people hold simultaneously, keeping those in mind as I navigate this world. Reflection helps prevent us from engaging in a "sense of urgency," which is a characteristic of white-supremacy culture (Okun 2000). Reflection also helps us to "challeng[e] dominant ideologies of color blindness, objectivity, neutrality, and meritocracy" (Leung and López-McKnight 2021, 14).

Library Cultures—What's Geography Got to Do with It?

XAN'S PERSPECTIVE

In my view, a practice of cultural humility demands consideration of the political and historical context of libraries. Understanding the historical, social, and economic context allows us to identify and comprehend the underlying structural and systemic issues that influence the present (Leung and López-McKnight 2021, 15). The impact of geography on me as a librarian has affected my entire library career because I was born and raised in Detroit, Michigan. Being from a northern city that is deeply segregated by race has heightened my sense of community, white supremacy, and classism. White supremacy shaped the response of Detroit's surrounding communities to the city and its residents. Similar to Brooklyn, Queens, Chicago, and other cities nationwide, Detroit had redlining policies (McGhee 2021). Redlining restricts where people may purchase a home or even rent. Homes in redlined areas were usually deemed high risk and not eligible for mortgage loans, or if eligible, loan rates were higher and home values were less. Because libraries are publicly funded, the legacy of redlining has an effect on library funding. Libraries in Detroit were built within a historical and political context that supported redlining.

The legacy of the 1943 and 1967 riots loomed large in the city of my birth. These riots were racialized and political, and have left a long-lasting imprint on the 134 square miles of Detroit. Learning about the historical and political context of communities might reveal the reasons a library may be in a certain community, or why the patrons are of a certain or particular racial or ethnic group. Place has everything to do with libraries, and libraries have everything to do with place. In my practice of librarianship, I strive to have humility and possess an awareness of the political and historical environment of libraries where I work. This is important to me in my thinking and practice of cultural humility.

TWANNA'S PERSPECTIVE

From thinking about the Indigenous land we are located on due to settler colonialism, genocide, the establishment of borders and states, and government and state-sanctioned violence, to the current geographic makeup of the now United States of America, geography is critical to this work. I am a visitor on this land. Cultural humility gives us the lens to see and understand that our relationship to the earth is interconnected, along with our relationships to one another. What is mentioned above is mirrored in library cultures. The social, political, and historical contexts affect the place of employment. The climate, weather, location, landmass, borders, urban/suburban/rural setting, and so on are distinct and vital factors. The movements, battles for justice, fight for climate change, dismantling environmental racism, and more are being woven into these places every second. Geography has always impacted and always will influence my practice and how I approach, navigate, and engage with my work and personal life. Where you live in the country, where you were raised, how long you've lived there, whether you are a local or transplant, whether you are familiar with the seasons, and know how to navigate the area is a part of your relationship with the geography.

Where We Have Worked

XAN'S PERSPECTIVE

I began my professional librarian career as a consortia librarian. Sales as a culture is its own world. Library school did not prepare me to work in sales. There were no courses on database licensing, vendor negotiation, or managing database deals; these key skills were necessary as a consortia librarian. Once in my position, I was welcomed into the workplace and even provided with opportunities to attend training (Scholarly Kitchen 2020). My workplace also had a history with Black women like myself: Black women did not last long (Kendrick 2017; Kendrick and Damasco 2019). If the organization had made an effort to determine why Black women did not last long at the agency, this might have resulted in an organizationally humble practice of reflection to determine why Black women were not retained.

A key incident that had the potential to incorporate cultural humility was when a white, gay, male identified colleague sexually harassed me offsite. I considered my colleague to be a work friend, and I trusted him. On a day trip a few hours from our town, this person made sexual overtures to me in a manner I found offensive and frightening. As we were only a few hours away from our town, we had lunch. At lunch he drank too much and became intoxicated, so I had to drive his car through rural Michigan towns; this was also traumatic (Dunbar 2006). The history of policing in rural towns along with the history of white men assaulting Black women because of stereotypical ideas about our sexuality was foremost in my mind during this situation. This self-proclaimed white, gay male thought he should have access to my Black body, and it was terrifying (Civitello and McLain 2017; Napson-Williams 2008; Collins 1998). At the end of the day, I survived this encounter. I had to do the calculus for my career while carrying the weight of the incident and history. I did not report him, due to my belief that I would not receive support from my coworkers who knew how this person identified. Also, sharing might have impacted my career beyond that organization. Years later, when I shared this story with the former leaders of the organization, one remarked, "When did [person's name] swing that way," incredulous about the colleague's interest in a woman. This demonstrated a lack of awareness of the historical and current cultural knowledge about Black women in this workplace. There was a lack of cultural humility on the part of the organization while seeing this visible shift in my relationship with this colleague. A white male colleague who was at the same level as me noticed the change and mentioned it without asking any questions, yet his notice was appreciated. My coworkers were nice, yet the unspoken rules, lack of action, and other behaviors were crippling to me as Black woman in the workplace (DiAngelo 2021). My situation highlights the continued silencing of acknowledging and taking action about how Black women might be treated in the workplace and, tragically, it exemplifies the weighty historical dynamics that can show up in organizations.

Moving from sales to my first professional academic librarian position was refreshing. I entered academic librarianship hopeful, and as the only Black person on the library staff. After only a few months into the job, I became director of the library. Cultural humility might have improved my staff interactions. Even though I was the interim director, many of the all-white staff engaged in microaggressions. During staff meetings, some staff expressed themselves with eye-rolling being one example of many microaggressions; on one occasion, a white female library colleague yelled at me and hit my desk. These were unprofessional workplace behaviors. An incident of outright insubordination from the white female administrative assistant led to a meeting with the office of the vice president of Academic Affairs. Later, this led to a meeting with me and the vice president where I was counseled, wisely, to not allow someone to so upset me (Kendrick and Damasco 2019). After I spent nine months in the role of interim library director, a new director was hired and some healing began. Critical cultural humility, where one examines one's advantage in the workplace and positionality of being a member of the dominant culture, might have improved some of the interactions.

I moved from a small private library to a large public university in the Southwest. This public university earned government status as a minority-serving institution during my time there. Initially, I was filled with hope that a working environment with underrepresented students might offer opportunities for growth and new experiences as a librarian. Those opportunities were present; however, there were forms of neglect by superiors, overassignment of work, and outright attack, again, from white female coworkers. Cullinan (1999) describes how BIPOC persons are not afforded the benefits of innocence, worthiness, or competence in the workplace. There were instances in this library where I experienced not being seen as worthy or competent or being given the benefit of doubt, or innocence.

TWANNA'S PERSPECTIVE

I worked for a year as the inaugural diversity resident librarian at the University of Utah, a public land-grant university; this is a historically, traditionally, and predominantly white institution (PWI). "The university is located on the traditional and ancestral homelands of the Shoshone, Paiute, Goshute and Ute tribes; the state of Utah is home to eight distinct tribal nations" (University of Utah 2020). Prior to this job, I worked at only one PWI research library, so my experience and exposure were minimal. I was the only Black librarian and most times would be the only Black person in certain spaces. Race is a social construct that impacts all aspects of life. Racism is normal and deeply ingrained in American society through its systems and institutions (Leung and López-McKnight 2021, 13). I was very conscious of this and turned to embodying and presenting whiteness wherever I could, not knowing that I was sacrificing pieces of myself as I did so.

"Whiteness and white racialized identity refer to the way that white people, their customs, culture, and beliefs operate as the standard by which all other groups of people are compared. Whiteness is also at the core of understanding race in America" (National Museum of African American History and Culture 2021). I felt and knew that if I wanted to "succeed," I needed to hide or minimize my Blackness and Caribbeanness. "When in an effort to be accepted a Black person is constantly leaving parts of their personality or life outside of where they work, their overall well-being suffers" (Jackson and Flash 2021). As an early-career librarian of color, I was focused on demonstrating to everyone, including myself, that I deserved this job and that I had what it took to be successful. "Also, the expectation to 'fit in' culturally strengthens the idea that in order to be present in certain workplaces or even more so, in order to have our achievements recognized, we have to exist in a particular way that matches the interests and cultural mores of those in power" (Jackson and Flash 2021). I experienced cultural isolation and tokenism due to being the only resident librarian, the only Black librarian, and the only US Virgin Islander.

I was born and raised on the island of St. Thomas, US Virgin Islands (USVI). I grew up on an island where socioeconomic status, kinship ties, where you lived on the island, and more shaped who you are. The island is thirty-two square miles. March 31 marks Transfer Day, commemorating the transfer of ownership from the Danish (Denmark-colonized West Indies) to the US (now 106 years under the US flag). The Indigenous populations were the "Caribs Kalinago, Arawaks, Tainos, and Ciboneys and possibly visitors from Africa" (Willocks 1995, 27). St. Thomas is mountainous. The local language is American Creole. The official language is English. I am a first-generation American with parents from different Caribbean countries. VI culture is a mixture of African, Caribbean, and American cultures. The transatlantic slave trade impacted music, food, language, cultural practices, and more in the Virgin Islands. Being physically removed from the mainland meant that people did not consider us American or US citizens. Our political and economic powers are recognized through the Revised Organic Act, and we are an unincorporated territory. It felt that we were a Black stepchild that other people unintentionally or intentionally forgot about. Erasure like this has been normalized. The experiences and knowledge of BIPOC are necessary to eradicating multiple oppressions (Leung and López-McKnight 2021; Matsuda et al. 1993; Yosso et al. 2009).

Power Imbalances in Libraries

There are many factors that account for power imbalances in libraries, but we describe only several in this chapter. In librarianship, there is a distinct preference for white people, whiteness, and those who adhere to white supremacy culture. The system is doing what it is designed to do. This is intentional and by choice. The evidence is countless and everywhere (Hudson 2017). It is in the laws, regulations, policies, procedures, and culture. We and many others have experienced racial battle fatigue due to the experiences we endure daily: the tokenism; the cultural, racial, and ethnic isolation; minimal or glacial changes to addressing structural inequities such as the lack of BIPOC representation in leadership; othering; inconsistent application of a human-centered approach; and an absence of the widespread application of cultural humility in librarianship. Racial justice has never existed, and it is a constant fight for Black people to be recognized as human. The structure is rooted in anti-Black racism, capitalism, and misogynoir. The systems and structure do not allow for the recognition of our humanity or safety. "The profession's dangerous and toxic alliance to White Supremacy and the impact of structural racism on the LIS workforce" continually need to be addressed (Leung and López-McKnight 2021, 26).

XAN'S PERSPECTIVE

My experience in libraries began as a library worker without an MLIS degree. I spent many years working in libraries without an MLIS or MLS degree. In order to punch the ticket of library success, a degree was required. Libraries in my experience were filled with many BIPOC workers who did not have library degrees. The demographics of nondegreed library workers meant that I found camaraderie and friendship with workers who had similar positions (Espinal, Hathcock, and Rios 2021). While many of my library-worker colleagues were diverse, supervisors were most often white. Two supervisors at this stage in my library career practiced cultural humility in ways that addressed power imbalances by being fair. This was refreshing. One supervisor was patient and explained expectations for work without being punitive or passive-aggressive. Another supervisor also acted with fairness to create an environment without inequity. Cultural humility with colleagues might look like an environment where a supervisor is patient rather than punitive and acknowledges their power while acting to create an equitable environment. DiAngelo (2021) describes the use of passive-aggressive behavior, silence, or smiles as a way to mask white fragility or discomfort with Black people. Power misuse or power imbalances were most often on display with white supervisors who were sometimes capricious with rules and not applying work expectations fairly while insisting on white-supremacy standards of dress, comportment, staying in one's place, and other hidden-curriculum practices (Okun 2000; Sue 2013). Using cultural humility as a framework to dismantle power imbalances and to encourage reflection might have improved workplaces where misuse of power was an issue and reflection was not a usual practice.

TWANNA'S PERSPECTIVE

I felt that, in order to be successful, I needed to prove my humanity, my existence, and my worth. My experiences in librarianship have been marked with success through a white, heteronormative, capitalistic cisgender, classist male lens. Whiteness is where the racial and social power, privilege, and advantage exist in libraries, so when I am the only one or one of few Black librarians employed at an institution, on a committee, with my title, rank, or status, this is due to the systems and structures that were designed, built, and maintained this way. There has never been a race war because whiteness was the paper, ink, and hands that this country was created by and for, which was based on anti-Blackness, anti-Indigeneity, and more.

Within the US, libraries are predominantly Eurocentric, ethnocentric, individualistic, and meritocratic, with deep assimilationist roots. Patriarchy, sexism, ableism, and misogynoir are also embedded in libraries. These cultural orientations have impacted how we navigate and experience libraries. For example, with regard to positionality related to degrees and credentials, there are requirements and preferences for those with master's degrees (MLIS, MLS, and their equivalents) or doctorates. Xan and I both have master's degrees in library and information science. My degree is from the University of Washington, a PWI, where I was one of two Black students in my residential cohort of more than sixty students. People treat and view me differently when they learn about my credentials. My words and actions might be perceived as more credible and authoritative. I may even be perceived as less trustworthy and knowledgeable, depending on the space—though my other identities, particularly visible ones, influence the power dynamics in any given situation, redressing the power imbalances is needed. Our identities impact our lives, and our stories matter.

Factors at Play

In this section of our chapter, we will not break out our experiences with the perspective headings used in the earlier sections of this work. Instead, we will share our counterstories in narrative form. Both of us have experienced themes of power imbalances in our careers; these include socioeconomic factors, rank/status, and kinship ties.

SOCIOECONOMIC FACTORS

Librarianship is designed for the middle-class-income brackets and higher, with a reimbursement culture which includes service and scholarship commitments that incur significant time and financial costs. The expectation is that the person already has the financial capital to pay up front for onsite finalist interviews, conferences, institutes, workshops, and so on. This includes monetary expenses such as registration fees, membership fees, transportation costs, lodging, incidentals, and other expenses such as child care or pet care. The reimbursement period can take anywhere from a few weeks to several months, which puts a financial strain on people and/or prevents them from participating to begin with. One conference can cost upward of $1,500, which, if you use a credit card, puts the total cost at $1,691.85 with a 12.79% interest rate, or even more with a higher interest rate. We cannot assume that everyone has the same access to credit cards or reasonable interest rates. Regardless of the rate, the individual typically faces a temporary but lengthy money deficit. Xan's experience of pursuing and earning tenure at a public university highlights the unspoken costs to her as a Black, working-class, professional woman (Ossom-Williamson et al. 2021).

In academic libraries, librarians are expected, as a part of our job, to travel and present. This is part of an academic role. However, the challenges around this travel are fraught with historical legacies of inequality and socioeconomic factors that do not consider equity. Everyone does not start at the same point, and to require travel, presenting, and involvement in professional organizations while also not making the process easier for librarians needs to be redressed. We each experienced the burden of having to pay for things up front. After Xan left a previous academic librarian position, newly hired librarians were given credit cards to pay for travel expenses. Changing policy is an example of a humble practice when a library policy around travel expenses is revised to redress a power imbalance.

RANK/STATUS FACTORS

Contemplate how words such as *paraprofessional*, *support staff*, and the like may give the perception that people with these titles are considered inferior or substandard, and their contributions are deemed less or not valued. Within the faculty ranks (nontenured, tenure track, tenured) are the more privileged; but power differentials exist within and outside the library. Power differentials, such as monitoring restroom breaks, hypersurveillance, or passive-aggressive practices around time-clock usage, can be countered with humble practices of empathy, giving colleagues the benefit of innocence and worthiness.

KINSHIP TIES FACTORS

The dominant culture views kinship ties through the nuclear family model. Other family compositions and kinship experiences might extend beyond the nuclear family (Taylor et al. 2022; Taylor et al. 2021). Within the library, this impacts employees and patrons. Library workers who have extensive kinship ties beyond nuclear families might have greater responsibilities that are not understood by leadership. Likewise, patrons might also have kinship ties that are unfamiliar to dominant cultured persons. In Xan's experience within libraries, there was no way for her to take advantage of federal leave policies to care for sick siblings who were unmarried. In this case, her white female supervisor acted from a place of critical cultural humility. The supervisor acknowledged her position of power, did not create excessive barriers to impede Xan's ability to care for loved ones, and organized a flexible work policy for Xan, which allowed her to care for sick siblings. This includes examining leave policies and how family is legally defined and assigned. Also, assessing how kinship ties are culturally influenced.

The themes of power imbalances with socioeconomic, rank/status, and kinship ties are several of many factors that exist. A key part of cultural humility is engaging in constant and consistent self-reflection, which can be applied to the policies, procedures, and regulations within institutions and organizations. Creating time for this to take place is necessary. Being other oriented takes intentional effort.

How to Redress Power Imbalances

Below are actions you can take to redress power imbalances that exist in your personal and professional lives.

INTERPERSONAL/INDIVIDUAL ACTIONS

Take several implicit association tests; identify and assess your identities, their power, privilege, and positionalities; take bystander intervention classes to aid in intervening and disrupting injustices whenever possible; report, document, and follow up about instances of discrimination, bias, and the like. Create accountability groups with trusted individuals. Fail forward (failure is a part of this work). Continue to learn about others and yourself. Do not treat others as walking encyclopedias. And recognize this is lifelong work and commitment.

GROUP/TEAM ACTIONS

Engage in thoughtful decision-making. Assign roles intentionally and with care. Be aware of and acknowledge the power dynamics in groups. Know when to lead, but, more important, know when to follow or get out of the way entirely.

SYSTEM/INSTITUTIONAL ACTIONS

Review and update policies and procedures routinely, asking the question "Who is helped or harmed by this?" Additionally, use an equity, diversity, and inclusion (EDI) lens, formally documenting unspoken, unwritten, or hidden policies, to provide support for ongoing education in regard to cultural humility, EDI, social justice, trauma-informed approaches, healing-centered approaches, anti-oppression practices, liberatory frameworks, and creating and holding spaces for this work to take place.

Summary

In this chapter, we have excavated the personal to inform workplace awareness and action, using counterstories as a tool to demonstrate ways to redress power imbalances. As we have detailed, oppression, anti-Blackness, sexism, and more are embedded in librarianship culture. However, using cultural humility to redress power imbalances can change personal, organizational, and systemic practices. Cultural humility demands us to know, understand,

and continue to educate ourselves in regard to the importance of culture in library workspaces.

Questions for Reflection and Discussion

1. How does the history of the place where your library is located affect your workplace?

   ____

   ____

   ____

2. How are issues of power imbalances addressed in your workplace?

   ____

   ____

   ____

3. What reflective practices can you adopt to help you develop an orientation of cultural humility?

   ____

   ____

   ____

4. What identities and roles do you hold, what are their power/privilege/positionality, and how do these impact redressing power imbalances in the workplace?

   ____

   ____

   ____

5. What is your responsibility for disrupting and dismantling structural inequities and embedding cultural humility?

   ____

   ____

   ____

6. Who are the most affected/vulnerable (sometimes you are included in this) in the room? And how can you center their needs (maybe yours)?

____

____

____

7. How would you describe mainland American culture to someone visiting or not raised on the US mainland? What do you think influences your answer?

____

____

____

Resources

Network of the National Library of Medicine (NNLM). 2019. "Integrating Cultural Humility into Practice." YouTube video, posted June 13, starting at 27:57 of 1:03:14. https://www.youtube.com/watch?v=4uE4PIW2CDk.

Project Implicit. 2011. https://implicit.harvard.edu/implicit/.

Unlearning & Divesting from the White Colonial Mind. https://www.dismantlingracism.org/white-supremacy-culture.html.

White Supremacy Culture. 2021. "White Supremacy Culture Characteristics." https://www.whitesupremacyculture.info/characteristics.html.

REFERENCES

Civitello, A., and K. McLain 2017. "It's Not Just Part of the Job: Speaking Out About Sexual Harassment." *ILA Reporter* 35, no. 6: 4–7.

Collins, P. H. 1998. "The Tie That Binds: Race, Gender, and US Violence." *Ethnic and Racial Studies* 21, no. 5: 917–38. https://doi.org/10.1080/014198798329720.

Crenshaw, K. W. 2011. "Twenty Years of Critical Race Theory: Looking Back to Move Forward." *Connecticut Law Review* 43, no. 5 (July 2011): 117. https://opencommons.uconn.edu/cgi/viewcontent.cgi?article=1116&context=law_review.

Cullinan, C. C. 1999. "Vision, Privilege, and the Limits of Tolerance." *Multicultural Education* 1, no. 2: 3–5. https://vetvoicenational.files.wordpress.com/2018/10/cris-cullinan-visions-privilege-and-the-limits-of-tolerance.pdf.

DiAngelo, R. 2021. *Nice Racism: How Progressive White People Perpetuate Racial Harm.* Boston: Beacon.

Dunbar, A. W. 2006. "Introducing Critical Race Theory to Archival Discourse: Getting the Conversation Started." *Archival Science* 6, no. 1: 109–29.

Espinal, I., A. M. Hathcock, and M. Rios. "Dewhitening Librarianship: A Policy Proposal for Libraries." In *Knowledge Justice: Disrupting Library and Information Studies through Critical Race Theory*, edited by S. Y. Leung and J. R. López-McKnight.

Hudson, D. J. 2017. "The Whiteness of Practicality." In *Topographies of Whiteness: Mapping Whiteness in Library and Information Science*, edited by Gina Schlesselman-Tarango, 203–34. Sacramento: Library Juice.

Jackson, L., and K. Flash. 2021. "Surveillance and Captivity of Black Excellence under the White Gaze: What the Treatment of Black Celebrities Can Tell Us about Black Librarianship." WOC+lib. https://www.wocandlib.org/features/2021/10/26/surveillance-and-captivity-of-black-excellence.

Kendrick, K. D. 2017. "The Low Morale Experience of Academic Librarians: A Phenomenological Study." *Journal of Library Administration* 57, no. 8: 846–78. https://10.1080/01930826.2017.1368325.

Kendrick, K. D., and I. T. Damasco. 2019. "Low Morale in Ethnic and Racial Minority Academic Librarians: An Experiential Study." *Library Trends* 68, no. 2: 174–212. https://10.1353/lib.2019.0036.

Leftwich, A. M. 2019. "Reflecting Journaling: A Daily Practice." *Librarian Parlor*, February 1. https://libparlor.com/2019/01/30/reflecting-journaling-a-daily-practice/.

Leung, S. Y., and J. R. López-McKnight, eds. 2021. *Knowledge Justice: Disrupting Library and Information Studies through Critical Race Theory.* Cambridge: MIT Press.

Matsuda, Mari J., Charles R. Lawrence III, Richard Delgado, and Kimberlé W. Crenshaw. 1993. *Words That Wound: Critical Race Theory, Assaultive Speech, and The First Amendment*. Boulder: Westview Press.

McGhee, H. 2021. *Sum of Us*. London: Profile Books.

Napson-Williams, T. "Violating the Black Body: Black Women, White Men and Sexual Violence, 1920–1952." PhD diss., University of Michigan, Ann Arbor, 2008.

National Museum of African American History and Culture. 2021. "Whiteness." *Talking About Race*, April 7. https://nmaahc.si.edu/learn/talking-about-race/topics/whiteness.

O'Connell, T. S., and J. E. Dyment. 2013. *Theory into Practice: Unlocking the Power and the Potential of Reflective Journals*. Charlotte: Information Age Publishing.

Okun, T. 2000. "White Supremacy Culture." *Dismantling Racism: A Workbook for Social Change Groups*. Durham, NC: Change Work. http://www.dismantlingracism.org/Dismantling_Racism/liNKs_files/whitesupcul09.pdf.

Ossom-Williamson, P., J. Williams, X. Goodman, C. I. J. Minter, and A. Logan. 2021. "Starting With I: Combatting Anti-Blackness in Libraries." *Medical Reference Services Quarterly* 40, no. 2: 139–50. https://doi.org/10.1080/02763869.2021.1903276.

Reale, M. 2017. *Becoming a Reflective Librarian and Teacher: Strategies for Mindful Academic Practice*. Chicago: American Library Association.

Scholarly Kitchen. "Revisiting—On Being Excluded: Testimonies by People of Color in Scholarly Publishing." *Scholarly Kitchen*, June 18, 2020. https://scholarlykitchen.sspnet.org/2020/06/18/revisiting-on-being-excluded-testimonies-by-people-of-color-in-scholarly-publishing/.

Schon, D. A. 1984. *The Reflective Practitioner: How Professionals Think in Action*. Vol. 5126. New York: Basic Books.

Sealey-Ruiz, Y. 2021. *Racial Literacy: A Policy Research Brief*. James R. Squire Office of the National Council of Teachers of English. https://ncte.org/wp-content/uploads/2021/04/SquireOfficePolicyBrief_RacialLiteracy_April2021.pdf.

Sue, D. W. 2013. *Race Talk and the Conspiracy of Silence: Understanding and Facilitating Difficult Dialogues on Race*. Hoboken: Wiley.

Taylor, R. J., L. M. Chatters, and C. J. Cross. "Taking Diversity Seriously: Within-group Heterogeneity in African American Extended Family Support Networks." *Journal of Marriage and Family* 83, no. 5 (2021): 1349–72. https://doi.org/10.1111/jomf.12783.

Taylor, R. J., A. D. Skipper, C. J. Cross, H. O. Taylor, and L. M. Chatters. "Racial/Ethnic Variation in Family Support: African Americans, Black Caribbeans, and Non-Latino Whites." *Journal of Marriage and Family* 84, no. 4 (2022): 1002–23. https://doi.org/10.1111/jomf.12846.

University of Utah. 2020. "Indigenous Land Acknowledgment Statement." Office of the President, October. https://president.utah.edu/indigenous-land-acknowledgment.

Watson, J. 2001. "Autoethnography." In *Encyclopedia of Life Writing: Autobiographical and Biographical Forms*, edited by M. Jolly. New York: Routledge.

Willocks, H. W. 1995. *The Umbilical Cord: The History of the United States Virgin Islands from Pre-Columbian Era to the Present*. 2nd ed. Harold W. L. Willocks.

Yosso, T., et al. 2009. "Critical Race Theory, Racial Microaggressions, and Campus Racial Climate for Latina/o Undergraduates." *Harvard Educational Review* 79, no. 4: 659–91.

3

Getting Past "Approachability"

What Cultural Humility Brings to Library and Information Education

LILIANA MONTOYA AND SARAH POLKINGHORNE

PROVIDING LIBRARY SERVICE MEANS INTERACTING WITH PEOPLE IN particular ways. How do library workers *learn how to interact* with people? Just as important, how do library workers *learn how to think about* their interactions at work? As students, many begin to explore these questions in their programs of study, including (but not limited to) ALA-accredited master's degrees. Learning about interpersonal interactions in a service context is core for students, whether their program teaches "reference services" as traditionally understood, or "information services" more broadly. In this chapter, we argue that both students and instructors benefit when cultural humility is incorporated into learning about information services.

Learning about cultural humility is beneficial for two reasons. First, it problematizes narrow, conventional ideas about what makes good service, such as the amorphous quality of "approachability." And second, a cultural humility approach provides students with practical, engaging ways to think about interpersonal interactions in a service context. Discussing cultural humility in class is a way to discuss matters of power and privilege that are always functioning in information services, but are also largely absent from the most influential guiding documents often encountered by students. After providing some background to begin this chapter, we each share our experience of discussing cultural humility within the context of a first-year required graduate course on information services. Liliana writes from the point of view of a student, while Sarah writes as the course instructor.

"Approachability": Service Is Not as Straightforward as It May Seem

Certain qualities and practices—such as a welcoming tone and body language, and open-ended, nonjudgmental questioning—are traditional elements of good library service. These qualities are codified by professional bodies and in mainstream textbooks. We discuss them briefly here in order to contextualize cultural humility as an important intervention in, and alternative to, predominant articulations of good service. The most prominent example of a codification of good service is the Reference and User Services Association's *Guidelines for Behavioral Performance of Reference and Information Service Providers* (2013). The RUSA *Guidelines*, as they are known, do not formally regulate service, but they do influence library workers' and administrators' notions of normal, good library service. This influence certainly extends beyond American borders into our Canadian context.

Whether in library technician programs or graduate information studies programs, instructors who teach about the *Guidelines* should offer opportunities for students to question, and not just absorb, RUSA's advice. An important example here is the concept of "approachability," enshrined in the first guideline, "Visibility/Approachability." The current *Guidelines*, like the previous version from 2004, are unequivocal on approachability's importance: "It is essential that the reference librarian be approachable" (para. 8). We are advised that "the librarian's first step in initiating the reference transaction is to make the patron feel comfortable in a situation that can be perceived as intimidating, confusing, or overwhelming" (para. 8). Approachability is framed as so important that it can make or break a reference conversation: as RUSA emphasizes, "the librarian's initial response in any reference situation sets the tone for the entire communication process and influences the depth and level of interaction" (para. 8).

Have you ever tried to define *approachability*? If we are to become approachable, we must know what this means. According to RUSA's *Guidelines* (2013), approachability is multiple things. First, it is a *quality* one can embody, emerging from library workers' placement ("highly visible"), posture ("poised"), and appearance ("easily identifiable"). This quality is also embodied through *action*, or, more precisely, a series of actions. RUSA reminds us that library workers must "make the patron feel comfortable," provide an appropriate "initial response in any reference situation," and "approach patrons and offer assistance." In other words, RUSA indicates that in order to *be approachable*, one must *approach patrons*. According to RUSA, approachability is something that we *do* as well as something that we *are*.

Similarly, approachability is emphasized in mainstream textbooks, such as *Reference and Information Services: An Introduction* (Bopp and Smith 2011; Wong and Saunders 2020). In this textbook's fourth-edition chapter on "The Reference Interview" (2011), the authors Kathleen Kern and Beth Woodard echo the RUSA *Guidelines*. They frame approachability as a matter of "first impressions" and "how the librarian first appears to users," which "will affect their attitude toward the librarian and may shape the phrasing of their questions; it may sway a user's decision to ask a question at all" (62). As with the RUSA *Guidelines*, approachability is framed as essential, but the resulting advice seems easy by comparison: make eye contact, and remember that "a smile goes a long way" (62). It would be understandable if this advice strikes you as not just easy, but perhaps *too easy*. Crucially, Kern and Woodard hint at the core issue with approachability, the one that cultural humility helps us discuss in the classroom—that is, approachability is not just about what we do and how we are, but how we are perceived. They rightly advise that approachability is not simply how we appear, but how we "first appear *to users*" (62; emphasis added).

This is a really important point, but Kern and Woodard do not unpack it, nor do they expand on their advice to "smile." Their straightforward advice does make sense in a basic operational way. As Laura Saunders (2020, 51) points out in the latest edition of this same textbook, "Most reference interactions begin with a patron approaching the reference librarian with a question." In other words, in order for patrons to receive service, they must (generally speaking) decide to approach a staff member. Therefore, library workers should do what they can to encourage and enable this moment of first contact. This is not a point of contention.

However, as Kern and Woodard hint at, what all this advice avoids is that approachability is determined not by staff, but by patrons. As a quality that library workers may embody, approachability exists only if it is perceived as such by other people. Related qualities, such as "visibility," are more objective: here we can ask (and answer), are library workers located in a physical or digital space where they can be found, or are they not? By contrast, when a patron is determining whether or not a library worker seems approachable, it is very unlikely that they're making this determination only on the basis of whether or not they receive a smile. Being approachable is like being intimidating—whether or not I am intimidating, regardless of my intent, depends on whether or not somebody else feels intimidated. By glossing over the central role and potential challenges of patron perceptions and biases, the advice of RUSA, and of related textbooks, is not only partial, but also reductive, in ways that are potentially harmful. It is one thing to advise students to "be approachable" and quite another to have a substantial, inclusive conversation about what it means *to be perceived as approachable* by patrons. For students, an unquestioning introduction to guidelines such as RUSA's, and strictures such as "approachability," leaves them less prepared than they should be to face interpersonal interactions with patrons. This is true for both racialized and white students.

This is where cultural humility comes in. Our experience in class is that cultural humility encourages sensitivity to power dynamics and to the diversity of people's experiences, including both staff and patrons. Incorporating cultural humility into a conversation about what it means to provide good information services leads to richer discussions and, for students, the beginning of an ongoing practice of reflecting on their own positionality and the partiality of their expertise.

Our Context: A Required Graduate Course, during the COVID-19 Pandemic

In the fall session 2020, Sarah, as professor for the course, proposed the reflection and discussion on cultural humility within the context of the course Information Resource Discovery in the University of Ottawa's School of Information Studies. This required core course provides a theoretical and practical basis for students to interact with different user communities, to identify and learn about information needs, and to search strategies and techniques, ethical issues, and evaluation methods. Within this frame, cultural humility was presented as a key resource in the information-mediation process and services to facilitate information access. Cultural humility was discussed in the first week devoted to information services, just after fundamentals of information searching (e.g., search techniques) and information behaviour* (e.g., concepts such as relevance and uncertainty) had been introduced. This course was offered online due to the COVID-19 pandemic. Its structure was mainly asynchronous, with students partaking in activities and discussions most weeks.

*Canadian spelling has been retained in this chapter.

The following sections offer, on the one hand, a student's perspective on the significance of learning about cultural humility for her professional practice. On the other hand, we also present the instructor's reflection on teaching about cultural humility and challenging students to incorporate this theoretical approach in their future information service interactions. By sharing these experiences, we aim to spark curiosity for other instructors and students who might have an interest in exploring cultural humility in their teaching and learning processes.

Liliana's Student Experience

When I enrolled in the class Information Resource Discovery, I assumed that the course content would be mainly learning about information search techniques and information topics focused on locating and using information and library resources. After glancing at the course's syllabus, I also thought we were going to discuss how to provide service by professionally engaging with patrons and showing credibility. As the course progressed, we started to have discussions about deeper ethical aspects involved in the information service interaction with patrons and the concept of cultural humility. I felt profoundly touched by how meaningful this concept was, since I am part of a minority and I have experienced situations where my cultural and linguistic backgrounds have influenced how others relate with me in biased ways.

The following paragraphs highlight three key elements that I have learned from cultural humility for my future professional practice. First, while the concept of cultural humility originated in healthcare, it is a relevant concept to be applied in the information studies field, given the diverse populations that we serve and the power imbalances that are potentially present in any service-providing interaction. Cultural humility has taught me to expect and appreciate diversity in my profession. We need to use a culturally humble approach to patrons' unique identities (e.g., race, class, culture, language, sexual orientation, immigration status) if we want to establish clear communication, pay close attention to their information needs, and cultivate respectful partnerships with them. It is unproductive to assume that we understand others' cultural backgrounds or experiences based on our prior knowledge, experience, or training.

Second, since cultural humility entails self-awareness and openness, it helps us look closely at our thoughts and behaviours and recognize how they can be related to our (sub)conscious learned values and attitudes. When these latter clash in some way with those of our patrons, we may have the tendency to limit our thoughts and interactions, still based on our biases and assumptions. Having discussions related to information service interaction in class, we had the opportunity to reflect on how often we tend to judge others when we do not agree with them or do not understand them, and, by doing so, we close opportunities for effective communication and partnership. Cultural humility allows one to be "flexible and humble enough to let go of the false sense of security that stereotyping brings" (Tervalon and Murray-García 1998, 119). Rather, approach the user with a sense of listening and openness; for example asking questions when uncertain, expressing curiosity and interest about their cultural worldview to help us understand their information needs and develop a strong working alliance with patrons who may be socioculturally different from us and have different personal experiences from ours.

Lastly, I learned that cultural humility represents a constant process with continual self-observation and reflection to grapple with our attitudes and prejudice. As the authors propose, cultural humility "incorporates a lifelong commitment to self-evaluation and critique, to redressing the power imbalances in a relationship, and to developing mutually beneficial and non-paternalistic partnerships with communities on behalf of individuals and defined populations" (Tervalon and Murray-García 1998, 123). Continually reviewing our internal thoughts in any service interaction, we may be able to acknowledge and work on putting aside our judgments and biases towards our patrons. Therefore, we can positively concentrate on assisting our patrons' information needs. As a student, discussing cultural humility helped me articulate theory, content, and practice to develop an ethical practice in my future service-providing career.

Sarah's Instructor Experience

Preparing to teach in fall 2020, the notions of good service that I learned as a student—"approachability" being a prominent example—seemed pointedly inadequate for 2020. I knew that there must be a fresher, more sophisticated way of thinking about the interpersonal interactions that form the basis of information services. Further, avoiding ubiquitous structural concerns such as power and privilege seemed impossible, or at least, unpalatable.

Knowing that librarianship is still predominantly made up of white women, I wanted to introduce students to a heuristic that would give them a way to discuss the inherent partiality of expertise and the fact that people have very different life experiences and positionalities, and further, that acknowledging these facts makes our services better, in the sense that it becomes more sensitive, responsive, and responsible to our communities. No matter how virtuous and appealing we perceive librarianship to be as a profession, we must become comfortable with the fact that our expertise is inherently partial, and commit to developing and maintaining an interpersonal stance that is other-focused. This is important if we are to unlearn and interrupt ways of making assumptions and interpreting other people's words and actions in unhelpful and potentially harmful ways.

I assigned Hurley, Kostelecky, and Townsend's paper on cultural humility (2019) as a required reading in the same week that I assigned the RUSA *Guidelines*. This was our first week discussing information services, week five of a twelve-week course. I introduced the RUSA *Guidelines* as exemplifying current, mainstream thinking about what makes a person good at providing information services. I introduced cultural humility alongside the *Guidelines*. I framed a cultural humility mindset as preferable to the behavioural mindset apparent in the *Guidelines*, and as preferable to the idea of "cultural competence" that has been more prominent in libraries. As always, I asked students to think about the conceptual underpinnings of our readings—the assumptions, values, and worldviews reflected in them. The third element this week was a guest lecture from Kirk MacLeod, a colleague who spoke about his journey to librarianship and his experiences providing information services. Students completed these two readings and attended MacLeod's lecture. Next, following our usual process, I asked students to complete a creative activity, crafting a three-slide deck, on the question "What, in your view, is the most important lesson to take away from this week's readings and lecture, and why?" Students shared their slide decks online, perused one another's work, and discussed their observations and insights for the rest of the week.

Although I make a point of not "helicoptering" over asynchronous online class discussion, it did become immediately clear to me that this week's discussion was richer for the inclusion of cultural humility than it would have been without this concept. Some students—in particular, racialized students—spoke generously about their experiences of having been disempowered in the past, and they often voiced distinctive perspectives on cultural humility. The concept of cultural humility sensitized many students to the varying circulation of power within service interactions. Students noted that applying a cultural humility approach to information services may involve situations where they, as the librarian, are the more powerful person in the conversation, such as if they are working as a public librarian supporting members of the public in a downtown branch. However, students observed, they might also find themselves providing service in circumstances where they held less power than their patrons—working as a librarian in a law firm was mentioned as a context in which the distribution of power would tend to favour the patrons rather than the librarians. What role can cultural humility play in these different service contexts? Why and how should we enact cultural humility in contexts where we need to establish, rather than relinquish, our authority as experts? These thought-provoking questions fueled the week's discussion and enriched the rest of the course as well.

Benefits of a Cultural Humility Approach

Considering that new information professionals will interact with multicultural populations from diverse ethnicities, genders, religions, socioeconomic statuses, sexual orientations, and more, we foresee several distinctive benefits of implementing a cultural humility approach, including:

PROMOTES SELF-REFLECTION

Information service providers have opportunities to practice cultural humility in every interaction with the users. Learning about cultural humility prepares information professionals and students to engage in an active process of self-awareness and self-evaluation to recognize preconceived notions and ideas that we may hold. Rather than assuming we understand others' cultural backgrounds or experiences based on our prior knowledge, experience, or training, we should approach patrons with a full engagement to listening and openness. For instance, instead of jumping to conclusions of what we think we understand, we could ask questions when uncertain, express curiosity, and show interest in the client's cultural worldview to help us understand their information needs and develop a strong working alliance with them. Cultural humility encourages us to look inward to our own response when providing information service. We can then realize that cultural stereotyping will only hinder our goals in helping patrons find information and resources that meet their educational, professional, and recreational needs.

PROVIDES NEW WAYS TO THINK ABOUT SERVICE QUALITY AND IMPROVEMENT

Service is widely codified as a core value of librarianship. Library workers provide the "highest level of service [and] strive for excellence in the profession by maintaining and enhancing our own knowledge and skills" (ALA 2006). Practicing cultural humility allows emerging information professionals to think about good service as reflected in the presence of ethical relationships grounded in empathy, respect, and critical self-reflection. Cultural humility "involves the ability to maintain an interpersonal stance that is other-oriented (or open to the other) in relation to aspects of cultural identity that are most important to the [other]" (Hook et al. 2013, 354). By focusing on an attitude of openness and a willingness to listen, learn, collaborate, and negotiate with others, students can practice communicating and offering holistic services that are patron-centred. These values, in turn, can ground new perspectives in service assessment and improvement. Rather than solely counting interactions or documenting reference conversations in terms of information exchanged transactionally, a cultural humility approach encourages different metrics, such as adequate staffing (so staff are not rushed or endangered) and the quality of patron experiences across all groups and needs.

ENCOURAGES AWARENESS OF PARTIAL EXPERTISE

Acting with cultural humility allows information professionals to cultivate the awareness of having partial expertise when we interact with patrons. While the information service professional's mission is to help users in their information search, our perspective is not the only one we should consider, since the user is the expert in his own culture, values, and information needs. Recognizing partial expertise helps us put into perspective our mission: to be a resource for patrons not only in that moment, but also for their ongoing learning. It is essential to engage with the user with an interpersonal stance of humility and openness, rather than from a superior role as the expert. Lacking cultural humility can lead information professionals to make quick judgments on users' information needs, which, in turn, will affect our relationship with patrons. Asking questions to better understand and engage with the user, we can determine what is important to them; we can work on power imbalances and motivate them to feel they are equal participants in the interaction.

Conclusion

A discussion of cultural humility in a graduate information services course raises two more key issues: safety and expertise. It is important to note that, when introducing cultural humility to students, adopting a cultural humility approach to service does not mean that library staff should be so patron-focused as to neglect or compromise their fundamental workplace safety. For example, all library staff deserve to work free from patron-perpetrated sexual harassment, which is widespread but rarely documented (Oliphant et al. 2021). Similarly, a cultural humility view, with its focus on understanding others' perspectives, does not imply that library workers' professional expertise does not matter. In fact, awareness of cultural humility within class discussions enables more complex discussions about topics such as boundaries and authority. This is because any careful, honest discussion about cultural humility is in part a discussion about power and privilege.

In this chapter, we've argued for the enriching benefits of incorporating cultural humility into a required graduate course on information services. Cultural humility is a distinctly helpful approach because it provokes and centres our consideration of others, including ways of being and communicating during interactions where we may share little in common with our counterpart. Cultural humility is user-centredness in action, articulated in a way that does not reduce the complexities or challenges of this way of working. Even as cultural humility does focus on the work and relations of individual librarians, it remains very compatible with more structure-focused lenses, such as critical race theory, which some students did discuss and explore in this course. Even as students undertake important exploration and critique through approaches such as critical race theory, they still, simultaneously, need everyday ways to think about relating to others within their professional work. Cultural humility provides this. And it does so by enabling reflection, introspection, and other-focused insights, rather than by dispensing ambiguous behavioural prescriptions like "approachability." In other words, cultural humility represents, and enables, progress. It belongs in LIS curricula, now and in the future.

Summary

- Cultural humility is an approach that should be introduced to LIS students learning about interpersonal interactions (stance) in the information services context.
- Cultural humility enables discussion among students about their varying subject positions and the diverse challenges they face in becoming a provider of information services.
- Cultural humility provides a bridge from inwardly, individually focused introspection toward sensitivity to larger structures as required and encouraged by other important approaches, such as critical race theory.

Questions for Reflection and Discussion

1. How does the process of embodying a cultural humility approach differ depending on one's identity, past experiences, and present context?

2. How does the adoption of a cultural humility approach vary depending on how much power different people have within any given interaction?

Resource

Hodge, T. 2019. "Integrating Cultural Humility into Public Services Librarianship." *International Information & Library Review* 51, no. 3: 268–74. https://doi.org/10.1080/10572317.2019.1629070.

For another reading on cultural humility that would work well as a basis for discussion with LIS students, we recommend this paper by Twanna Hodge.

REFERENCES

American Library Association (ALA). 2006. *Core Values of Librarianship.* http://www.ala.org/advocacy/intfreedom/statementspols/corevalues.

Bopp, R. E., and L. C. Smith. 2011. *Reference and Information Services: An Introduction.* 4th ed. Santa Barbara: Libraries Unlimited.

Hook, J. N., D. E. Davis, J. Owen, E. L. Worthington Jr., and S. O. Utsey. 2013. "Cultural Humility: Measuring Openness to Culturally Diverse Clients." *Journal of Counseling Psychology* 60:353–66. https://doi.org/10.1037/a0032595.

Hurley, D. A., S. R. Kostelecky, and L. Townsend. 2019. "Cultural Humility in Libraries." *Reference Services Review* 47, no. 4: 544–55. https://doi.org/10.1108/RSR-06-2019-0042.

Oliphant, T., D. Allard, A. Lieu, and K. Mallach. 2021. "Naming Patron-Perpetrated Sexual Harassment in Libraries." *Proceedings of the Annual Conference of the Canadian Association for Information Science*, May. https://journals.library.ualberta.ca/ojs.cais-acsi.ca/index.php/cais-asci/article/view/1207/1043.

Reference and User Services Association. 2013. *Guidelines for Behavioral Performance of Reference Service and Information Service Providers.* Chicago: American Library Association, May 28. https://www.ala.org/rusa/resources/guidelines / guidelinesbehavioral.

Tervalon, M., and J. Murray-García. 1998. "Cultural Humility Versus Cultural Competence: A Critical Distinction in Defining Physician Training Outcomes in Multicultural Education." *Journal of Health Care for the Poor and Underserved* 9, no. 2: 117–25. https://doi.org/10.1353/hpu.2010.0233.

Wong, M. A., and L. Saunders, eds. 2020. *Reference and Information Services: An Introduction.* 6th ed. Santa Barbara: Libraries Unlimited.

PART II

REFLECTIVE PRACTICE

4

Reflections on Culturally Humble Practice in Bibliography, Scholarship, and Readers' Advisory

A Case Study

MICHAEL MUNGIN

Background and Self-Reflection on Cultural Humility

In my practice of library instruction, I have started discussing positionality at the top of instruction sessions. Academic librarians are frequently asked to do one-shot lessons, often centered around an assignment or a few specific library tools. As effective as these sessions can be, they are also occasionally mystifying to students. We expect them to trust our expertise and intentions despite sometimes meeting us just once. The students don't necessarily know anything about their librarian, even our credentials. Indeed, I am still met with surprised reactions when I communicate that librarians usually require a master's degree as a point of entry into the profession. To address this, I enjoy opening sessions with new students by briefly discussing myself, my background, my education and employment history, and my reasons for becoming and staying a librarian. Finally, I address how all that lived experience informs what I teach and how, and I ask them to practice reflecting on how their own positionality might affect how they receive what I teach.

For sure, some students seem bemused by this approach. It must confound their expectations. They think they are going to receive a highly specific lecture, only to encounter a librarian talking about himself for two to three minutes. Indeed, culturally humble practice is often characterized by *avoiding* self-focus (Tangney 2000; Hurley, Kostelecky, and Townsend 2019). However, I conclude by posing the rhetorical question: "So, why do you think I'm going into all of this?" Students and professors pick up pretty quickly that I'm opening the door for dialogue, participation, even disagreement with what I'm presenting. Hurley, Kostelecky, and Townsend (2019) describe how a librarian's own positionality can complicate our efforts to center the communities we serve. In my experience in academic libraries, college and university students are generally up to the task of approaching that consideration head-on. Anecdotally, I have found that students and professors generally appreciate peeling away the fallacy of library or librarian "neutrality," and the acknowledgment that we each bring all our lived experiences into the classroom. Not only does this practice give students a chance to participate in a self-reflection of how all our "backgrounds, experiences and expectations impact [the] situation" (Rogers 2018) we're in, but I generally find that students are more eager to participate in the active learning process after this introduction, and they are also seemingly more likely to contact me afterward.

So—why am I going into all of this? Reflective practice, characterized by ongoing rumination and self-appraisal of how one's experiences, thoughts, and behaviors affect one's work, is a crucial aspect of bringing humility into one's practice (Hodge 2019; Tervalon and Murray-García 1998). This chapter will detail the conception of a bibliographic online resource I created that engages with and centers the history of American cinema for, by, and about queer and trans people of color (QTPOC). For the context of this chapter to be effectively communicated—especially through the lens of cultural humility—I feel compelled to provide some autobiographical information in order to clearly address my own positionality, not unlike my classroom primer.

I grew up in south Seattle in the 1980s and '90s, lower-middle class with two working parents and two older siblings. The area was a vibrant, fairly progressive, diverse space. My schools were full of different languages and cultures. Though I'm Black and my parents are Baptist, for a number of complicated reasons, I attended a predominantly Japanese American Methodist church. The opportunities to experience and appreciate cultural and ethnic diversity were omnipresent in my formative years, which I've always felt grateful for.

However, as many opportunities as I had to build both self-awareness and humility with regard to race, religion, and ethnicity, I was not so fortunate when it came to another important aspect of my identity and experience: my sexual orientation. Even though Seattle was progressive compared to most American cities, I was still surrounded by homophobia. It was present at home with my family, at school with my classmates, in religious settings, and certainly all over the media. Even in the news, when queer* people did appear, it was frequently through the traumatic lens of HIV/AIDS, a disease that has taken family and friends; it was through the violent lens of assault, like the beating of Matthew Shepard, whose murder became international news just as I was beginning the process of coming out to family and friends; it was through the lens of hatred, as political, religious, and community leaders freely and casually slandered and vilified entire swaths of queer people with little significant or meaningful censure outside the queer community itself.

Hurley, Kostelecky, and Townsend (2019) discuss how mainstream media and depictions of marginalized groups often perpetuate false, painful, and traumatic narratives that are all too easy for people, marginalized *and* mainstream, to internalize to potentially great harm. In moments of self-reflection, I *still* find remnants of those spurious narratives that I am forced to continue to unlearn before they damage my mental health or guide me down any number of paths that might be destructive to my personal and professional lives. Reducing the harm of these stigmas, stereotypes, and misrepresentations is one of the natural and beneficial outcomes of culturally humble practice. To this end, Hurley, Kostelecky, and Townsend also point out that libraries are uniquely situated to "lead the effort to dismantle these dominant stereotypical narratives through the provision of accurate information thus supporting both cultural pride and culturally humble practices" (552).

This resonates with my experience significantly. What I like about this facet of cultural humility is that it draws attention to the significant importance of representation. "Representation matters" has become a common rallying cry in recent years. Though the phrase is increasingly misapplied (Jackson 2020), it speaks to some crucial aspects of the services that librarians and libraries provide to our user communities. The collections that libraries and librarians build must speak well and speak fairly to the experiences of the user population. In fact, when I reflect on my career, it is clear to me that my "librarian origin story" is something of a natural outgrowth of good cultural humility practice, though no one involved would have necessarily called it that at the time.

*I want to honor and acknowledge that *queer* as an identifier is still controversial. Many in the LGBTQ+ community have negative, and even traumatic, connotations attached to this word. I use it as a reclaimed term of empowerment and solidarity, but I do not want to disregard the potential aversion to this identifier.

Most, if not all, of my initial counterprogramming against those traumatic mainstream narratives of LGBTQ+ and QTPOC folks came in the form of books and films I discovered at the library. I discovered the life-changing books of Black, Latinx, and Asian American writers like James Earl Hardy, Michael Nava, Justin Chin, Alice Walker, and E. Lynn Harris. Crucially for me, I soon discovered the Seattle Public Library (SPL) actively collected feature films and documentaries. I found the seminal films of creators like Marlon Riggs, who discussed those traumas like HIV/AIDS and homophobia not through the detached or hostile gaze of the "mainstream," but through the lens of members of the communities I imagined I would someday navigate and belong to. The library was, in many ways, my only point of access to these worlds as an early teenager. I had few openly gay peers. I had no money to buy the books I self-consciously and surreptitiously perused at Borders and Barnes & Noble. The library was my gateway, allowing me to see the lives other QTPOC had built so I could project into the future the kind of life I wanted to build. Representation facilitates opportunities for thought, reflection, challenge, and validation. "Representation matters" because it allows one to imagine futures for one's self—a powerful feeling that QTPOC people don't often get to take for granted.

Devine and colleagues (2012) discuss how individuation (seeking out individual voices from within an outgroup as opposed to relying on stereotypes of that group) and perspective-taking (an empathetic attempt to view the world through the perspective on an outgroup in the first person) are key techniques in reducing bias and discrimination. Reflecting on my formative years, I believe these techniques were what I was using books and films for—as a kind of salve for the internalized homophobia that far too many cultural and societal influences cultivate in the minds of LGBTQ+ youth. My love and passion for cinema in particular grew out of this self-empowerment and expansion of perspective that the art form instilled in me. The Pulitzer Prize-winning film critic Roger Ebert stated in a 2005 speech that he believed films were "empathy machines":

> If it's a great movie, it lets you understand a little bit more about what it's like to be a different gender, a different race, a different age, a different economic class, a different nationality, a different profession, different hopes, aspirations, dreams and fears. It helps us to identify with the people who are sharing this journey with us. (RogerEbert.com 2018)

I would add that great films also help you understand yourself a little bit more. A character you identify with grows in the way you hope to grow; an incisive line of dialogue sticks in your brain, its depth of meaning unfurling over time as you have newer and more complex life experiences; a breathtaking piece of cinematography makes you see the world through, literally, a different lens. Films featuring QTPOC, as difficult as they could be to find, opened worlds to me when I had few other options available.

And I had help along the way. Libraries and librarians helped me find the doorways to those worlds. The staff at the local branch of the Seattle Public Library soon noticed the frequency of my visits and the insatiably rapid pace with which I consumed media. At first, I was trepidatious. I had to be judicious in who I told about my sexuality. The threat of violence, humiliation, or exclusion was very real. (I will sheepishly admit to sneaking a few books out of the library to avoid anyone knowing what I was reading . . . and then sneaking them back in at a later date.) To my great benefit, the staff still chose to engage me. Some of them made wonderful recommendations based on my interests and taste. One of the librarians, to my everlasting gratitude, showed me that all media had subject headings attached to them and that I could plug those into the online public access catalog and uncover a treasure trove of similar works. As exciting as serendipitous discovery was, the techniques the librarians taught me were different—they felt like power. I hesitate to say this about a profession already too prone toward vocational awe, but those librarians were part of a tremendous change for the better in my life.

As I suggested, I think these library staffers were engaging in some aspects of culturally humble practice. I see a stark contrast between these SPL librarians and the behavior of some school librarians, teachers, and adult influences of my youth. As I expanded my horizons as a young man, I was often presented with media that I was "supposed" to consume. I remember working up the courage to ask my middle school librarian if there were books with more diversity than the ones I was seeing. I received a baffling little lecture about how, if I really wanted to "branch out" in my reading, I shouldn't confine myself to books about people like myself, but I should "branch out" into various "classic" novels, which tended to have limited applicability to my life. When I dove into the world of cinema, I was routinely pointed toward deeply troubling "important" films like *Gone with the Wind*, *Birth of a Nation*, and *The Jazz Singer* as important touchstones. I was always deeply disappointed with these suggestions when I read and watched them. If one of the main benefits of cultural humility is its tendency to encourage lifelong learning (Tervalon and Murray-García 1998), encouraging a fourteen-year-old Black kid to watch a racially illiterate film like *Gone with the Wind* to further his appreciation of cinema is a misstep. As Hurley, Kostelecky, and Townsend (2019, 550) write, "Cultural humility . . . asks us to recognize the significance of context in our interactions." This was not accomplished in these situations.

In contrast, the SPL librarians seemed to have recognized and understood that I was on a kind of journey of self-discovery, and they identified and performed their roles in that journey. These positive formative experiences with libraries have been influential in my own goals and practice within librarianship. I have sought ways to explore and expand the small but lastingly meaningful interactions and services librarians can offer patrons who don't always feel seen by such institutions. When the opportunity arose to create a vital resource that could fulfill this goal, I decided to go for it. Ultimately, I believe the experience represented the success of a culturally humble practice of librarianship on a personal, professional, and institutional level. The rest of this chapter will focus on that project.

An Intersectional Lens: Toward a QTPOC Film Canon

BACKGROUND

At the American Library Association (ALA) Annual Conference in 2012, Kimberley Bugg, then a librarian at Villanova, presented an exciting project she had cocreated. The finished project was a thoughtful online guide to enlightening and seminal works on the topic of Black popular culture, intended to connect students to these resources (Daniel and McRae 2020). This ambitious project was funded by a Carnegie-Whitney Grant, which are monetary awards given out by ALA each year to support the creation of a bibliographic resource built around a theme (ALA, n.d.). Many of us in the session were impressed by the care and effort that had gone into the creation of this resource (now titled the Fade 2 Black Popular Culture Index). Bugg strongly encouraged those of us inspired by this work to consider pursuing such grants in the future, built around our own personal passions. Though it would be years before I could find the inspiration, time, and energy to meet that challenge, the idea had taken root.

More specific inspiration arrived with the publication of Slate's Black Film Canon in 2016, a curated list that drew attention to the seminal, influential, and unique works of Black filmmakers about Black lives—works that are frequently overlooked by awards and "mainstream" audiences, but that have been so meaningful to so many (Harris and Kois 2016). Many of the films on Slate's list had been personally meaningful to me in my own exploration of cinema (and my own self-exploration), and the project pointed me toward many cinematic gems I had yet to discover. When I discovered that no such curated, annotated resource appeared to exist for films focusing on QTPOC lives and filmmakers, the idea for my own project solidified. After applying for and securing a Carnegie-Whitney Grant of my own, I started the long, ambitious process of creating what became the QTPOC Film Canon—an annotated bibliography (or filmography) of seminal, powerful, and inspiring films that focus on the lives of queer and trans people of color (Mungin 2019a). On a personal level, this was the project that would have proven invaluable to the younger version of myself I described earlier. These films would have illuminated, taught, enriched, and radicalized that kid. I hoped it would do the same for a new generation of QTPOC youth. As much progress as we have made toward making life safer for QTPOC, there are still countless people of all ages who are looking for the voices represented in these films.

The QTPOC Film Canon went live in late 2019. After reviewing more than 170 films, I whittled the list down to about 60 of the best examples of films centering on QTPOC lives. The list has been well received by librarians, users, and even a couple of the films' directors who have discovered the resource. In order to facilitate the connection to libraries, I included resources to aid collection of the films, as well as a widget for WorldCat, the union catalog connected to the world's library holdings, so visitors could find copies of the films for free at their local library. Thus far, it has received more than seven thousand unique visitors. Though I still consider the site a work in progress, it has been modestly successful thus far. The canon can be viewed at: https://qtpocfilmcanon.squarespace.com.

Connections to Cultural Humility

Two pioneers of the study of cultural humility, Melanie Tervalon and Jann Murray-García, have discussed the concept as having three broad tenets: lifelong learning and self-reflection; recognition and redress of power imbalances; and accountability for practicing and modeling humility, at both an individual and an institutional level (Tervalon and Murray-García 1998; Chávez 2012).

LIFELONG LEARNING AND SELF-REFLECTION

Certainly, this project represents a culmination of my own dedication to self-reflection and learning. As much as this project was intended as a service to librarians and library users, it was tremendously important to me in my own journey of self-discovery that began in my teenage years. As an example, many of the films included in the canon deal with deeply disturbing subject matter, including some of the same topics that were so traumatic for me in my youth. Watching the 170-plus films I considered for inclusion in quick succession had significant impacts on my own worldview and mental health, for better and for worse. For me, one of the limitations of humility is its close connection to empathy, which can be deeply draining for those in public service roles like educators and librarians. Cultural humility can have radically positive impacts on our users and students, but it's impossible to ignore the toll that this kind of investment can take on those working in those roles.

On a more positive note, however, the canon has already drawn attention to films about issues facing QTPOC for some who weren't aware. Colleagues and friends who have watched some of the featured films have provided feedback that often touches on their ignorance of much of history and issues discussed in the films they found through the canon. Though the project was initially aimed at QTPOC and the librarians who serve them, this self-reflection and self-recognition of privilege that this project has inspired among others is another noted benefit.

RECOGNITION AND REDRESS OF POWER IMBALANCES

"Canon" is a fraught concept. Almost automatically, it assumes an imbalance of power and authority because someone or some group must declare something to be so quintessential, valuable, or seminal that its worth exists almost beyond question. Who gets to make such a determination? Midway through the project, I worried that this film canon was an overreach for one person to undertake alone. As a cisgender man, how well could I evaluate films that touched on issues affecting trans and nonbinary folks? How well could I determine if films that decentered cis men were worthy of addition to "the canon"? As a Black man, could I responsibly judge the veracity or appropriateness of a film about, for example, Chinese Americans? A misstep would put me in the same precarious position as those who canonized and recommended *Gone with the Wind* to me.

This realization inspired several additions and adjustments to this resource. Foremost among them was my inclusion of a "positionality statement." Much like I contextualize my role as an instructor in the classroom (and as the author of this chapter), it was clear to me that I likewise needed to contextualize my role as creator of this resource (Mungin 2019b). In this statement, I also invited comment, contribution, disagreement, and even collaboration—all of which I have received since the publication of the canon, ultimately to the great benefit of the resource. Tangney (2000) writes that humility, by definition, involves an ability to acknowledge one's limitations, errors, and knowledge gaps. This aspect of humility has ultimately been a boon for the project.

In fact, a prime example of a change that arose from feedback was the reframing of the entire project. "The QTPOC Film Canon" became "*Towards* a QTPOC Film Canon," which better represents the features of cultural humility I hoped would be present in this project. Interestingly, the positionality statement is one of the most visited links on the canon website. There are many possible explanations for this, but I noticed a lack of relevant examples of similar statements. It is possible that, as understanding of cultural humility and self-reflection around positionality increases in libraries, others are looking for models of how to discuss it in their educational artifacts.

INSTITUTIONAL ACCOUNTABILITY

This project could not have been completed without direct support from my professional institution. My colleagues, supervisor, and library director believed in the value and validity of this project from inception to publication. For cultural humility to gain traction in an organization, I believe this must be the case or, even better, the norm.

In order to bestow a Carnegie-Whitney Grant, ALA requires an attestation from a supervisor that the person completing the work can fit this into their work burdens, as well as an additional attestation from a colleague that the scope and labor of the work are within the abilities of the applicant. These can be potentially high bars to clear, depending on the level of support within an organization; yet, no barriers were presented to me in this process. In addition to those hurdles, I requested technology to help me view the films I hoped to review for the canon, some of which existed only in various physical media forms that require hardware to use. Furthermore, I requested two days of telework each week in the summer of 2019 to complete this work. These ambitious requests were met not with resistance, but with enthusiasm and even offers of further assistance if necessary.

This institutional response was incredibly important. An initial concern was that my colleagues and administrators, none of whom identified as QTPOC, would not fully appreciate the need for such a resource. That fear was not unfounded. There were occasional incidents of confusion or dismissal of the project. However, in general, my colleagues' own abilities to decenter themselves and their own specific lived experiences led them toward supportive action. Further, various colleagues within the University of Washington library system actively promoted the project via LibGuides, social media, displays, and word of mouth, culminating in it being featured in the university's alumni magazine. More recently, an institutional working group dedicated to digital scholarship collaborated with me in determining various aesthetic, accessibility (also related to recognizing and redressing power imbalances), and marketing improvements and initiatives that will constitute the next stages of this project. Even further, several items included in the canon were not in my library's holdings, and I was repeatedly encouraged to use a portion of my allotted collections funds to purchase them for the library.

This level of institutional support sends a message that such culturally responsive projects can find support and facilitation in our library and potentially encourages others toward such pursuits. In academic librarianship especially, scholarly projects like this are expected and often required activities for maintaining employment and attaining promotion or tenure. Yet scholarship focused on underrepresented and marginalized communities is often devalued and dismissed in academia (Riley-Reid 2017; Swanson, Tanaka, and Gonzalez-Smith 2018). Libraries must commit, as mine did, to making space for their staff to explore these scholarly avenues.

Conclusion

The creation of this scholarly resource represents one example of the kind of output that librarians in numerous different settings can create when (1) they are given the opportunity to use professional time and resources for this end, and (2) they use the model of cultural humility to analyze the potential needs of users who have been marginalized and underserved. This particular project and book chapter speak to the aspects of cultural humility that can manifest in the job responsibilities of instruction, collections, readers' advisory, professional development, and scholarship inherent to many different librarian positions. Though this one project is unique, my hope is that readers draw connections to their own work and actively seek to incorporate the lessons and concepts discussed here in their own innovative work. Librarianship lends itself to reflective and culturally humble practice, if librarians are supported in such endeavors.

Summary

- Successes and failures of cultural humility in librarians' own lived experiences can be powerful inspiration for providing innovative services.
- Power imbalances manifest in more subtle ways in library services than in other professions, but they exist nonetheless. Mindfulness and reflection around those imbalances are necessary in order to offer the highest-quality service.
- Acknowledging and reflecting on one's own positionality create opportunities for improved user engagement, innovative services, and culturally responsive practice.
- Institutional support is vital to practicing cultural humility, especially in scholarship and collections work.

Questions for Reflection and Discussion

1. Which of the cultural humility concepts discussed in this chapter can you incorporate into your practice of librarianship? Who among your colleagues can help you facilitate that? What institutional barriers exist?

___

___

___

2. Who is not reflected or represented in the collections, artifacts, and staff at the libraries you work at or patronize? What can you contribute to improving those conditions?

____

____

____

3. To what extent does self-reflection on your own history with libraries affect the work you seek to do? What experiences can you draw from that reflect both good and poor cultural humility practice? Are there lessons that can spark improvement and innovation in your own work?

____

____

____

Resources

Chávez, Vivian. 2012. "Cultural Humility (Complete)." YouTube video, posted August 9, 29:28. https://www.youtube.com/watch?v=SaSHLbS1V4w.

Cultural Humility: People, Principles and Practices is a thirty-minute documentary featuring two pioneers of cultural humility principles, Melanie Tervalon and Jann Murray-García, reflecting on their experiences and on how awareness of cultural humility has grown in twenty years. Directed by V. Chávez.

SJSU School of Information. 2020. "Integrating Cultural Humility into Librarianship." YouTube video, posted October 19, 1:00:31. https://www.youtube.com/watch?v=-kHx2GE19tI.

This lecture by Twanna Hodge serves as a valuable primer on the connections between cultural humility and the work librarians do.

REFERENCES

American Library Association. n.d. "Carnegie-Whitney Grant." Accessed July 3, 2021. https://www.ala.org/awardsgrants/carnegie-whitney-grant.

Chávez, V., dir. 2012. "Cultural Humility (Complete)." YouTube video, posted August 9, 29:28. https://www.youtube.com/watch?v=SaSHLbS1V4w.

Daniel, J., and J. McRae. 2020. "Black Pop Culture Index." Accessed July 3, 2021. https://research.auctr.edu/c.php?g=197208&p=1297307.

Devine, P. G., P. S. Forscher, A. J. Austin, and W. T. Cox. 2012. "Long-Term Reduction in Implicit Race Bias: A Prejudice Habit-Breaking Intervention." *Journal of Experimental Social Psychology* 48, no. 6: 1267–78.

Harris, A., and D. Kois. 2016. "The Black Film Canon." *Slate*, May 30. http://www.slate.com/articles/arts/cover_story/2016/05/the_50_greatest_films_by_black_directors.html.

Hodge, T. 2019. "Integrating Cultural Humility into Public Services Librarianship." *International Information & Library Review* 51, no. 3: 268–74.

Hurley, D. A., S. R. Kostelecky, and L. Townsend. 2019. "Cultural Humility in Libraries." *Reference Services Review* 47, no. 4: 544–55.

Jackson, L. M. 2020. "When 'Representation matters' Becomes a Meaningless Rallying Cry." *Vulture*, February 8. https://www.vulture.com/2020/02/representation-matters-penguin-diverse-editions.html.

Mungin, M. 2019a. "Introduction/About." An Intersectional Lens: Towards a Queer and Trans People of Color (QTPOC) Film Canon. https://qtpocfilmcanon.squarespace.com/about.

Mungin, M. 2019b. "A Positionality Statement." An Intersectional Lens: Towards a Queer and Trans People of Color (QTPOC) Film Canon. https://qtpocfilmcanon.squarespace.com/a-positionality-statement (accessed 1 July 2021).

Riley-Reid, Trevar. 2017. "Breaking Down Barriers: Making It Easier for Academic Librarians of Color to Stay." *Journal of Academic Librarianship* 43, no. 5: 392–96.

RogerEbert.com. 2018. "Roger Ebert on Empathy," April 4. https://www.rogerebert.com/empathy/video-roger-ebert-on-empathy.

Rogers, A. 2018. "Cultural Humility in Librarianship: What Is It? (A Guest Post by Adilene Rogers)." Teen Librarian Toolbox. www.teenlibrariantoolbox.com/2018/11/cultural-humility-in-librarianship-what-is-it/.

Swanson, J., A. Tanaka, and I. Gonzalez-Smith. 2018. "Lived Experience of Academic Librarians of Color." *College & Research Libraries* 79, no. 7: 876.

Tangney, J. P. 2000. "Humility: Theoretical Perspectives, Empirical Findings and Directions for Future Research." *Journal of Social and Clinical Psychology* 19, no. 1: 70–82. https://doi.org/10.1521/jscp.2000.19.1.70.

Tervalon, M., and J. Murray-García. 1998. "Cultural Humility Versus Cultural Competence: A Critical Distinction in Defining Physician Training Outcomes in Multicultural Education." *Journal of Health Care for the Poor and Underserved* 9, no. 2: 117–25. https://doi.org/10.1353/hpu.2010.0233.

Cultural Humility and Evaluating Books for Young Readers

SILVIA LIN HANICK AND KELSEY KEYES

DEVELOPING AN ATTITUDE OF CULTURAL HUMILITY WHEN ANALYZING titles for young readers requires a commitment to three areas: accuracy, decentering yourself, and mitigating power imbalances by rejecting self-focused responses such as tradition, nostalgia, and inertia. For this chapter, we draw on our eight combined years of service, including terms as committee cochairs for Rise: A Feminist Book Project for Ages 0–18, a book list of ALA's Feminist Task Force and the Social Responsibilities Round Table. We also draw on our advanced studies in literature and our experience as professional librarians and parents.

Accuracy and Completeness

A first step in using the cultural humility approach to evaluate books for young readers is to consider both the factual accuracy and the completeness of a book. Part of this process requires us to acknowledge what we don't know. It asks us to fact-check, to research, and to seek help when we reach the limits of our knowledge.

Factual accuracy can be a straightforward process. Dates, names, places, and the like should be confirmed as accurate. But a cultural humility approach asks us to go further and consider the question: If the information is incorrect, does this inaccuracy cause harm? There could be a minor mathematical error in the background of an illustration. This is a factual inaccuracy, but does it cause harm?

In contrast, harmful factual inaccuracies often reinforce dominant narratives and stereotypes. *Beautiful Shades of Brown: The Art of Laura Wheeler Waring* (Churnin 2020) celebrates Waring as an artist of the Harlem Renaissance who prevailed against systems that sought to exclude her based on race and gender. As a young girl, Waring dreamed of seeing her art in a museum. "That," the text declares, "was a crazy idea for a 10-year-old in Connecticut in 1897. . . . Nobody was going to put paintings of African Americans on museum walls!" (n.p.). This sentence is factually inaccurate: prior to 1897, the African American landscape painters Robert S. Duncanson (1821–1872) and Edward Mitchell Bannister (1828–1901) exhibited celebrated works throughout the United States and Europe. The text goes on to claim that "maybe there weren't portraits of African Americans in museums yet, but she could turn her room into a gallery." Portraits of African Americans may have been rare, but this statement is not entirely accurate either. Henry Ossawa Tanner's *The Banjo Lesson* (1893), a tender portrayal of an older Black man teaching a child to play the banjo, was admitted into the Paris Salon in 1894, then purchased and donated to the Hampton University Museum in Virginia later that year. These factual inaccuracies in *Beautiful Shades of Brown* contribute to the ongoing erasure of Black contributions to American art and culture. These sentences also illustrate how questions of accuracy contribute to power imbalances. Suggesting that Waring was "crazy" to trust in her own talent, to strive beyond her social position, and to imagine the possibility of Black liberation trivializes mental illness while promoting harmful stereotypes. Waring's ambition in the face of segregation could instead be characterized as inspiring, bold, or courageous.

A cultural humility approach, however, pushes us to consider not just whether the information presented is accurate, but also if it's complete. This is especially important in biographical profiles. Does a book present all of the person's many identities? Are some aspects left out because they may be considered unsavory, controversial, or difficult? *Rosa's Animals: The Story of Rosa Bonheur and Her Painting Menagerie* by Maryann Macdonald (2018) is a lushly illustrated middle-grade biography of the nineteenth-century artist. Though the biography carefully contextualizes Bonheur's life and work, noting her unconventional education, habit of dressing in trousers, and feminist legacy, it fails to fully acknowledge the nature of her relationships with Nathalie Micas and Anna Elizabeth Klumpke. With Micas, Bonheur became "friends for life" (31) and with Klumpke, "trusted friends" (54). Using the language of close friendship rather than decades-long romantic partnership is an act of queer erasure. Similarly, picture-book biographies of Sally Ride and Billie Jean King celebrate their accomplishments but don't often celebrate their queer identities; as librarians, we should select books about notable figures that honor the person's full story.

A cultural humility approach also asks us to question who is being promoted or included in books. There are numerous "feminist" abecedary books, and Coco Chanel is a common "C" entry. While Chanel was undoubtedly a remarkable businesswoman and fashion designer, she also collaborated with and spied for the Nazis during World War II. Is she really a figure we want a new generation of children to admire? Anthologies profiling notable women—which have become extremely popular in recent years—are another fraught area requiring careful reading. *Women in Art: 50 Fearless Creatives Who Inspired the World* (Ignotofsky 2019) offers an opportunity to consider how we balance factual accuracy against respectful treatment of trans identities. The entry for the composer Wendy Carlos makes the choice to reference her deadname while noting in the same sentence that "she always knew she was a trans woman" (Ignotofsky 2019, 99). Indeed, Carlos has long shared that she was certain of her gender identity from childhood; by age five, she reported, she was "*convinced* [she] was a little girl" (Bell 1979, n.p.). Deadnaming, or using a trans person's birth name, in this instance negates Carlos's gender identity and contributes more harm than accuracy.

A cultural humility approach to assessing books asks us to fact-check fastidiously and to locate the limitations of our ready knowledge. This approach also encourages a healthy skepticism of information published in books for young readers. We can't know everything or catch every error. Adopting an attitude of humility allows us to learn and grow. It allows us to say, "I didn't know that, but now that I do, I will handle this book differently."

GUIDING QUESTIONS: ACCURACY

- Are facts, dates, and translations accurate?
- For nonfiction books, are biographical profiles presented with full acknowledgement of a person's many identities? Are historical events recounted without white supremacy or Eurocentrism? Is there inaccuracy by omission?
- For fiction books, are the characters accurate to their time, place, culture, and identity?

Decenter Yourself as a Reader

A second step in using a cultural humility approach is to decenter yourself as a reader. S. R. Ranganathan proposed in 1931, "Every reader his or her book" and "every book its reader." As librarians selecting books for young readers, we read not only for ourselves, but also for our communities, in all of their visible and invisible diversities. To meet our communities' needs, we must decenter our own reaction to a book to consider how someone unlike us might receive it. Too often books assume a white, male, neurotypical, middle-class, able-bodied, cisgender, or heterosexual audience. All readers become accustomed to this default, regardless of how different our own nexus of identities might be.

Consider a modern storytime classic, *Ten Little Fingers and Ten Little Toes.* Published in 2008 by the author Mem Fox and the illustrator Helen Oxenbury, the picture book is celebrated for its racial diversity. The book travels between urban and rural settings, introducing babies with a range of skin tones from many countries, with an ideal rhythm for reading aloud. There is much to love—for white, able-bodied audiences. In an interview with *Reading Rockets,* Fox gives an origin story for the book. During a signing event, she looked out at her audience, noting that "all the babies, you know, had ten little fingers and ten little toes. It didn't matter who they belonged to or what color they were" (Reading Rockets 2014, 0:58:00).

However, more than two thousand babies born in the United States every year have congenital limb differences (CDC 2020). That means not all babies *have* ten little fingers and ten little toes. To suggest otherwise denies the experience of those parents and children while stigmatizing, rather than normalizing, limb differences to able-bodied children. Further, the text and illustrations exoticize Black, brown, and Asian babies. A baby of Asian descent, drawn with slanted slits for eyes, "was born far away," while a white baby "was born on the very next day," setting up whiteness as local and familiar. A dark-skinned baby in a shalwar kameez "was born in the hills." Another baby, likely meant to be Inuit, was "born on the ice" and stands next to an emperor penguin chick, though the Inuit people inhabit the Arctic and emperor penguins the Antarctic. A dark-skinned baby in a tunic was born "in a tent." In contrast, babies from Western settings (including one Black baby) appear in jeans, dresses, or other modern clothing and are not placed in distant, rural locations.

At the close of the book, the narration shifts from third person to first person, with the narrator revealed to be the mother of the last baby introduced, a "sweet little child" who is "mine, all mine." This expression brings the reader (and their child) into the story; this story is about and for *you*. That the audience is represented by a white mother and white baby reinforces this book's limitations. We are supposed to see ourselves in this mother and baby, just as we see Black, brown, and Asian babies as foreigners, trapped in time and place.

Global Baby Boys (2014), and others in the series, takes a different approach to representing diversity. Each of the board books features photographs of babies from around the world. Using photographs ensures that racial facial features are neither flattened nor exaggerated as a part of an illustration style. While babies are dressed in clothing typical of their culture, they occupy the same contemporary time period. Most babies wear cozy pajamas or variations on shorts and a T-shirt. Where deviations occur, they are not isolated to a specific country: a baby from Mexico is photographed with a tasseled straw hat, a baby from Guatemala is wrapped in a colorful blanket, and a baby from the United States smiles from under a red firefighter's helmet. Boys are presented as real children, from specific countries; their depictions do not rely on stereotypes.

Other excellent examples of books that challenge these "default" categories can be found in the All About Clive and All About Rosa book series by Jessica Spanyol. The books have a simple art style and short, basic text, but they do a wonderful job of including children who have a wide variety of skin tones, hair textures, and names that suggest nonwhite backgrounds. Children who wear glasses and who use wheelchairs are included. Moreover, the books normalize all toys (dolls, trucks, dinosaurs) and all kinds of play as being for *all* children, regardless of gender. Rosa, a girl, crashes cars, makes noise, stomps, digs, and yells. Clive, a boy, takes care of baby dolls, feeding them, taking them for rides in a stroller, and tucking them into bed. The stories are not *about* diversity, ability, or gender. They simply illustrate a variety of children playing, imagining, and living.

Thus far, we have analyzed books to show the value of cultural humility. Below, we share personal reflections on how the cultural humility approach has helped us, as librarians and as people, build a habit of decentering ourselves as the reader.

CULTURAL HUMILITY IN PRACTICE: KELSEY

While I think of myself as an astute reader, especially when it comes to issues of gender and sexism in books, I am still constantly learning. A book I struggled with, *How Mamas Love Their Babies* (Fitzgerald 2018), is an excellent example of how I still, without realizing it, habitually revert to the middle-class, religious ethos I was raised in. I thought the book was nice enough; I appreciated the diversity included in the illustrations and thought the message was lovely, although I did wonder if the '70s-photo-pastiche illustrations, with their muted colors, would interest children. However, when I got to a page that showed a woman outside of a strip club with the text "Some mamas dance all night long in special shoes. It's hard work!" (n.p.), I was shocked. It felt so out of place. I instantly imagined reading this book to my own children and then having tricky conversations with them about stripping and/or sex work. I could not imagine this book being read out loud for storytime at my local public library. Parents would be outraged! I had a hard time even imagining the book lasting long on the shelves—surely my conservative state would challenge the book. While I would disagree with such a challenge, I did question the appropriateness of casually including sex work in a children's picture book.

What I was doing here, of course, was centering *myself* in reading the book. Even though I consider myself sex-positive, my knee-jerk reaction was to shield my children from the book and question its appropriateness for any child. What I was not considering was the number of families who might appreciate having their lived experiences included in a children's book without shame or stigma attached. I was not considering the children who might read the book and excitedly recognize their own mamas in it, who might happily say, "Like your special shoes, Mama!" and see this as a way their mama works hard and loves them. When this different perspective was pointed out to me, I became embarrassed by how puritanical my own reaction to the book had been. I questioned my class privilege and assumptions about sex work. This wasn't bad—it was a useful opportunity for me to listen, reflect, and learn so that I would improve. We all have biases, but we can strive to decenter our own reaction to a book and consider how people unlike us might experience it.

CULTURAL HUMILITY IN PRACTICE: SILVIA

Think back: When did you first see yourself on the cover of a book? When did you look at a character on the cover of a book and think, "Oh, that could be me"? This did not happen for me until I was in my thirties.

In my practice of cultural humility within librarianship, I strive to select books that deliver moments of recognition and belonging for readers who seldom see honest stories written about themselves. As someone who has not, until recently, seen my Taiwanese American identity centered in literature for young readers, I can empathize with, and speak to, this experience of erasure. Growing up without seeing myself reflected in books meant that I always attempted to fit myself into a white default: Could I see myself in Ramona Quimby? Anne Shirley? Lyra Belacqua? Or, I could look to certain close approximations, like Japanese American Claudia Kishi from the Baby-Sitter's Club series (1986) and Shirley Temple Wong, a nine-year-old recent immigrant from China on the cover of *In the Year of the Boar and Jackie Robinson* (1984). While dozens of ethnicities make up the Asian American and Pacific Islander (AAPI) community, we are often treated as a bloc; specificity is set aside for, at best, solidarity and, at worst, monolithic stereotyping. My lived experiences are often grouped with those of Chinese and Japanese Americans, reflecting Taiwan's colonial history. Even the US Census does not recognize me in its race and ethnicity category. I check "Other Asian" and write in "Taiwanese."

Then, I picked up Gloria Chao's young adult debut, *American Panda* (2018). Mei Lu, a seventeen-year-old Taiwanese American college freshman at MIT, is not thin enough, not pale enough, and loud. Mei's efforts to balance her resentment for the patriarchal expectations of her culture with the love she feels for her tradition-minded parents may be a struggle familiar to many. Still, *American Panda* is undoubtedly a novel written for a Taiwanese American audience. The book does not assume a white reader; it does not explain Mandarin phrases and idioms, describe food items, or contextualize references to Chinese school, wedding traditions, or folk dances. This was not a didactic book meant to teach others about my culture; this was a rollicking romantic comedy for someone like me. Before the mentions of stinky tofu and arguments with her mother about how "there are no ugly women. Only lazy women" (1) (something I grew up hearing from my own mother), there was the cover of the book. With a deeper complexion, coarse hair, broad nose, short eyelashes, and low eyelid crease, this image of Mei met an unexpected emotional need: it disrupted the image of the slender, pale, sleek-haired sylphs that typically represent Asian American women in media, and it introduced the possibility that someone who looked like me, with my specific cultural experiences, could be a main character.

Similarly, the first time I read Joanna Ho's *Eyes That Kiss in the Corners* (2021) to my son, I was overcome with relief and gratitude because of the language with which Asian eyes were described and the use of the Taiwanese word for grandmother, *amah*. This book was for *us*. On the first page, the protagonist waves at her friends, observing that "some people have . . . big eyes, long lashes. Not me." When we read this book together, my son chants, with excitement, "Not me! Not me!" He delights in his difference and the way the coming pages will celebrate his eyes. Reading with him, I feel something mend within me. Books cannot resolve all the evils of systemic injustice and institutional racism, but they need not contribute to such ills either. Find a reader their book and offer a path to healing and hope.

GUIDING QUESTIONS: DECENTER YOURSELF AS A READER

- Who is the assumed audience for this book?
- What does the book treat as default or familiar? This question can be asked about racial identity, food, customs, physical or neurological ability, and ease of access to systems of power.

Recognize and Mitigate Power Imbalances

Finally, a cultural humility approach to evaluating books requires us to recognize and mitigate power imbalances, starting with an acknowledgment that, historically and today, publishing reinforces hegemonic power and privilege. Classic and contemporary books are made, overwhelmingly, by white, straight, cis people. How do we redress this power imbalance?

It is understandable that many of us fall back on tradition, nostalgia, and inertia when selecting books, personally and professionally, for young readers. As librarians, however, we should do better. A cultural humility approach asks us to question our reliance on canonical books or self-focused responses, as they are imperfect methods for selecting culturally sensitive titles.

Tradition and ALA Book Awards

Representation matters. Angela Bronson argues, in her 2016 article "Mirrors and Windows: Diversity in Children's Picture Books":

> Having children only see one type of race shown in picture books can affect them deeply. That is why I believe books should be used as "mirrors and windows" reflecting who kids are, but also showing them someone who is different to expand their views. . . . Diverse characters allow children to mirror themselves and have windows to others. (28)

Illustrations are powerful, especially for prereaders. When the majority of protagonists in children's literature are white people and when nonhuman animals are more common than BIPOC, many children will not see themselves or their families represented in their reading world.

Representation in children's literature reflects and reinforces existing power structures, including white supremacy, especially in award-winning books. Most libraries with a children's collection prioritize purchasing and displaying award-winning books. Teachers frequently choose to teach or share these books in classrooms. Parents and other caregivers looking to buy quality books are more likely to be aware of or to seek out award winners. Librarians, teachers, and caregivers then reiterate that quality books feature white or nonhuman-animal protagonists. Publishers, driven by a profit motive, select books that are likely to succeed on the market, which often means publishing books that look like the books that have recently won major awards. ALA book award committees, composed mostly of librarians, choose books to win awards from what has been published in the last year or so. Power perpetuates power. This ties into what we call *inertia*—the idea that similar books continue to be published once they've been established as popular (which will be discussed further below).

The Newbery and the Caldecott are the most well-known and recognizable awards given by the American Library Association. Both are the namesakes of white European men. The Newbery Medal was named for the eighteenth-century British bookseller John Newbery. The Association for Library Service to Children awards it yearly to "the author of the most distinguished contribution to American literature for children" (ALA, n.d.). In analyzing the ninety-nine awards given since 1922, we found that sixty-six were awarded to women and thirty-three to men, and only twelve of the ninety-nine awards went to BIPOC authors.

Named after a nineteenth-century English illustrator, the Randolph Caldecott Medal has a similar history. The Caldecott annually honors the preceding year's "most distinguished American picture book for children." Our analysis found that female illustrators won twenty-four times, male illustrators won fifty-four times, and male/female couples won the Caldecott six times. Only eleven Caldecott awards have gone to BIPOC illustrators, and three of these won while working with white partners.

As shown in figure 5.1, the protagonists of Caldecott-winning books are overwhelmingly white. Only eight books feature BIPOC protagonists drawn by BIPOC illustrators (and three of those winners are from the past five years). More than three times this number of books feature nonhuman animals than BIPOC protagonists.

Worse, several books featuring characters of color were written by white people, often employing problematic or racist stereotypes and imagery. For example, Gerald McDermott, a white man, won a Caldecott for his work on *Arrow to the Sun* (1974), which features a Pueblo boy; however, the story digresses from the spirit of the Acoma tradition from which it was taken. Likewise, Blair Lent, well known for *Tikki Tikki Tembo* (1968), won the Caldecott for *The Funny Little Woman* (1973). Lent's work frequently featured inaccurate and insensitive depictions of Asian characters. Though *The Funny Little Woman*

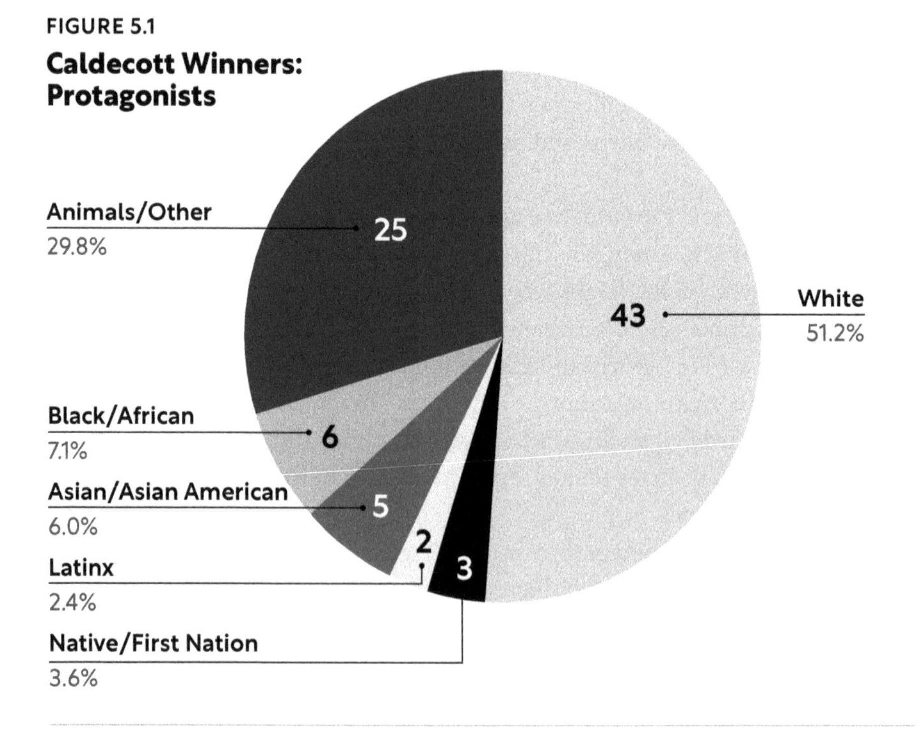

counts in figure 5.1 as featuring an Asian character, not all representation is positive representation.

A more difficult consideration is of the books that don't exist at all. We think here about Judith Shakespeare, Virginia Woolf's hypothetical, equally talented, but unpublished sister to William. Which books were never written because BIPOC children never saw themselves reflected in books and therefore never imagined that they could grow up to be writers or illustrators? Which books were written or illustrated by BIPOC but never published widely? If books by or representing BIPOC aren't written, or aren't promoted by publishing houses, they don't enter the cycle of winning awards and cannot secure a place in tradition and canon.

Below, we will draw again on personal reflections to illustrate how principles of cultural humility have shaped how we relate to tradition, nostalgia, and inertia, in our personal lives and as librarians.

CULTURAL HUMILITY IN PRACTICE: SILVIA ON NOSTALGIA

My relationship with books for young readers changed dramatically after having a child. I anticipated maternity would amplify my ability to evaluate and select books for children. Instead, the opposite happened. As I built my son's home library, the objectivity, curiosity, and critical lens with which I typically approach titles fell away in favor of coziness, sentimentality, and nostalgia. Above all, I looked forward to sharing J. K. Rowling's Harry Potter series with him. My entire childhood was wrapped up in the pages of this series. As is true for many in my generation, the books retained their charm well into adulthood, with our House affiliations and the forms of our Patronus becoming a sort of shorthand for the children we were and the people we became.

Then, of course, after years of transphobic dog whistles, Rowling removed all doubt about her views in a 2020 essay (Rowling 2020). It is not as if the books, or Rowling, were ever unimpeachable. The book series reinforced painful stereotypes about enslaved people, Jewish people, and those living with HIV/AIDS. Characters of color appear only in tertiary roles. And queer representation began and ended with Albus Dumbledore, revealed by Rowling to be gay only after the series was complete. Yet, for well over two decades, I was willing to look past these betrayals in exchange for the crackling, electric memory of thoroughly loving a book.

Nostalgia is powerful and hard to overcome. Even with a well-practiced attitude of humility and a deep commitment to respectful representation in books for young readers, you may find yourself wondering, as I did, "Can we make an exception?" How do you acknowledge the imperfect, insensitive parts of a beloved title from your childhood without negating the real joy you experienced? Is there a way to cherish and share a book with racist, sexist, homophobic, or ableist themes without perpetuating those attitudes?

The answers to such questions are deeply personal. As for me, I am, with equal parts reluctance and resolve, setting aside Harry Potter. Using the cultural humility approach, I asked myself: Are there reader identities I would caution about or away from this series? Yes. How do I treat books that are insensitive to my culture? I do not include Dr. Seuss books in my personal life or professional work due to his history of illustrations that dehumanize Asian characters; there are no rhymes clever enough to offset the pain of a racist caricature. For me, this pain is personal. Keeping Harry Potter because of nostalgia, and because the pain is not personal (Cho Chang's implausible name notwithstanding), is not a comfortable exchange. Adopting an attitude of cultural humility means that I need to set aside nostalgia in order to center the experiences of young trans patrons, queer patrons, Jewish patrons, or patrons of color. Their humanity is more important than my nostalgia.

I do not think that keeping Harry Potter for your children or in your library programming automatically makes you complicit in transphobic oppression. Likewise, letting go of Harry Potter does not invalidate my reading journey or the series's importance to me as a reader. Rather, nostalgia should be acknowledged and then set aside in favor of clear-eyed evaluations based on a commitment to redressing power imbalances. Remedies will vary based on your personal journey and the needs of your community, but it may be helpful here to return to a familiar script: "I didn't know that when I read (and loved) this book, but now that I do, I will handle this title differently."

CULTURAL HUMILITY IN PRACTICE: KELSEY ON INERTIA

When I was pregnant with my first child, the first book I purchased was *Just for You* (Mayer 1975), part of the Little Critter series. This book held a special place in my heart and was the first book I learned to read. Clearly, nostalgia motivated my buying this book decades later, but inertia played an important role too—when I shopped for my own copy of *Just for You*, I was happy to find that it was easily available. Nearly forty years later, it was still being published. I wouldn't have to scour eBay or my childhood bedroom to try to find a copy. This is what we mean by inertia in this section—it's the fact that it is still very easy to find and purchase books that have achieved a certain status of "classic" or "popular." This status keeps the books in print, accessible to purchasers, and continued purchases maintain the classic status of the book.

When I reread *Just for You* as an adult, my experience was different. Luckily, I did not find *Just for You* hugely problematic in any way. That is, I didn't feel disgusted by things I hadn't noticed as a child reader, so I didn't have to choose whether to share it with my child. *Just for You* isn't perfect: it has heteronormative gender roles (the mom usually wears an apron and frequently does household chores, and the little sister wears a bow on her head) that bother me. There may be other issues with the book that I'm not noticing because of my own fondness for it.

My story is an example of how inertia, combined with nostalgia and tradition, often play a powerful role in selecting books for young readers. Books like the Berenstain Bears series, *Pat the Bunny*, or *Peter Rabbit* are fondly remembered by adults, which keeps these books in print and makes them more popular purchases. That's the power of inertia: it leads to purchasing books that may be fine but might also be outdated. These kinds of books may not be bad or offensive in any real way, but some are. For example, I enjoyed the Babar books as a child, but now, as an adult reader, I find the overt colonialism and racial caricatures unacceptable, so I won't be bringing them into my home. Inertia may have us supporting hegemonic power structures rather than seeking out something new that might be both wonderful and more reflective of contemporary times and families.

• • •

Selecting books that you already know and love for young readers is easy. Relying on tradition, nostalgia, and inertia to guide book purchases overlooks newer, high-quality, culturally relevant books. A cultural humility approach can help us break the cycles that ultimately reinforce a white hegemonic view of the world.

Tradition, as it plays out in books for young readers, is a long game that begins now. As discussed above, award-winning books have a chance at leapfrogging the nostalgia and inertia cycles. If a book has won prestigious awards, it is more likely to be promoted by school curriculums, libraries, and bookstores, and it may be more likely to end up on the radar of parents or caregivers. We hope, for example, that *We Are Water Protectors* (Lindstrom

2020), which won the 2021 Caldecott, will be brought into many households. As children read this passionate call to action for climate justice, they may fall in love with it, recall this fondness as adults, and buy it for their own children. Depending on when folks start their families, it will, unfortunately, be twenty to thirty years before a lovely book like *We Are Water Protectors* benefits from the cycles of nostalgia and inertia and becomes a "classic." Given the challenges in place for even this title, it is all the more important that librarians advance the legacy of culturally sensitive books without a gold sticker on the cover.

To be clear, we are not advocating for the dismissal of all classic books; many of them have timeless themes and remain wonderful for contemporary audiences. Not all are problematic in their portrayals of gender, race, or culture. While we have been focusing largely on problematic books thus far, *The Snowy Day* (Keats 1962) stands out as a positive example of a Caldecott winner that is still culturally relevant today. *The Snowy Day* was the first time "that a picture book with an African American main character was published" (Bronson 2016, 29). The author, Ezra Jack Keats (who changed his last name from Katz after facing antisemitism), intentionally made the main character a Black boy. Keats said of this experience:

> None of the manuscripts I'd been illustrating featured any black kids—except for token blacks in the background. My book would have him there simply because *he should have been there all along*. (Alderson 1994, emphasis added)

By acknowledging the impact of white supremacy in publishing and choosing to redress this power imbalance by depicting a Black child at play, Keats created a classic we can still feel good about reading to children sixty years later. The point is not to abandon all classics or all award-winning books, but to question them and review them with modern eyes. We should not embrace them because they once won an award or because we liked the book as a child. Many classic books stand the test of time and can be introduced at storytime without issue. Still, a cultural humility approach asks us to question all books, especially those that have long enjoyed the shine of being considered a "classic." We encourage librarians and other book purchasers to think critically about awards and to recognize their primary use as marketing tools. This provides a more nuanced approach in which librarians are asked to recognize the use of book awards as well as the limits of their use. When we rely on tradition, nostalgia, and inertia, we inevitably replicate outdated social values. A cultural humility approach encourages us to push back against the appeal of self-focused responses when selecting books and to pause and consider whether other books are better for a particular reader or situation.

GUIDING QUESTIONS: RECOGNIZE AND MITIGATE POWER IMBALANCES

- Do you take shortcuts when selecting books that reinforce power imbalances?
- Are there reader identities that you would caution away from a particular title? If so, what makes that title acceptable to those who don't share that identity?

Conclusion

In offering critical readings of beloved titles in this chapter, we are not advocating for their removal from library shelves or in programming, displays, or readers' advisory. However, many books discussed in this chapter already have plenty of cachet and do not need further promotion. We should instead use our professional power to advocate for lesser-known or more recent titles that better represent diverse identities. The cultural humility approach is one way to make difficult decisions about the books we elevate.

A cultural humility approach to evaluating books for young readers requires a commitment to accuracy, decentering yourself, and mitigating power imbalances by rejecting self-focused responses such as tradition, nostalgia, and inertia. This approach can uncover how books for young readers cause harm, requires us to confront the consequences of this harm, and then asks us to *act* on this new knowledge ("I didn't know that, but now that I do, I will handle this title differently").

Reading, recommending, and loving imperfect books need not be a judgment on your character. Once we are able to find comfort in an attitude of humility and reflection, we can also find comfort in adjusting our stance based on new information, acting as appropriate for our audience. Where one librarian may remove a title from their storytime rotation, another might include that title with a fact sheet or alongside discussion questions. As professionals, we have an obligation to use the cultural humility approach outlined above to make decisions regarding which books to purchase, promote, and display. We must acknowledge the power we use when choosing a book for our communities; the books we elevate today will become tomorrow's classic, canonical texts, shaping the literary experiences of young readers to come.

Summary

- Children's literature both reflects and reinforces existing power structures. Librarians can disrupt power imbalances by elevating accurate, culturally sensitive books in place of superficially diverse books or outdated classics.
- A cultural humility approach to selecting books for young readers asks that you take on fact-checking; decentering yourself as the reader; and mitigating power imbalances based on tradition, nostalgia, and inertia so you can say, "I didn't know that, but now that I do, I will handle this title differently."

Questions for Reflection and Discussion

1. As librarians, the boundary between our personal and professional reading is likely porous. What aspects of cultural humility do you find easier to adopt in your professional life than your personal life? What aspects are the reverse?

2. Using the cultural humility approach, you may find that some books you've selected for young readers may contain problematic content. What strategies do you have for reducing harm and redressing power imbalances?

3. When did you first see yourself on the cover of a book?

____

____

____

____

Resources

Bronson, A. 2016. "Mirrors and Windows: Diversity in Children's Picture Books." *Public Libraries* 55, no. 6: 28–30.

Rise: A Feminist Book Project for Ages 0–18. "Rise Book Criteria," last modified January 26, 2020, https://risefeministbooks.wordpress.com/criteria/.

REFERENCES

Alderson, B. 1994. *Ezra Jack Keats, Artist and Picture-Book Maker*. New Orleans: Pelican.

American Library Association. n.d. "John Newbery Medal." Last modified March 24, 2021. https://www.ala.org/alsc/awardsgrants/bookmedia/newbery.

Bell, A. 1979. "Playboy Interview: Wendy/[. . .] Carlos." *Playboy* 26, no. 5 (May): 75–110.

Bronson, A. 2016. "Mirrors and Windows: Diversity in Children's Picture Books." *Public Libraries* 55, no. 6: 28–30.

Centers for Disease Control and Prevention (CDC). 2020. "Data & Statistics on Birth Defects," October 26. https://www.cdc.gov/ncbddd/birthdefects/data.html.

Chao, G. 2018. *American Panda*. New York: Simon & Schuster Books for Young Readers.

Churnin, N. 2020. *Beautiful Shades of Brown: The Art of Laura Wheeler Waring*. Illustrated by F. Marshall. Lerner. Berkeley: Creston Books.

Fitzgerald, J. 2018. *How Mamas Love Their Babies*. Illustrated by E. Peterson. New York: Feminist Press.

Fox, M. 2008. *Ten Little Fingers and Ten Little Toes*. Illustrated by H. Oxenbury. Boston: Houghton Mifflin Harcourt.

Global Fund for Children. 2014. *Global Baby Boys*. Global Babies. Watertown, MA: Charlesbridge.

Ho, J. 2021. *Eyes That Kiss in the Corners*. Illustrated by D. Ho. New York: HarperCollins.

Ignotofsky, R. 2019. *Women in Art: 50 Fearless Creatives Who Inspired the World.* Berkeley: Ten Speed.

Keats, E. J. 1962. *The Snowy Day*. New York: Viking Press.

Lindstrom, C. 2020. *We Are Water Protectors*. Illustrated by M. Goade. New York: Roaring Brook Press.

Macdonald, M. 2018. *Rosa's Animals: The Story of Rosa Bonheur and Her Painting Menagerie*. New York: Abrams Books for Young Readers.

Mayer, M. 1975. *Just for You*. New York: Random House Books for Young Readers.

Reading Rockets. 2014. "A Video Interview with Mem Fox." YouTube video, posted April 23, 5:05. https://youtu.be/UuJiM8UiRiw.

Rowling, J. K. 2020. "J. K. Rowling Writes about Her Reasons for Speaking Out on Sex and Gender Issues." June 10. https://www.jkrowling.com/opinions/j-k-rowling-writes-about-her-reasons-for-speaking-out-on-sex-and-gender-issues/.

6

Learn, Act, Connect

Thriving as an International Librarian and Global Citizen

MEGGAN HOULIHAN, DINA MEKY, AND AMANDA CLICK

THIS CHAPTER WILL EXPLORE CULTURAL HUMILITY IN THE CONTEXT OF international librarianship. We are three American academic librarians who have lived and worked outside of the United States. Meggan, Dina, and Amanda worked together at the American University in Cairo (AUC) more than a decade ago. But the things we learned while living in Egypt—and other places—stay with us and inform our perspectives on cultural humility. Meggan accepted a position at the AUC in 2009. After four years in Cairo, she took a position at New York University (NYU) Abu Dhabi in the United Arab Emirates (UAE), where she spent five years working with students from more than 175 countries. Meggan is a white, cisgender, able-bodied female who grew up in the suburbs of Chicago. Dina was an undergraduate student at the AUC and worked with Amanda and Meggan as a student assistant in the library. She graduated and left to pursue her MLIS at Syracuse University. She's currently working in Boston for Northeastern University and recently completed her MEd in instructional design and e-learning. Dina grew up in a multiracial, multiethnic household and spent her life shuttled between the US and Cairo. Amanda completed her MLIS in 2008 and accepted her first librarian position at the AUC. After three years in Egypt, she returned to the US to enter a PhD program. Her doctoral fellowship focused on library and information science education in the Middle East and North Africa (MENA), and so she split her time between coursework in the US and conducting research and developing LIS professional development opportunities in MENA. Amanda is a white, cisgender, able-bodied woman who was raised in the American South by non-Southerners.

During our time living outside of the US, we were not familiar with the phrase *cultural humility*. But after reading about, discussing, and reflecting on the concept, we realized that it is integral to our experiences. Cultural humility is an essential part of everything from shopping for groceries to teaching information literacy.

This chapter is organized around four topics; the last three are inspired by Tangney's (2000) dimensions of humility:

1. Preparing to live in an unfamiliar culture
2. Appreciating the new and unfamiliar
3. Being open to new ideas
4. Acknowledging our mistakes

Each section will include our observations and experiences, as well as those shared by other international librarians in informal conversations that helped shape this chapter. In addition, this work is influenced by Xan Goodman's (n.d., 1) three pillars of cultural humility:

- Commit to learning: "a commitment to being a lifelong learner who deliberately and bravely establishes a practice of rigorous self-reflection and critique."
- Act to remove power imbalances: "a willingness to acknowledge and dismantle power differentials or imbalances based on authority or position."
- Commit to connect: "a commitment to connecting to the community you support."

Any librarian would be well served by using these pillars in a cultural humility practice. But they are particularly relevant if, as an international librarian, you find yourself immersed in a new and unfamiliar culture and wish to succeed in the workplace and adapt socially.

Preparing to Live in an Unfamiliar Culture

COMMIT TO LEARNING

While it is impossible to be fully prepared to live in a new culture, there are plenty of ways to collect information and learn from others prior to arrival. This is a time to embrace the first pillar, commit to learning. In the context of international librarians, this might initially look like learning from others who already live in the country or region. Connect with future colleagues, friends of friends, people with international experience—anyone who can help you understand what to expect. Ask questions about housing, neighborhoods, language, transportation, what to bring and what not to bring. AUC provided a list of contacts for newcomers, and Amanda wrote to several future colleagues for advice. The responses she received provided helpful advice on everything from voltage adapters to footwear to learning Egyptian Arabic. She also bought and read several travel guides from cover to cover.

Once you arrive, your commitment transfers from learning on your own at a distance to learning from new friends and colleagues. Spend time listening and asking questions—about workplace culture as well as the social and political environment. Learn about the students, communication norms, and institutional structure. Talk to your local colleagues and neighbors, and observe the world around you with an open mind. It is useful to learn from other foreigners who are fairly new to the country and are still learning, as well as those who have years of experience living in the culture. Perspectives shift throughout the cultural adaptation process, so it is important to consider a variety of viewpoints.

COMMIT TO CONNECT

The third pillar, commit to connect, is also a key part of preparing to live in an unfamiliar culture. Some international librarians already have a personal connection with the country and culture in which they've chosen to live. For example, an American librarian in Egypt had already lived in Morocco and Sudan, and held a master's degree in teaching Arabic. Another described an existing interest in the region; in preparation for a move to the UAE, he continued his language study and started watching Arabic television shows. In the summer before moving to Cairo, Amanda took a course on the Quran at a university in her hometown. These efforts and experiences helped the librarians understand the culture before becoming immersed in it and made it easier to connect with the community they would soon be supporting.

Appreciating the New and Unfamiliar

COMMIT TO LEARNING

One of the most exciting aspects of international librarianship is the opportunity to immerse yourself in "newness." The transition might not be easy, but it is important to remain open and commit to learning about the new and unfamiliar. Amanda recalls that learning to grocery shop in Cairo permanently changed the way she cooks. In many places in the US, most types of produce are available throughout the year, as fruits like mangoes and bananas are shipped in from warmer climates. In Egypt, however, the grocery stores and produce stands sell what is in season. Initially, Amanda found this to be a bit of a challenge, but eventually she learned to cook "in season," which generally results in more flavorful meals. This is a lesson she carried with her back to the States.

As a child living in Cairo, Dina learned that there are local ceremonies that involve marking the new transition and "blessing" a new space for the family. She experienced this as she moved with her family to new apartments in the city. Part of this ceremony involves having the local imam or priest pray over the house with incense, with new and old neighbors coming to visit. The family is expected to provide beverages and snacks to the visiting group. The ceremonial aspect of this marked new beginnings and offered Dina opportunities to meet new people in a context where being welcomed was the central focus.

The commitment to learn about your new city and country of residence continues once you're on the ground. All the preparation in the world cannot prepare you for your first cultural experiences in a new place. Several former AUC librarians recalled their first view of the pyramids and chaotic walk through bustling Tahrir Square. The authors recommend taking an old-fashioned print map out into your new city—go and explore to the best of your ability. Get lost. Find your way home. Be vulnerable and open. On the suggestion of a colleague, Meggan spent her weekends in Cairo exploring the city by foot using a print map to guide her. She was able to navigate one of the largest cities in Africa by identifying Metro stops and cultural landmarks and relying on the kindness of strangers. Her friends and colleagues appreciated her willingness to explore, and she became the default navigator for adventures both in- and outside Cairo.

Sometimes the things you have committed to learn change suddenly. Amanda arrived in Cairo in mid-August and set out to learn about day-to-day life in her new neighborhood. Two weeks later, just as she was beginning to feel settled, Ramadan began. Life is very different during Ramadan: work schedules shift, people are more focused on family obligations, and shops maintain different hours. During this month, Cairo is filled with colorful lanterns, iftar tents, and a palpable sense of community. In some ways, it felt like adapting to a new culture all over again. This experience serves as a reminder that cultural humility is a journey and not a destination.

REMOVE POWER IMBALANCES

The new and unfamiliar may challenge you in unexpected ways. Being an expatriate in a foreign culture can be a privilege or a disadvantage, depending on your passport, accent, skin color, nationality, and identity. We the authors, as Americans, acknowledge our place of privilege in Egyptian society. Foreigners experience this day-to-day privilege in many ways. Experiences such as receiving preferential treatment at a doctor's office or bypassing a line at a government office illustrate their elevated status. Cultural humility calls for all of us to act to remove power imbalances. It is important to realize, however, that sometimes there is little you can do legally to dismantle positions of power within a country. But it is still critical to acknowledge them, and push back on them if possible: "Passport-privileged" foreigners (i.e., those who are able to move freely between countries with few restrictions) living in some Gulf countries expressed concern about the treatment of construction workers, who are often paid poorly, work in unsafe conditions, and have little ability to advocate for change. In some cases, higher-education professionals have been barred or deported for their role in advocating for change in labor laws. Librarians and other faculty may find their perspectives on international issues and/or research agendas have evolved upon returning to the US, due to witnessing such power imbalances.

COMMIT TO CONNECT

Language is key in connecting with your community, but this will look different from one culture to another. For example, in Cairo, many Egyptians speak at least basic English and are keen to practice it with a native speaker. In France, however, the expectation is usually that conversations will take place in French. A German librarian explained that his main focus upon moving to Paris was on learning the language, and he spent several years mastering French. We found that speaking with the people you regularly interact with in day-to-day life is an essential piece in cultural humility. Some of our most informative and enjoyable conversations took place with friendly strangers in taxis, grocery stores, and bus stops. Cairo taxi drivers are full of information about the neighborhoods and history of the city. Ask thoughtful questions and take the time to listen carefully.

In addition to language, there are social cues and etiquette that you learn only while interacting with locals. A colleague living and working in Paris had to learn the "proper" way of slicing certain types of cheeses. He recalls his friends bursting into applause once he mastered properly cutting the Camembert. His friends celebrated his achievement and dubbed him a "true Frenchman."

Being Open to New Ideas

COMMIT TO LEARNING

An essential component of cultural humility is self-reflection, a tool that supports the commitment to learning. Apply this framework to your new work environment and commit to learning from everything around you—from colleagues, exciting new life experiences, and everyday encounters. Self-reflection takes time and mindful effort. Traffic in Cairo is terrible, and we found that a long bus ride home was a great place to reflect on the day's conversations, interactions, and topics. Others kept journals to document their time living outside of their home countries and as a space to reflect on their experiences.

Learning about and accepting new ways of doing things are central to living and working in a new culture. For example, ideas and teaching strategies used in your country might be different or even unwelcome in your new host country. Our German colleague in France noted that the expectation for teaching is a lecture-style experience rather than classes that involve active learning or group work. Lectures were something the students expected and respected. An American librarian in particular might find this to be jarring, but it's necessary to adapt and be open to changing your perspective.

You may also find that your understanding of a historical or political event is colored by your cultural background. Meggan quickly learned that many Egyptian students selected research topics related to Palestine and Israel, which is a particularly controversial topic in MENA. Despite her master's degree in history, Meggan did not have a thorough understanding of the complex history of the region. Acknowledging this gap in her knowledge led her to explore the topic, engaging in meaningful conversations with her students and colleagues about historical perspectives and personal experiences. Dina found that while attending primary and secondary school in Egypt, she had learned history from a different lens than is usually taught in US schools. World history tended to be very Middle Eastern- and Africa-centric, with a different set of vocabulary associated with events. For example, there was a larger focus on the history of the Dutch invasion of the Congo or British colonialism in India, rather than on World War II; Idi Amin was a name more readily recognized than Adolf Hitler. As an international librarian, being consistently open and willing to acknowledge your biases and lack of context will help you adapt and connect better with your new host country.

REMOVE POWER IMBALANCES

Trust is a vital component in the removal of power imbalances. During the Arab Spring, Meggan built trust with her students by starting her library instruction sessions with tea and cookies, as well as a student-selected "song of the day." As a foreigner, she realized that it was not possible to fully understand the emotions of a student body that was actively participating in a revolution. The "song of the day" gave everyone a moment to reflect quietly and start class on a positive note. Other strategies to build trust with patrons include attending campus-wide events and student shows, employing culturally relevant examples in the classroom, and using language that resonates with your patrons.

In the classroom, take notice of the power imbalances between yourself and your students, and also between the students in your class. As an undergraduate student at AUC, Dina was privy to the social dynamics of different social classes and hierarchies. On campus, different Egyptian social classes are present in the same space, but there is little effort made to integrate, network, or socialize. To the instructor's eye, there might be a measure of equality in the classroom; but among students, this is not the case. Cliques among students are common, and equity issues arose between upper- and lower-income students. For example, there is a "accent hierarchy" among Egyptian students; wealthy Egyptian students often attend international K–12 schools and thus speak English with American or British accents, and tend to speak it in social situations. In addition, as an instructor, you are also afforded a measure of authority and innate power by your students. Acknowledging these dynamics is critical to becoming an effective instructor and learning about inconspicuous social cues and social structures.

There may be larger power imbalances that are not easily disrupted. The AUC Main Library is the largest English-language print library in Egypt, with access to a plethora of electronic resources. The many public universities in Egypt were not as well resourced, and their graduate students were given extremely limited access to the AUC Library. These students could complete an onerous process to apply for access, which was then allowed only on Saturdays. Librarians who did not speak Arabic sometimes struggled to provide research assistance to these students, who were struggling with English-centric resources. These interactions were good opportunities to practice cultural humility and to be intentionally open to the experiences of others.

COMMIT TO CONNECT

As an American librarian, it can be a bit shocking to discover that our field is not necessarily highly respected elsewhere in the world or that some libraries are primarily focused on protecting resources from the public instead of providing access. Amanda learned a great deal about the state of librarianship outside of the US, especially while working to create professional development opportunities for librarians in MENA. This allowed her to connect with academic, government, school, and public librarians from all over the region. These relationships and the things she learned from these librarians still inform Amanda's practice. For example, she is a strong open-access advocate in part because of her connections with researchers in MENA who cannot access the resources they need because of prohibitive pricing.

Acknowledging Our Mistakes

COMMIT TO LEARNING

When it comes to acknowledging our mistakes, the key term in *cultural humility* is *humility*. A large part of the culture shock you face when moving to a new country, institution, and culture is a comparison (whether intentional or unintentional) to your home culture. Acknowledging your mistakes, stereotypes, and preconceived notions about a region or culture is the first step in a long "unlearning" process. As much as possible, try to enter your new situation as free from expectations as you can. However, understand that you are going to make mistakes. You will misunderstand, you will say or do the wrong thing. And, most important, you must acknowledge and learn from these mistakes.

This might sound counterintuitive as a part of this chapter offering guidance on how to adapt to a new culture using the tenets of cultural humility, but a key step is to actively avoid comparisons to your home country or culture. While you may learn as much as you can in order to arrive feeling informed, there is a limit to what you can learn remotely. For example, a librarian who had worked in the UAE and studied Arabic was engaged in conversation with Emirati colleagues. When he used the term *bedouin* as learned in his study of Modern Standard Arabic, the Emiratis were amused by his response and informed him that, locally, the term was more nuanced and the connotation was different.

Learning and perhaps even adopting your new country's slang terms, understanding social hierarchies (even when they make you uncomfortable), and learning appropriate social cues or dress are all a part of adapting to a new culture. We the authors quickly learned not to assume that American or English-language influences, jokes, or references would be understood or appreciated. Even though the internet and satellite television have provided some common cultural foundations around the world, cultural context is subjective. Dina recalls an instance in which an American professor made a reference to the American breakfast cereal Froot Loops and used GIFs of an American television show as a part of a presentation. None of the local Egyptian or international students understood either example, and the professor was left scrambling to make himself understood.

Learning about your new environment also means learning about your limitations and privilege. As a foreigner, you might be relegated to a certain social status, and you are often given a "pass" while you are new in many cases. But not always. Amanda recalls serving on a planning committee for the conference of an international librarian association. Attendees would come from American-style institutions from all over the world, speaking English with varying levels of proficiency. Amanda was excited to plan a pecha kucha session, a format that was becoming very popular at the time. In a pecha kucha talk, the presenter shows exactly twenty slides for exactly twenty seconds each. It is a very precise format; the slides are supposed to be set to advance automatically. The presenters hated the format. Most ignored Amanda's carefully crafted instructions, few adhered to the twenty-slide guideline, and almost no one set the slides to advance automatically. Presenters found the format frustrating for a variety of reasons: Some chafed at what they saw as overly strict requirements. Some were less confident presenting in English and needed flexibility in their session. Others were simply not familiar enough with PowerPoint to follow the pecha kucha format. As the third presenter in a row glared at her from the stage, Amanda realized that her excitement about a hot new presentation style had caused her to ignore the cultural realities of the conference.

REMOVE POWER IMBALANCES

Part of acknowledging—or perhaps avoiding—mistakes is to actively identify and remove power imbalances that exist between you and your students. Language barriers are an excellent example of this. An American librarian in Cairo noted that, as someone with a background in second-language teaching, he was sensitive to his students' varied experiences with English and made a point to use clear diction, expressions, and examples.

For international librarians, there are usually two main types of language-based power imbalances: one in which you are in a position of power (as an English speaker teaching in English, for example); and one in which you are not, because you are unfamiliar with the local language and cannot explain things in ways that help your students better understand you. Realize that optics in this case sometimes matter, as your students might be reluctant to reach out for clarification or help and might be isolated or offended. For example, a librarian teaching a class of non-native English speakers once referred to the group as "guys," which is an American slang term often used to refer to a group of people, regardless of gender. The female students took offense and assumed that they were being excluded from the lecture. Reeducating yourself, adjusting your language, and reflecting on different kinds of language barriers is a key in cultural humility. Amanda experienced a minor but interesting language barrier while taking a graduate-level course at AUC, in which she was the only non-Egyptian student. Although the course was taught in English, the professor and students would often sprinkle conversation with Arabic idioms. The hospitable students made a particular effort to include Amanda and would always pause to explain the Arabic phrase: "Oh, *bokra fil mish mish* means 'and tomorrow there will be apricots,'" similar to the English "Sure, when pigs fly."

COMMIT TO CONNECT

Finding a community in your host country also plays a part in your commitment to connect. It's important to widen your social circle beyond your colleagues and/or other foreigners. Befriending locals will help you recognize and learn from your mistakes, normalize social cues, and learn about the subtleties of local culture. An American librarian living in Morocco described being invited to a colleague's wedding. While he was exhausted after the all-night celebration, he fondly recalls all that he learned about local traditions, family dynamics, and social etiquette. The experience helped him feel integrated into Moroccan culture.

Think about how you might get involved at the local level. Keep in mind, though, that gender differences might need to be taken into consideration—in some cultures, mixing genders might be considered inappropriate in certain situations. And in some countries, there might be other social barriers or hierarchies (defined by a colleague as "categories of interaction") according to which you might not be able to befriend a person who might be seen as a different social class than you. For example, in Egypt, each building has a bawaab (a security guard/doorman) who is responsible for upkeep of the building and who may run small errands for residents. While bawaabs are treated with respect and formality, it's generally frowned upon to socialize with them, especially for a woman. Before she understood this dynamic, Amanda invited the bawaab's son into her apartment for a cold drink, causing quite a stir. Likewise, aha'wey (roadside coffee shops) are the primary centers of socialization in the Middle East, but are traditionally male spaces. Women might be separated, actively discouraged, or viewed with surprise and suspicion in most of these spaces. It's important not to be discouraged or disappointed, and to have a sense of humor when learning.

Returning to the US

Meggan's experiences working in Cairo and Abu Dhabi have greatly impacted her librarian practices since returning to the US two years ago. In the library classroom, Meggan uses global examples to illustrate search techniques. She is mindful to include examples that demonstrate different perspectives on historical and current events, while highlighting diverse authorship. Both in the classroom and during reference consultations, Meggan eliminates library jargon and general slang in order to make her outreach efforts accessible to all.

Amanda's experiences outside of the US heavily influenced her research agenda. She returned to the States and entered a PhD program, engaging with coursework in both LIS and Middle East studies. The aftermath of the Arab Spring disrupted her plans to conduct her dissertation research in Morocco, Egypt, and Lebanon, so she turned her attention to studying the experience of international students in the US. Her research explored cultural adaptation and the research process (Click 2018). An interest in evidence-based practice led her and Meggan to collaborate on a systematic review of the LIS literature on academic libraries and international students (Click, Wiley, and Houlihan 2017).

As someone who was raised between Egypt and the US, and in a Hispanic, Arab, and American household, transitioning between different cultures is easier than most for Dina. Living abroad exposed her to different cultural norms than are prevalent in the US; identifying as a librarian of color, she finds herself connecting to underrepresented student populations more readily. While teaching in the classroom, she is extremely aware of the examples and the slang used and actively tries to keep them to more neutral examples. Living and working abroad have also taught Dina flexibility, patience, and appreciation for inclusionary practices in meetings and classrooms.

Conclusion

Living internationally is a study in making mistakes, embracing humility, and learning from new experiences. There are so many factors to consider while living outside your own culture that it's easy to become overwhelmed and anxious. This chapter does not claim to represent the experiences and perspectives of all international librarians. Instead, the intent of the stories shared here is to give the reader some idea of what it takes to succeed as a librarian and an informed and humble global citizen.

Acknowledgments

We would like to thank our colleagues from across the US, MENA, Europe, and Asia for sharing their stories, thoughts, and comments while we wrote this chapter. Our experiences and opinions are uniquely our own.

Summary

- You can prepare, to a certain extent, to live and work in a new culture. Take the time to learn about your new host country and workplace through research, readings, and conversations.
- Focus on appreciating the new and unfamiliar when immersing yourself in a new culture. Explore your surroundings and connect with your new neighbors, colleagues, and friends.
- Remain open to new ideas, and accept that you may not be able to truly understand some aspects of the unfamiliar culture. Engage in self-reflection.
- As you adapt to a new culture, accept that you will make mistakes. Be kind to yourself, but take the opportunity to reflect on and learn from these experiences.

Questions for Reflection and Discussion

1. How might you apply the three dimensions of cultural humility highlighted in this chapter (appreciating the new and unfamiliar, being open to new ideas, and acknowledging mistakes) in your current work context?

____

____

____

____

____

2. Reflect on your past responses to change. What might be the biggest challenge for you in adapting to a new culture?

____

____

____

____

3. How would you begin to orient yourself in a new work environment? For example, if you are an instruction librarian, how would you approach adapting your pedagogy?

____

____

____

____

Resources

Cooke, N. A. 2016. *Information Services to Diverse Populations: Developing Culturally Competent Library Professionals.* Santa Barbara: ABC-CLIO.

Phillips, L. S., and K. G. Holvoet. 2017. *Taking Your MLIS Abroad: Getting and Succeeding in an International Library Job*. Santa Barbara: Libraries Unlimited.

REFERENCES

Click, A. B. 2018. "International Graduate Students in the United States: Research Processes and Challenges." *Library & Information Science Research* 40, no. 2: 153–62. https://doi.org/10.1016/j.lisr.2018.05.004.

Click, A. B., C. W. Wiley, and M. Houlihan. 2017. "The Internationalization of the Academic Library: A Systematic Review of 25 Years of Literature on International Students." *College & Research Libraries* 78, no. 3: 328–58. https://doi.org/10.5860/crl.78.3.328.

Goodman, X. n.d. *Cultural Humility in Action*. California State Library. https://www.library.ca.gov/Content/pdf/services/toLibraries/mhi/Cultural_Humility_in_Public_Libraries.pdf.

Tangney, J. P. 2000. "Humility: Theoretical Perspectives, Empirical Findings and Directions for Future Research." *Journal of Social and Clinical Psychology* 19, no. 1: 70–82. https://doi.org/10.1521/jscp.2000.19.1.70.

7

Cultural Humility in Instruction on Health Outreach Projects

Revising a Course on the Grant-Writing Process

JARROD IRWIN

THE PROJECT DESCRIBED HERE WAS COMPLETED WHILE I WAS AFFILIATED with the National Network of Libraries of Medicine, Southeastern/Atlantic Region, headquartered at the Health Sciences and Human Services Library of the University of Maryland, Baltimore. The organization is now known as the Network of the National Library of Medicine and has different regional divisions.

This project has been funded in whole or in part with federal funds from the Department of Health and Human Services, National Institutes of Health, National Library of Medicine, under grant no. UG4LM012340 with the University of Maryland, Baltimore.

In late 2019, while working for the National Network of Libraries of Medicine (NNLM), I was tasked with updating an online, asynchronous course that NNLM offers called Grants and Proposal Writing On Demand. Among the charges I was given was to find ways to incorporate principles of cultural humility into the course. The course focuses on grants for health outreach and education projects, including those that the NNLM supports through their own funding programs. It covers the process of researching health needs to be addressed by such a project; the process of planning a grant-funded project; selecting an appropriate grant to apply for; and, of course, the process of writing a grant proposal itself. This chapter will look at the changes made to this course to incorporate principles of cultural humility and how these principles might improve the effectiveness of grant-funded health outreach projects and library instruction.

There are two reasons I have chosen to discuss a course on grant writing in these pages, even though this is not a subject many librarians will find themselves teaching. First, because it is a specialized topic, I use it as an example of how principles of cultural humility can fit into library instruction, even for topics that may not seem to have obvious connections to equity, diversity, and inclusion. Second, a major part of grant writing for health outreach projects is planning the project itself, which often includes working with partner organizations that represent a wide range of different communities. Cultural humility is a valuable practice for this work; it can help project staff members maintain an openness to learning about health disparities that members of these groups face in local and individual contexts, in addition to general health disparities faced by these groups as a whole.

The Relevance of Cultural Humility to This Course

The biggest challenge I encountered in updating Grants and Proposal Writing On Demand was figuring out how cultural humility concepts could improve participants' understanding of grant writing. The previous version of the course was, expectedly, focused on the process of researching and writing a grant proposal, along with key terms to know while working through this process. But isn't this sufficient for the goal of the course? If the whole point of writing a grant proposal is following the directions from the people offering the grant, what can grant writers gain from thinking about cultural humility?

The greatest impact that cultural humility concepts had on the revised course was not in the content describing the parts of a grant proposal or how to read a request for proposals. Instead, cultural humility was most relevant in sections dealing with planning and executing the grant-funded project. This includes discussions of how to identify a health need to address, since many grant opportunities for health outreach aim to address health disparities. It was also relevant for collaborating on a health outreach project with partner organizations. The sections of the course dealing with specific details about grant proposals did benefit from changes to make the instruction more culturally humble, but these were mostly smaller changes to how existing course content was presented.

A key reason that a cultural humility approach enriched the course's treatment of these topics is that disparities in health outcomes often affect members of marginalized groups—the same groups that a cultural humility approach to library work aims to include more fully in the life of the library. These health disparities are frequently discussed in the public health literature, and their causes are often described with a paradigm known as social determinants of health. Healthy People 2030, an initiative of the US Department of Health and Human Services (2020), describes these determinants by defining the categories they fall into:

- Economic Stability
- Education Access and Quality
- Health Care Access and Quality
- Neighborhood and Built Environment
- Social and Community Context

Notably, social determinants of health highlight ways that members of a given group might experience different health disparities or other challenges related to health or wellness. For example, in a rural library context, health disparities faced by Black community members might be related to the demands of agricultural work facing the nation's forty-eight thousand Black farmers (US Department of Agriculture 2019), while in urban areas, health disparities might be driven by inadequate infrastructure in neighborhoods that were redlined and left to decay. Rather than treating Black Americans as a monolith facing the same health disparities, social determinants of health provide a way of accounting for local and even individual nuances in health needs. As such, an awareness of the social determinants of health complements a cultural humility approach to grant writing for health outreach projects because it forces grant writers to consider local and individual needs and conditions when planning health education and outreach.

A second reason that cultural humility is relevant to this course is the frequent situation where a grant-funded project is a collaboration between a library and another organization. While cultural humility is important for any type of partnership, it is especially relevant when a library partners with a community-based organization run by and for those who suffer from racism or other forms of oppression. There is much potential for health outreach work in these collaborations. Principles of cultural humility were important in the course's recommendations for how libraries can form and conduct these partnerships, particularly by ensuring that partners have a meaningful stake in planning and completing the project. They must not be simply tokens or a stamp of approval to make the grant proposal look better, and the library must not treat them as merely a means of winning a grant or of furthering the library's own agenda.

Next, I will discuss the specific changes made to Grants and Proposal Writing On Demand to incorporate principles of cultural humility and address the concerns detailed above. These changes are discussed in sections devoted to course material on planning, implementing, and evaluating a project that might be supported by a grant. I will also touch on smaller-scale changes to the course content intended to make it more culturally humble and inclusive of participants from a wider range of backgrounds and identities.

Changes to the Course Material

COURSE CONTENT ON PROJECT-PLANNING

As discussed above, working with a partner organization that is part of a health outreach project's intended audience can be valuable for planning an effective and relevant project. The updated version of Grants and Proposal Writing On Demand emphasizes that these prospective partner organizations must be equal partners in planning the project, instead of being invited to take part in a project that library staff have already designed. Doing otherwise risks exploiting the partner organization for their labor, resources, or credibility that they could give to the project. One way to reduce the risk of this problem is for libraries to partner with organizations that they already have an established relationship with. This prior relationship can make it easier to work together in a constructive and mutually beneficial way. If a library does not currently have relationships with potential partners who would be suitable for the health outreach work in question, the best time to start forming such a relationship is before library staff even start seeking grant opportunities.

Similarly, the updated course recommends including members of the project's intended audiences in every step of the process, from planning to evaluation. Otherwise, staff who work on the project might act on misinformed assumptions about what their community members need or want. Cultural humility is especially valuable at the project-planning stage because it requires an open-ended learning process regarding other people's needs and perspectives. Planning a project in this way makes it easier to understand local health needs and effective ways to perform outreach or education related to those needs.

Cultural humility can also inform the way that the project staff identify and interact with experts to better understand the health needs that staff want to focus on. In this context, expertise should be understood broadly, not as the exclusive possession of people in specific positions of influence or authority. Scholars, activists, and community leaders can certainly provide important insights about your intended audience as a group, but their expertise does not extend to the experiences of individuals who will participate in the project. These individuals are the experts on their own life experiences, values, and needs. Participants' social and community contexts are important to consider, but a culturally humble approach requires understanding how both social factors and individual factors influence ways the library can best function as a health resource.

When you consult a researcher, community leader, activist, or other expert, they should not bear the entire burden of educating library staff on the needs of the project's intended audience. Respect their time by acquiring basic information from other sources to the extent possible. This information includes demographic data about the community, evidence of health disparities that you might cite in a grant proposal to show the need for the project, and similar projects that have been done in the past. In general, the role of experts is working with the library staff to interpret some of this more basic information and determine how it should inform the project plan.

Besides planning for the project itself, the updated course recommends planning for the project's conclusion, which raises additional considerations for partnerships. Library staff can commit to a continuing relationship with their partner in a variety of ways, even if the specific work that took place as part of the project does not continue. For example, the library might agree to maintain and periodically update some of the information resources that were developed for the project. Alternately, a regular discussion group at the library might continue as a community-driven event focused on the topic of the project. Grant writers should also consider what future collaborations might be possible between the library and any partner organizations. Not only does this leave the door open for future partnerships, but it also helps communicate that the library values the partner organization and their constituents.

COURSE CONTENT ON IMPLEMENTING THE PROJECT PLAN

Although the most extensive changes to the course dealt with the project-planning process, cultural humility also provides insights into the implementation process. Library staff will have to continue learning about the audience's needs and preferences while the project is ongoing, and then adapt accordingly. For example, they might learn that one aspect of their project should be modified to be more useful to their intended audience, or that a particular term that library staff have been using is inaccurate or insensitive. Such discoveries should be embraced as essential learning experiences when performing health outreach work. A useful analogy is the concept of agile project management, which emphasizes the ability to adapt quickly to changing requirements and the willingness to pursue an iterative process of improvement, rather than the expectation of a perfect product (White 2008). Cultural humility, similarly, can help create a more inclusive environment by allowing space for project staff to learn, accept correction if they say or do something insensitive, and implement any needed changes quickly.

This emphasis on an ongoing learning process is one advantage of cultural humility over a cultural competence approach because situations where someone receives correction are seen as normal and beneficial. Such an approach is particularly helpful when considering how to address microaggressions, such as a remark that reinforces a stereotype but that a person made without the intent to offend. Cultural humility can foster a work environment where microaggressions can be readily addressed and corrected, since they are not treated as a failure of one's cultural competence but an unavoidable part of an important learning process.

COURSE CONTENT ON PROJECT EVALUATION

Program evaluation is a topic within grant writing where cultural humility might seem to have only tangential relevance, since it mostly involves following instructions from the sponsor or sharing the evaluation data that you promised in the grant proposal. Indeed, the course content on these aspects of evaluation in Grants and Proposal Writing On Demand did not receive the type of drastic revisions seen in the material about project planning. This content still centers its discussion on developing high-quality goals that can be used to evaluate the project, using the acronym SMART: goals for a health outreach project must be specific, measurable, achievable, relevant, and time limited (Siegert and Taylor 2004).

However, specifying goals and collecting data to assess their completion are only one-half of evaluation. The other half is using evaluation data to make changes to the project and to direct future projects—and this is where cultural humility is most important to an evaluation strategy. Having a process for changing your program in response to feedback is a key part of giving program participants a meaningful say in shaping the program. This is especially important for programs whose intended audiences are affected by systemic oppression: a grant-funded project must not become yet another space where community members find their voices ignored. Acting on evaluation data to make meaningful changes helps establish the program as a space where the participants' perspectives and priorities matter.

In situations where this requires changing the project plan that was originally described in a grant proposal, libraries that receive funding for health outreach projects should advocate for the interests of project participants when communicating with the funding organization. Sponsors of grants usually require periodic reports or check-ins throughout the grant's funding period. These provide good opportunities to discuss challenges encountered with the project, feedback from participants, and adjustments that need to be made. If major issues or revisions to the project plan arise, be proactive in communicating with the sponsor about these and explaining why they are necessary.

The evaluation plan is not typically something you can change significantly because the project objectives represent what the sponsor looks at to judge the project's success. However, this does not mean that project staff are restricted to collecting only data described in the evaluation plan, or that no other sources of feedback deserve to be heeded. A culturally humble approach to evaluating the project can allow for recording and recognizing less-formal sources of feedback that participants might direct to you, and potentially finding ways to measure them. For example, if a participant in a program about mental health and wellness tells you that they went to your library's reference desk to ask more questions about the topic, you might check your library's records of reference conversations to see if there has been an increase in questions about mental health. In addition to helping identify necessary changes to the program and shape future programming, these supplementary anecdotes and other types of data can be described in the project's final report, as well as in materials that the library produces to describe its outreach work.

CHANGES TO LANGUAGE IN THE COURSE

Although the most significant changes to Grants and Proposal Writing On Demand were new content related to planning, implementing, and evaluating a grant-funded project, there were smaller changes intended to make the course more inclusive. These were mostly changes to wording to recognize a fuller range of the backgrounds and life experiences of the course participants. The two examples I discuss here relate to professional backgrounds and assumptions that were made about participants' language abilities.

The first change deals with how the course describes the wide range of individuals who might be working on grant projects. Originally, the course used the word *librarian* in several places. However, NNLM members who might take the course also include healthcare professionals, educators at all levels, staff of community-based and faith-based organizations, and others. In the context of grant-funded projects, the wide variety of potential partners means that the range of roles and job titles is more expansive still. Even confining the discussion to libraries, though, there is a tapestry of staff with different positions, credentials, and professional backgrounds who make libraries run successfully, including volunteers. For that reason, the updated course uses very general language, such as *project staff*, when referring to all those who might work on writing a grant proposal and running a grant-funded project. This terminology helps acknowledge the important contributions made by people with different forms of education and professional experience to a grant-funded project, in addition to those who hold MLIS degrees and have the word *librarian* in their job title.

Another change was to a reference to participants' first language that appeared in the original course in a discussion about proofreading grant proposals. Previously, the course recommended that a native English speaker should complete the final phase of proofreading to find any issues with spelling, grammar, and clarity. The updated course recommends "someone who is fluent in the language of the proposal." This change is important because the relevant qualification for a proofreader is proficiency with the language. Although someone whose first language is English might indeed be a strong proofreader of English writing, the fact that English is their first language is not a relevant requirement in itself. Someone who has learned English as a foreign language can also be a skilled proofreader, but such a person would be excluded by the previous recommendation. This change also reflects that a grant proposal might be written in a language other than English. Courses taught by NNLM have some international participants in countries with official languages other than English, so this is not merely an abstract possibility.

Improvements in terminology will continue to be considered during future updates to the course. NNLM courses are reviewed once a year to determine if any changes need to be made, such as adding the most up-to-date values for statistics cited in the course. These annual updates are an ideal time to reevaluate the language used, which is valuable because inclusive language in health outreach is a topic of active discussion and sometimes a lack of consensus. For example, one possible change in future updates to the course would be the replacement of the phrase *vulnerable communities*. Katz and colleagues (2020) argue that the phrase is sometimes used to avoid naming the reasons some communities are vulnerable—particularly, racism and other systemic forms of oppression. However, this phrase remains in common use in public health contexts so far. The practice of cultural humility in instruction on health outreach requires ongoing awareness to changing understandings of accurate and empowering ways to discuss health disparities.

Conclusion

If your library works primarily with students or the general public, grant proposals might not be a topic that will interest most of them, and you will not likely be teaching a course about it. Nonetheless, as I updated Grants and Proposal Writing On Demand to incorporate principles of cultural humility, two important ideas became apparent about where these concepts can be beneficial for library instruction and outreach, even on topics that do not seem to have direct ties to equity, diversity, and inclusion. This project also suggested ways that these cultural humility concepts can be beneficial for libraries when defining their missions and evaluating potential partnerships, whether grants are involved or not.

First, instruction on any topic that involves collaboration between different organizations or teams can fruitfully incorporate cultural humility concepts. These situations can benefit from participants maintaining an ongoing practice of openness to learning and changing behavior to ensure a positive and welcoming environment. Instruction on these topics should stress that the partners must have meaningful input in every step of your shared work, from defining the problem that the project team will tackle to evaluating the team's success. Additionally, a key idea when working with partners who are members of marginalized groups is to avoid behaviors that might further entrench power imbalances in your interactions, such as treating these partners as simply a means to advance your own goals. Strategies for fostering positive partnerships can include establishing relationships before any project is even at hand, as well as seeking other opportunities to pursue a shared mission.

Second, for any type of health education and outreach that your library might pursue, cultural humility is valuable because many pressing health disparities are influenced by various forms of discrimination, including racism, transphobia, homophobia, and sexism. Concepts like the social determinants of health can aid the practice of cultural humility by helping library staff recognize how local context, an individual's life experience, and society-wide forms of systemic oppression all influence people's health needs, as well as effective ways of providing information relevant to these needs.

Instruction and outreach are not the only areas of library work where the ideas discussed in this chapter could be beneficial; library staff can apply them to the full range of the library's activities. One way to begin doing so is to extend these ideas to the library's process for developing mission statements, strategic plans, and library policies. Beyond simply including cultural humility concepts in these documents, members of the community could take an active role in shaping these documents from their inception and driving changes as needed. Additionally, the project-planning considerations discussed here can be used to evaluate partnerships that are proposed to the library, whether a grant is involved or not. When deciding whether or not to take one of these opportunities, you and your colleagues can ask questions about culturally humble practices for partnerships and outreach work. Will your library and its users have a meaningful say in how the project is planned and implemented? Will feedback from participants be collected and acted upon? In these ways, cultural humility can become a guiding principle of your library's activities across the board, which in turn can establish your library as a trusted resource where all community members have a place and a voice.

Summary

- Cultural humility concepts can be productively incorporated into library instruction, even when the topic is not directly related to equity, diversity, and inclusion. This is especially true when the topic of instruction relates to collaborative work.

- For health education and outreach work by libraries, concepts like the social determinants of health are valuable complements to cultural humility because they encourage recognizing local and individual factors in health disparities, in addition to the effects of society-wide patterns of systemic discrimination.
- Cultural humility in library programming, whether grant funded or not, requires that members of groups you intend to reach have every opportunity to explain their own needs and shape the project. This includes members of your intended audience, project partners, and experts who are familiar with ways that library activities should account for local social contexts.

Questions for Reflection and Discussion

1. What ideas do you have for how principles of cultural humility could fit into instructional content that you have taught before?

____

____

____

2. What are some concrete ways you can give members of marginalized communities more influence over your institution's work related to equity, diversity, and inclusion?

____

____

____

3. What relationships or connections does your library already have with organizations run by and for members of your community, and how can your library be an effective partner in working to promote the health and wellness of these organizations' constituents?

____

____

____

Resources

Network of the National Library of Medicine. n.d. "Clinical Conversations Training Program." https://nnlm.gov/guides/clinical-conversations-training-program.

Includes modules on cultural humility, social determinants of health, and related topics.

US Department of Health and Human Services, Office of Disease Prevention and Health Promotion 2020. "Social Determinants of Health." Healthy People 2030. https://health.gov/healthypeople/objectives-and-data/social-determinants-health.

Information about social determinants of health from Healthy People 2030, an initiative from the Department of Health and Human Services' Office of Disease Prevention and Health Promotion.

REFERENCES

Katz, A. S., B. Hardy, M. Firestone, A. Lofters, and M. E. Morton-Ninomiya. 2020. "Vagueness, Power and Public Health: Use of 'Vulnerable' in Public Health Literature." *Critical Public Health* 30, no. 5: 601–11. https://doi.org/10.1080/09581596.2019.1656800.

Siegert, R. J., and W. J. Taylor. 2004. "Theoretical Aspects of Goal-Setting and Motivation in Rehabilitation." *Disability and Rehabilitation* 26, no. 1: 1–8. https://doi.org/10.1080/09638280410001644932.

US Department of Agriculture 2019. 2017 Census of Agriculture Highlights: Black Producers. National Agriculture Statistics Service, October. https://www.nass.usda.gov/Publications/Highlights/2019/2017Census_Black_Producers.pdf.

US Department of Health and Human Services, Office of Disease Prevention and Health Promotion 2020. "Social Determinants of Health." Healthy People 2030. https://health.gov/healthypeople/objectives-and-data/social-determinants-health.

White, K. R. J. 2008. *Agile Project Management: A Mandate for the Changing Business Environment*. Conference paper, Project Management Institute Global Congress 2008, Denver, Colorado, October 19. https://www.pmi.org/learning/library/agile-project-management-mandate-changing-requirements-7043.

PART III

COMMUNITY

8

Embedding Diné Culture in Individual and Institutional Cultural Humility Practices

A View from the Tribal College Library

RHIANNON SORRELL

> *A complete total Navajo understands the brotherhood of man and can cope with both cultures—thus being able to use his skills and his understanding for the benefit of his people.*
>
> —"Navajo Educational Goals," *Stories of Traditional Navajo Life and Culture*

WHAT DOES CULTURAL HUMILITY LOOK LIKE IN A TRIBAL COLLEGE LIBRARY? What role does cultural humility play in a predominantly Indigenous institution? How can cultural humility be embedded into a tribal college institutional policy, when there is no word for "humility" in the local language? Demographically speaking, Diné College—the first tribally chartered and controlled college in the US—is essentially homogenous, with Diné (Navajo) students making up over 90% of the student population, where the average enrollment is around 1,500 students across eight campuses. However, anyone who has stayed long enough on Diné Nation will witness a range of diversity, norms, protocols, and contradictions in Diné social and cultural interactions, as well as differences in language and dialect. At an institution of higher education rooted in the Diné language and culture, the varied experiences of Diné students, faculty, staff, and local communities come to meld, mix, and even clash. There is no better place to experience the range of diversity and experience than the Diné College Libraries, which, despite being classified as "academic" libraries, serve the needs of the Diné people, regardless of whether they are affiliated with the college or not. It is also a place where one can observe, experience, and engage with the institution's mission and policies, which are founded on Diné traditional values, and how they play out in both academic and general community contexts.

When I came back to the Navajo Nation in 2014 and began working at Diné College, I didn't think much about the myriad cultural differences of my people other than anticipating how they may affect my ability to do my job. *Cultural humility* as a term was unheard of to me, but conceptually, it had been a frequent topic of conversation among my mother and her sisters, who worked in Indian Health Services in the areas of pharmacy, nursing, and dentistry. At the time, cultural competency was emphasized more to incoming healthcare providers, with a focus on cultural protocols and competency checklists; but long-term local practitioners like my mother noted the importance of humility in working for the betterment of one's own people. Despite having the cultural competence advocated for in healthcare services, social services, and counseling, it wasn't as effective for dealing with the range of cultural attitudes and experiences of an Indigenous population spread across a geographic area the size of West Virginia. Rather, carrying oneself with humility had a greater effect, especially if one intends to make a lasting difference among one's people.

As I approach my ninth year at the Diné College Kinyaa'áanii Charlie Benally Library, there is much to share about the cultural diversity of a primarily Indigenous institution and the role cultural humility plays in making a difference in providing library and educational services to this underserved population.

Becoming Unselved

One of the most important lessons I've received in cultural humility came after returning to the Navajo Nation to work after spending eight years on the East Coast. It was the harsh reality that many young Navajo professionals face when returning to the reservation with the intention of putting their degrees and education to work for their people: that despite any level of education and expertise you may have gained and think you are bringing to the table when you come home, you will still have to start from square one, as an outsider, even if you've grown up in the community you are now serving.

I've always known that should I come back to work on the reservation, my arrival would be met with suspicion. I would have to begin the hard work of integrating myself back into the community, a process that would involve a great deal of patience and humility on my part. Any newcomer to a tribal community with a high degree of education is often perceived as possessing a certain level of arrogance that made it possible for them to get through the higher-education system. Accompanying this perception is the expectation that this newcomer's arrival to the community is only a temporary pit stop on the way to something bigger, higher paying, and off reservation. Coming back to serve your tribal community involves recalibrating and reorienting a number of internal survival mechanisms: individualism, competitiveness, and careerism are essential to success in mainstream schooling, but are seen here as destructive features of a Western education that is mostly concerned with material gain. Thus began my own journey in unlearning much of what I'd been taught in my graduate program in becoming an academic librarian.*

In coming back to work in a tribal college setting, I could not expect the same cultural, professional, and institutional infrastructures that are in place at larger state colleges and universities. The tribal college and its libraries are more community oriented than larger state university and research libraries. At the time, there were no ranking or promotion procedures in place for academic librarians, and the closest thing to a faculty librarian appointment was teaching as an adjunct instructor in a subject specialty. Coworkers and patrons were more interested in who my grandparents were and where I grew up rather than my professional experience. A few were more straightforward in their suspicions about my intentions at the college: Why are you here? When are you leaving? Don't you prefer the city?

The answers to these questions don't matter as much as how you spend your time on the reservation and your attitude. I spent the majority of my first year at the college working part time at the library help desk and adjunct teaching, as there was no full-time position for me at the time. This in and of itself was an incredibly humbling experience for me, as someone who worked and trained specifically for a career in tenure-track librarianship. My journey didn't begin with any fanfare or keys to my own office but with an intense help desk schedule and reintroduction back to my community.

*Among the first items to be "unlearned" soon after returning to the Navajo Nation was standards-based approaches to teaching, particularly information literacy. While the ACRL rescinded the Information Literacy Competency Standards for Higher Education in 2016, prior to that, I found myself working around such checklist-based assessment strategies to accommodate for and factor in Diné traditional knowledge and epistemologies in research at Diné College.

Diné Patrons at a Diné Academic Library

Given the history of American Indian education, whose goal was to eradicate Indigenous languages and cultures, the "help desk" does not necessarily symbolize service orientation or the intention of assistance. Even within Indian higher-education contexts, there are remnants of Bureau of Indian Affairs-era physical and administrative infrastructures and power imbalances that make tribal citizens uneasy. The literature alludes to this inherent power at the help desk: "The person behind the desk in the library has power in relation to the patron, but not necessarily status or authority. Different patrons will experience this power dynamic in different ways, influenced by their cultural position and experiences, and in ways that may not be clear to us as professionals" (Hurley, Kostelecky, and Townsend 2019, 15). Indeed, in addition to the "library anxiety" phenomenon that affects the broader library-user population (particularly in colleges and universities), the unease around approaching the library help desk by members of our tribal communities is palpable, even among frequent visitors.

The Diné College Libraries have a single help desk that serves as both a circulation and a reference desk. All library patrons approach this desk with their inquiries, no matter what they are. These desks are also located near the library entrances, so library staff are often the first and last points of contact for patrons entering and leaving the building. Most patrons who come through the library are students, but a significant portion of visitors are community residents who are not affiliated with the college. Our libraries also welcome children and allow for guest access for non–Navajo Nation residents. In adhering to the broader mission of tribal colleges, which are rooted in cultural preservation and the betterment of tribal communities from within, the tribal college libraries' service is geared toward the tribal nation as a whole, regardless of college enrollment status.

While racial demographics of Diné College paint a homogenous picture of primarily Navajo students and community members, there is no "typical" patron profile. Like many community-based higher-education institutions, nontraditional students make up a larger percentage in tribal colleges than the average four-year academic institution. Many of our students are older, returning, part time, GED recipients, or transferring; have dependents; or have other careers, or may be between careers or retired. Diné College caters to the needs of student parents through its on-campus family housing and incentivizes recruitment through dual enrollment. Many of these students are indistinguishable from our nonstudent community users. Therefore, library staff have to be mindful in how they address patrons and not assume they belong to either student/nonstudent category.

Working at the library help desk has allowed me to observe and work with a range of Diné patrons with varying degrees of shyness and interpersonal inclinations. Greetings and salutations (such as "How are you?" or "Thank you for coming in") may make some patrons self-conscious or uncomfortable (as demonstrated by several visitors preemptively telling me "I'm coming back" before I can bid them a "good day"). It is also important to note that common customer service language and responses do not have translations in the Navajo language, so an individual's friendliness or interpersonal abilities cannot be presumed to exist in standard service interactions. This is often a point of contention among non-Diné individuals who come to us from the South or other areas that place a heavy importance on that type of etiquette. Conversely, there are also situations that arise that may be considered too personal for the academic library help desk. Some patrons have come to know me so well that a visit to the library also means visiting with me and catching me up on the latest goings-on in their lives and communities. Some patrons will gently broach topics of personal hardship, which may eventually result in a request for assistance—ranging from loans to personal favors. Although such interactions may be considered inappropriate in a larger university setting, such scenarios do happen in the tribal college setting. While staff members may be limited in their abilities or willingness to intervene, listening with compassion is always encouraged and appreciated.

Working at the tribal college library service desk also means being open to and making mistakes in adopting Navajo cultural protocols. For example, depending on the age and familiarity with a patron, a simple handshake could be a point of delicate negotiation of Diné cultural protocol—a handshake is not expected in a service desk interaction, but being a member of the community means that a potential clan relative or elder might extend their hand to you after a long period of time since last seeing you. The Navajo handshake is not universally firm or strong, as it is in Western contexts; firmness of the handshake is dependent on one's closeness and relationality to the other person. While the likelihood of encountering this handshake scenario lessens with younger generations of Diné visitors, older individuals may utilize the handshake in many community-oriented social situations, even across the help desk.

While getting accustomed to serving both campus and general community patrons in an academic setting presented a smaller challenge in navigating the diverse needs of students, faculty, staff, and community populations at a tribal college, the larger challenge was critically contending with the cultural and language diversity of my own people. Although I was raised by parents from two different regions of the Navajo Nation and was familiar with the differences in dialect and spiritual beliefs, I tried to avoid conversations related to these differences, as they left me feeling unknowledgeable and inadequate. It was here that I'm grateful for the college's institutional principles and values, which are based in Diné education philosophy and that helped guide those early interactions. In keeping the college's mission rooted in the well-being of the Diné people, the institutional values drive everything from curriculum to human resources policies to off-campus collaborations. Although coming to Diné College challenges what you know about Diné culture, history, language, and teachings, it gives everyone—students, faculty, staff, community members, and so on—the tools to make their journey in and through the institution. At heart, these tools represent pride in Diné culture and teachings while maintaining a sense of humility with one another.

Humility's Roots in Diné Culture and Teachings

Humility has no easy translation in the Diné language, but as a concept and in practice, it is a part of the foundation that makes up the Diné system of living and provides the basis for Diné interpersonal values. Like other Indigenous knowledge systems, the Diné worldview sees human beings as only a small part of a larger whole and completely dependent on the harmony and balance of the whole in order to thrive. Schwarz (1997, 12) observed, "In the Navajo world, the complex network of effect makes the human individual part of and dependent on the kinship group and the community of life, including plants, animals, and aspects of the cosmos that share substance and structure." The essential belief that we are made by Diyin Dine'é (the Holy People) with elements and minerals from the earth—corn, water, sunlight, air, turquoise, white shell, abalone, and jet—establishes the initial connections between Nihokáá' Dine'é (surface people) and the earth/cosmos. From there, the system of K'é is established.

The system of K'é is an essential aspect of Diné culture that begets humility as it recognizes the interrelatedness of all things. Most people, Diné included, are introduced to K'é in contexts relating to clans and kinship among the Navajo. A familial relationship is established between two people when they introduce themselves with their clans; from then on, the two refer to each other in the appropriate kinship terms—younger/older brother/sister, mother/father, son/daughter, grandmother/grandfather, grandchild, and so on. However, as forms of Indigenous knowledges are incorporated in more contemporary institutional settings such as academics, healthcare, business/industry, and government, there has been a need to incorporate the critical discourse of K'é beyond its clan and family relationship contexts in order to facilitate more equitable and reciprocal partnerships between Indigenous and non-Indigenous institutions and people. In practice, this challenges us to critically consider the interrelatedness of all things and how our actions have resounding effects on the world around us—including relationships and interactions with non-Diné people who fall outside of our clan system. This makes us cognizant of how we conduct ourselves with those who do not necessarily share our racial or cultural background.

Humility in Diné Interpersonal Values

Those who grew up in traditional settings or in immersion programs are taught to carry themselves with a set of personal and interpersonal values that will empower the individual and foster success in cooperation and collaboration. The Office of Diné Culture, Language, & Community Service's (2000) "Empowering Values of the Diné Individual" outlines Hózhǫ́ǫ́jík'ehgo (Blessingway) Teachings and Naayée'eek'ehgo (Protectionway) Teachings that create a balance of personal and interpersonal values that ground the Diné individual in their culture while maintaining an openness to new ideas. The following are some examples:

Hózhǫ́ǫ́jík'ehgo Na'nitin
Blessingway Teachings

Há áhweenít'į́	Being generous and kind
K'ézhnidzin	Acknowledging and respecting K'é
Hazaad baa áhojilyą́	Having reverence and care of speech
Hazhó'ó ajísts'ą́ą́'	Being a careful listener
Ahééh jinízin	Being thankful
Há hózhǫ́	Showing positivity toward others

Naayéé'eek'ehgo Na'nitin
Protectionway Teachings

Doo hwił hóyéé'da	Never be lazy
Doo ádahozhdeeláa da	Never be impatient
Doo háníí jizh'ą́ą da	Don't be easily hurt
Doo ni' na'áhozhdiilté da	Don't be overly reluctant
Doo adááh yájiłti' da	Don't be overly argumentative
Doo njichxǫ' da	Don't get mad

The above teachings have been identified as instrumental in cooperation and request-making among Diné individuals and communities. These teachings are carried forward in policy planning in tribal institutions, particularly in education. Like the healthcare field, schools and colleges on the Navajo Nation rely on non-Navajo professionals who largely serve on a rotation basis. Many are given an overview of Diné cultural protocols and norms before they begin interacting with patients/students. The above teachings have been utilized in the Diné College employee orientation sponsored by its human resources office as an introduction to Diné culture and as a précis to the college's values and principles, which are also the values and principles that drive the library's approach to services and scholarship.

College Values and Policies

When Diné College (formerly known as Navajo Community College) was established in 1968, it was done so with the mission to advance postsecondary opportunities for the Navajo people while reinforcing and reintegrating traditional Diné educational philosophies in policy and curriculum. Today, the philosophy of Sa'ah Naagháí Bik'eh Hózhóón—the manner in which one lives in harmony and balance so as to live to old age—guides the college's curriculum, governance, operation, and identity. Every student and employee beginning their journey is guided through the four principles of the college's education philosophy, as they are expected to carry out their work and themselves within the guidelines of Sa'ah Naagháí Bik'eh Hózhóón. The principles are not prescriptive, standards based, or dogmatic; rather, they serve as a foundational framework that can be adapted by anyone, regardless if they are Diné or not:

Nitsáhákees—thinking
Nahat'á—planning
Iiná—implementation
Siihasin—reflection and assurance

Moreover, the college articulates a set of institutional values through which students and employees are expected to implement in their studies, classes, and operations in order to achieve the mission and purpose of the college. Although it is not made explicit in institutional language, the demonstration of the Blessingway and Protectionway Teachings are tools that help the individual navigate the institutional and cultural landscape of the college:

> T'áá hó ájít'éego—Excellence and self-initiative in problem-solving, compassion, setting clear goals, and establishing positive working relationships.
>
> Ahił na'anish—Cooperating and helping one another, keeping all employees well informed, using proper language for communication, respecting one another on equal terms, and honoring K'é.
>
> Ił ídlį́—Respecting the cultural, racial, and gender diversity of the Diné People, maintaining safe, courteous, respectful, and positive learning environments, and valuing inclusiveness.
>
> Ił éėhózin—Understanding, thoughtfulness, competence, confidence, conscientiousness, and reflectivity for serving the needs of the Diné People. (Diné College, n.d.)

The above values not only make clear the professional and interpersonal expectations of the institution but also provide a means for a historically underrepresented group to take pride in and perpetuate their culture without shutting others out. One of the concerns surrounding cultural humility is the implicit suggestion that minorities need to be culturally humble, thereby continuing a history of oppression (Hurley, Kostelecky, and Townsend 2019, 18). The values and principles of Diné College are grounded in traditional beliefs that place people in a state of always seeking and maintaining balance and harmony with other people, the natural world, and the cosmos. It is a lifelong endeavor to seek, restore, and maintain hózhǫ́—the state of balance, beauty, and harmony essential to achieving old age. Much in the way the practice of cultural humility is an ongoing effort rather than a skill set to be mastered, living in and maintaining hózhǫ́ is a constant, lifelong journey that requires continued practice.

Although cultural humility is described as an interpersonal endeavor with no discussion of what it looks like on an institutional level, Diné College's founding principles and values based on the Diné traditional system of living provide a framework for all individuals, regardless of background or place in the organization, to approach their work and social interactions with interrelatedness at its center.

Applying Diné Values in Implementing Cultural Humility Practices in the Library

Because cultural humility requires a consistent effort on the part of the practitioner in recognizing that there is no end goal for their endeavors—that it is a lifelong journey in which the reward is an appreciation for the beauty and diversity in cultures—the value of T'áá hó ájít'éego is an essential component of the cultural humility journey. The phrase *T'áá hó ájít'éego* roughly translates to "It is up to you" (sloganized as "If it is to be, it is up to me") and places a high value on self-initiative, drive, and self-accountability. Initially popularized as a fitness initiative to incite Diné citizens to take charge of their own health through exercise, diet, and holistic measures, it is now used in educational contexts to encourage students to own their education and to recognize that there's no more powerful drive than their own.

Within the Diné College library, the impetus is upon the library staff to meet patrons "where they are" and make sound judgments on how to assist them, taking into account the vast cultural, linguistic, gender, and racial diversity among the Diné people. Besides not automatically assuming that the patron is a student (or otherwise affiliated with the college), it's also important to be prepared to take into account the range of experiences that are behind the patron's visit to the library. For example, a simple question about the Kinaaldá ceremony has an exigence as varied as the Diné individuals asking about it. It may be a part of a course assignment that a student has to research. It may be asked by a young Diné couple from the community seeking to prepare for their own daughter's ceremony. It may be from a Diné individual who grew up in the city and is looking to juxtapose their own coming-of-age story. It may be from a transgender youth wanting to learn more about the roles two-spirit individuals play at various ceremonies. It may be a traditional practitioner who wants to dispute the information that has been transcribed by missionaries and anthropologists. It may be a clan relative who wants to personally invite you to a Kinaaldá and recruit your help. Because the context of most of these interactions are cultural, it requires the library staff to take care in how they assist the patron and approach these topics.

In responding to these types of inquiries, it takes a significant amount of self-initiative (T'áá hó ájít'éego) and openness to others' experiences (Ił ídlį́) to help Diné patrons navigate topics in the cultural context. It takes an honest accounting of the dimensions of humility (Tangney 2000) to break through the initial discomfort one may encounter while broaching the topic critically. In practice, this has required me to acknowledge my own gaps in knowledge, be open to contradictory information, and have an accurate assessment of my own abilities (all of which are described by Tangney)—that I don't know what the "right" way is to run a Kinaaldá, considering the variations based on region, language, and individual medicine person; that just because I had one myself, it doesn't make me an authority (and I have been chastised by some individuals who state that it isn't appropriate for me to talk about my own Kinaaldá); that just because I'm invited to help out at a Kinaaldá doesn't mean I won't be in the way and possibly be scolded or reprimanded in the fast-paced course of events. Although the exchanges don't always yield quick and easy answers, the conversations generated from working with the patron from a place of humility almost always end with gratitude, a plan for moving forward, and a stronger sense of community.

Oftentimes, library staff must exercise a certain amount of professional judgment and implement the Diné values when dealing with certain scenarios, particularly those that aren't as easily addressed with standard operating procedures. Such scenarios are commonplace at hybrid libraries such as tribal college libraries, where the lines between public and academic library policies intersect and need to be mitigated by the library staff. These scenarios may involve a relative or community member who periodically visits the library but does not want to get a library card and always requests a guest pass for computer privileges (guest passes are issued only to one-time visitors; they are not to be given out to anyone who qualifies for a library card—i.e., Navajo Nation residents who visit the library more than once). They may involve a student who has driven over an hour to make it to campus, only to realize they left their overdue books at home and need to check out more books to complete their finals (patrons must be in good standing—i.e., no fines or overdue materials—before checking out additional materials). They may involve a patron who needs assistance setting up a job interview via video conferencing (institutional IT policies do not allow for video conferencing in computer labs, and many lab computers have such conferencing functions disabled).

While standard operating procedures and policies would make it easier for staff to simply write off these scenarios and respond to each with a simple no, such a response is not in accordance with the mission of the institution, nor does it acknowledge K'é. The value of Ił ééhózin requires us to approach problems with thoughtfulness, compassion, and understanding, as well as ask ourselves if we are being reflective and conscious of serving the needs of the Diné people. It certainly requires extra effort on the part of the staff member to think through solutions that are within the bounds of reason as well as reinforcing K'é. With the case of the guest-pass requestor, it wouldn't be unreasonable to continue to allow them to request guest passes if their visits are increasingly infrequent, if they don't already have a library account with fines, and if they don't abuse computer privileges. The student who left their overdue books may be allowed to take more books out if they don't have a history of losing items. Arrangements may be made for the jobseeker by setting aside a room and loaning a laptop (often a personal one) so that the individual can proceed with their interview without breaking IT policies. Moving forward with such decisions also requires the value of Ahił na'anish, keeping colleagues informed and cooperating with one another. In order to implement the above solutions, cooperation, agreement, and planning are needed among colleagues so as to avoid confusion and scenarios in which patrons may consider such exceptions and accommodations as rule. Applying Ahił na'anish also requires working with and clearly communicating with the patron that the accommodations you are making for them is with the intention of helping them within the reasonable bounds of the existing rules/policies.

As with any institution, problems and disputes do arise both at the local level at the library and more broadly with and across different departments at the college. While standard operating procedures and policies are in place to mitigate many of the disputes, professional judgment and implementation of the Diné interpersonal values are needed to come to peaceful resolutions that avoid bureaucratic processes that mirror Western attitudes of conflict resolution that have historically disenfranchised Indigenous people.

Final Thoughts

The challenge of becoming unselved while maintaining a sense of cultural pride is a daunting and seemingly self-contradictory task, especially as a woman and minority. The current literature does not have easy answers for implementing cultural humility practices for those who do not come from the dominant culture and raises doubts about whether or not cultural humility can be practiced at the institutional level. My experience working at a tribal college library does not provide easy answers to these questions, but it does illustrate how Diné culture emphasizes and perpetuates service values and community-based practices without service-industry language or even words for "humility." It welcomes the variety of experiences in and out of Diné Bikéyah without diminishing the epistemologies and praxes that brought the Diné people here today. The Diné educator and founder of the Navajo Studies program at Diné College Ruth Roessel (1981, 173) stated, "As I look at Changing Woman and her two sons I see their emphasis on service. So I want to help and serve my people. . . . I want other Navajos to grow up and be taught that the higher values are service—not self!" The concepts of service to the community/people and humility are deeply embedded in the complex system of Diné cultural values, practices, and expectations. Navigating this system isn't easy; it can often be a source of frustration and disillusionment with popular rhetoric around "coming back" and helping your people. But more than anything else, it is a source of pride, and it ties its most dedicated practitioners back to the land and the community.

Summary

- Despite the homogenous picture of tribal institutions such as Diné College, there is great diversity in people's relationship to their cultures.
- Working with Indigenous populations from a cultural humility standpoint involves (re)integration into communities and unlearning certain practices that are standard in higher education.
- Elements of humility are embedded in traditional Navajo worldview, which recognizes the interrelatedness of all things.
- Rooting its mission in Diné language and culture, Diné College provides institutional-level guidelines informed by traditional Diné

teachings and values for professional and interpersonal interactions for all its employees.

- Traditional Diné teachings and values guide and inform the services provided at the Diné College Libraries, which serve a diverse Diné student and nonstudent population.

Questions for Reflection and Discussion

1. The terms *unlearning* and *becoming "unselved"* are used in the context of reintegrating into a tribal community. How can these practices inform cultural humility practices in predominantly white institutions (PWIs) and minority-serving institutions (MSIs) such as historically Black colleges and universities (HBCUs) and tribal colleges and universities (TCUs)?

____

____

____

____

2. How can institutions embed cultural humility into their institutional language and policies without crossing the threshold to a cultural competencies checklist?

____

____

____

3. At the heart of traditional Diné cultural teachings and values is the fundamental belief in the interrelatedness of all things. What forms of Indigenous knowledges, epistemologies, and ontologies inform and reinforce cultural humility practices?

____

____

____

____

REFERENCES

Diné College. n.d. "About DC." https://www.dinecollege.edu/about_dc/about-dc/.

Hurley, D. A., S. R. Kostelecky, and L. Townsend. 2019. "Cultural Humility in Libraries." *Reference Services Review* 47, no. 4: 544–55. https://doi.org/10.1108/RSR-06-2019-0042.

Office of Diné Culture, Language, & Community Service. 2000. "Empowering Values of the Diné Individual." *T'áá Shá Bik'ehgo Diné Bí Ná nitin dóó Íhoo'aah.* Division of Diné Education.

Roessel, R. 1981. *Women in Navajo Society.* Rough Rock, AZ: Navajo Resource Center.

Schwarz, M. T. 1997. *Molded in the Image of Changing Woman: Navajo Views on the Human Body and Personhood.* Tucson: University of Arizona Press.

Tangney, J. P. 2000. "Humility: Theoretical Perspectives, Empirical Findings and Directions for Future Research." *Journal of Social and Clinical Psychology* 19, no. 1: 70–82. https://doi.org/10.1521/jscp.2000.19.1.70.

9

Beyond Late Fees

Eliminating Access Barriers for Everyone

CARRIE VALDES

I NEVER INTENDED TO BE A PUBLIC LIBRARIAN. I FELL INTO WORKING IN libraries, starting as a work-study student at the circulation desk at my college library. It was an easy job. I checked materials in and out, maintained the reserve section, and stopped anyone who set off the security gate. I did not have the authority to actually prevent anyone from leaving, but we did have a security guard who would intervene if someone attempted to bolt or if they set off the gate twice in a row. I enjoyed working the circulation desk, until the day a young man about to graduate came up to me in tears. The university was blocking his graduation because he had an overdue library book. He had been in a car accident while driving home a few months prior and a passenger in his car had died. More important from the library's perspective was the fact that a library book had been damaged beyond repair in the accident. He explained he did not have any money, was in massive debt, and was facing a civil case from his friend's family. He asked how much he owed to replace the book. This was a situation way above my pay grade, so I called my supervisor. Lisa was sympathetic, but "policy was policy" and the patron needed to pay to replace the book before the library would release the hold on his graduation. The book had been purchased in the 1950s for about $20. Unfortunately, the replacement cost was over $300. The book was out of print and difficult to acquire. The patron needed to pay to replace it, not just cover the purchase price. Graduation was right around the corner, and if he wanted to walk, he needed to figure out a way to come up with the money. The interaction left such a bad taste in my mouth that I immediately applied for a job in another area of the library—government documents. It was extremely boring, but none of the items could be checked out, so that situation would not repeat itself.

Fast-forward five years and I am now married with two small children. We had recently relocated to Moab, Utah, and full-time jobs with benefits were hard to find. My husband wanted to open a restaurant, and I wanted health insurance for the girls. So, when the local library posted a full-time children's library assistant with county benefits, I applied. I was not remotely qualified for the position, but I had an interest and a small amount of previous library experience and was the mother of two young children. I was offered the position.

I had been the children's library assistant for about two months when a young woman came in with her three stepchildren. She wanted to get library cards for herself and the kids, but all three already had accounts that were restricted because of long-overdue materials. Their father had signed as guarantor, but the stepmom insisted the materials were in the biological mother's possession (or at least had been before she went to jail). The stepmom had no idea where the materials were or any reasonable hope of finding them. The total replacement cost was in the hundreds of dollars, and there was no way they could pay it. As I continued to talk to her, she became increasingly upset, to the point that she started yelling at me. Being new to the job, I did what any newbie would do and went to get the director. The director was sympathetic, but late fines and replacement costs were part of the county-fee ordinance, and she had no authority to waive them. Plus, she was a huge advocate of the library treating everyone the same: it was the only way to guarantee we were being "fair." The stepmom could get a card, but none of the kids could use their old card or get a new one with a different guarantor. Policy is policy. The woman left extremely mad, and all the kids were crying. (While this story is not unique, keep it in mind, as it plays an important role in future events.)

Within six months of being hired as the children's library assistant, I was promoted to assistant director. As the assistant director, one of my primary responsibilities was to file charges against patrons with long-overdue items totaling at least $40 in replacement costs. One of the first cases I had was a mom who was homeschooling four kids. Her teacher's card was maxed out at thirty checkouts, and each of the kids' cards had the maximum of ten checkouts. In total, she had seventy overdue library items. Library staff had completed the overdue process, which consisted of looking on the shelves for each item numerous times and contacting the patron at regular intervals to ask about the items. The last step of the process was a registered letter that indicated if items were not returned by a specific date, library theft charges would be filed. Within a few days, the patron came in to talk to me. She insisted the items had all been returned and it was not her fault they did not get checked in correctly. I assured her that we had searched the shelves many times already. She insisted we go look together. I had a printout of all the items, so we walked to the shelves. Almost immediately she pulled an item off the shelf, exclaiming that it was one of the books we were accusing her of stealing and here it was on the shelf! Despite my suspicion that she had brought it into the library and reshelved it herself, I told her I would check for the rest of the list later that afternoon. Unsurprisingly, I found well over half the items on the shelves. I contacted her and explained we still had an issue with about twenty-five items, with the replacement costs totaling approximately $500. She responded that she had returned them all and if we lost them, it was our fault, not hers, so she would see us in court. And that is exactly what happened. I filed charges with the Moab Police Department, an officer referred the case to the county attorney, and the county attorney's office filed charges. At the arraignment, the patron pleaded not guilty and asked for a trial in front of the judge. I testified to the steps we had taken in searching for the items, the numerous attempts to contact the patron, and how our check-in process worked. The patron insisted she put the items on the check-in counter and claimed someone else must have picked them up prior to check-in and walked out with them. The judge agreed it was a possibility and determined we had not proven our case. The patron was declared not guilty by the court.

Coincidentally, at about the same time, another patron debuted in the police blotter in the local newspaper as "Woman Spends Night in Jail Due to Overdue Library Books." What had actually happened was more complicated than that, but trust me, that headline was all we heard about for weeks. We had filed a police report for library theft; the patron had failed to show up for the hearing. The judge issued a bench warrant for her arrest due to failure to appear. She was pulled over for a traffic violation and arrested for the outstanding warrant. Nonetheless, the library was pegged as the cause for her incarceration.

I was promoted to library director in 2007 and spent the next ten years enforcing this status quo. After all, policy is policy. The library was committed to "fair" practices. But these events weighed on my mind—especially the stepmom's plight as she tried to get her stepchildren interested in reading—but I lacked the impetus to change anything.

Then, two things happened. First, we had an incident that required me to call the police. The responding officer's name was familiar to me, but I could not place him until he told me a story about how much his mom hated the library. Turns out, as a child he had come into the library with his stepmom and siblings to get library cards, but everyone at the library was really mean, and they all left crying. Sound familiar? Yeah, I was that mean old librarian. All three of those kids now had families of their own, and not a single one of them had stepped foot in the library in years. As the officer left, he remarked that everyone in this library was much nicer than the other one (we had built a new library building in the meantime) and he might bring his nephew in soon.

Then came the 2018 Public Library Association conference in Philadelphia. I heard from two different speakers on two different days, and their sessions resulted in a massive light-bulb moment for me. That moment has dramatically changed the way we do things at the library. At the conference I heard Steve Pemberton, author of *A Chance in the World: An Orphan Boy, A Mysterious Past, and How He Found a Place Called Home* (2012), talk about how the public library literally saved his life. He spoke of a childhood in an abusive foster family with an illiterate foster father who would beat him when he was caught reading. Pemberton shared about the safe space that was the library, offering solace during an abusive childhood. He visited there alone at a young age and was able to check out materials that sparked his imagination. Using the microfilm collection, he was able to identify his biological father and make connections with his "real" family. I don't know about the rest of the audience, but Steve Pemberton's presentation validated my entire existence. I left his lecture with a feeling of pride in my career and the value of public libraries. The problem? That feeling didn't last. I spent a sleepless night trying to reconcile the feeling of pride and the knowledge that a young Steve Pemberton wouldn't have been able to even use the Grand County Public Library as a child. We wouldn't have issued a library card to a child without a guarantor, and if he did manage to get a card, we would have restricted it due to overdue fines or lost/damaged materials. A child in his situation wouldn't have been able to follow the policies to use the library and would therefore be denied access to the library. How could I feel proud about that?

The next day I listened as the author Elizabeth Gilbert imparted words of wisdom from her mentor. To paraphrase her presentation, she asked, What are you willing to give up to be the library you keep pretending you are? Steve Pemberton spoke about what libraries could offer—diversity, inclusion, access, opportunity, new beginnings, breaking cycles, and building community. Elizabeth Gilbert asked why libraries were not doing what they said they were doing.

We claim we want people to use the library. We market our services, our programs, our collections, and then we throw barriers at people who try to use our services. We kick kids out if they are too young to be in the library unattended. We issue library cards only to those who can provide "proof" that they are members of our community. We refuse children library cards if their parents or guardians are not able to accept legal responsibility for overdue fines and/or lost items. We restrict patrons from accessing library materials if they have overdue fines and/or lost library items. We bring court actions or file debts with collection agencies for lost library materials. Are we a public library or not? As with most public libraries, we at Grand County did not provide library service to all community members. We provided certain library services to all community members but reserved full library service for only those who were willing (and able) to jump through the hoops we required. Essentially, we were providing full library services to local property owners, and our policies and procedures were entrenched in classism and racism. Think about it for a second: residency requirements ensure that library service is fundamentally for white, middle-class property owners in a specific geographical area. I sincerely believe that most librarians are good people with good intentions, but we must recognize our inherently racist past as well. History is a lousy excuse to continue doing what we are doing.

I went home and made a list of everything I was willing to give up to provide services to all members of our community: protecting "our" materials from patrons; my concept of fairness; teaching responsibility; and preventing "cheaters." It is not our business to teach people lessons. We are merely here to facilitate access to information. I decided three principal rules would govern our policies and procedures moving forward: (1) the public library is for the public; (2) people must be kept at the center of our policies; and (3) privilege is thinking that something is not a problem just because it is not a problem for you.

We immediately stopped legal recourse to recover overdue items. We originally had fears that the library would lose out on a lot of money. But once we considered the cost of library staff time, the police department's time, the county attorney's staff time, and the cost of the trial—with court resources accounted for as well—it was clear the taxpayers would be better served if the library simply replaced the overdue items. There was no reason to file theft charges. We spent thousands of taxpayer dollars for absolutely no reason. The cost/benefit analysis clearly showed that pursuing any kind of legal action was more expensive for the taxpayer. It was also a public relations nightmare. We really do not want to be seen as a heartless, insensitive, unforgiving institution; we want to be the local public library that everyone loves. We no longer file charges, nor do we turn over the account to a collection agency. We simply restrict the card from checkouts until the patron talks to us, and we immediately replace any needed item. (The timely replacement of needed items is very important for a reason I will explain later.)

Next, we eliminated overdue fines on children's materials, and soon after, we eliminated overdue fines altogether. There have been numerous studies that show overdue fines (and replacement costs) are a regressive method of raising revenue—they most penalize the families who can least afford to pay. We have a large donation jar at the front desk, and when someone feels guilty about returning items late or damaged, we offer the jar as a solution. The first year that we went completely fine free, the amount of donations actually ended up being higher than the previous year's overdue fine-collection amount.

The next issue we looked at was our policy on unattended children. As with most libraries, we had a hard-set rule that changed over the years. Prior to May 2018, a child had to be twelve years old to be in the library unattended. However, Utah became the first state to pass a "free-range" parenting law in 2018. The law changed the state's definition of neglect to allow children of "sufficient age and maturity" to "engage in independent activities" such as walking to and from school, going to nearby stores, playing outside, or visiting the local library. We now have a policy that addresses behaviors and not age. Of course, there is a commonsense interpretation of "sufficient age and maturity," but our policy does not reference a minimum age. Instead, we focus on what conduct is appropriate at the library. Our policy dictates consequences for unacceptable behavior, including asking a patron to leave the library for the day. Our policy simply states that if a child is too young to be asked to leave, then they cannot be in the library unattended. We have not experienced any increase in unacceptable patron behaviors based on removing the minimum age for unattended children.

Working on the unattended-children policy brought to the forefront another underserved population: children who want to utilize library services but were denied because a parent or guardian was unwilling or unable to sign as a guarantor. Our solution was a student card. We issue a student card to any child under the age of eighteen who can show us that they are a student at the local school district. We do not ask for a guarantor on the account. The card is limited to five items, and if they lose something, they are allowed to check out only four (or three, or two, depending on how many are lost or damaged). We reset the student's account at the start of each school year, meaning they start with a clean slate each year. Because these cards can be issued without guardian knowledge, we do not allow the student to check out R-rated movies or music CDs with explicit lyrics. We remain Children's Internet Protection Act (CIPA) compliant, as the school district requires guardians to sign off on acceptable-use policies each school year, and we have the same internet provider as the school district (Utah Education and Telehealth Network, or UETN). We send a letter home with each child who is issued a student card that explains how it works and offers the parent or guardian the option of closing the student card or changing the card to a regular juvenile card.

The next issue we tackled was residency for adults. The traditional requirement for proof of residency does not work in Moab. Many Moab residents do not have utility bills in their name. Some of them are couch surfers who lack a physical mailing address. There is also a large contingency of folks who camp and the unhoused who lack a physical address. We have a yearly influx of seasonal workers who reside within Grand County but often in vehicles, on friends' couches, or in a room in a shared house. We now offer an introductory card that limits checkouts to five items (the resident limit is twenty) but allows for the patron to utilize all other library services. Upon presentation of proof of residency, we change the patron type to resident. Our residency requirements remain the same: a utility bill, a tax statement, or a rental agreement. Some people bring in proof of residency; some people are content with a checkout limit of five. What matters the most is that library staff can now issue a library card immediately without proof of residency. During the COVID closure, we went a step further and started online registration. The system automatically assigns an introductory patron status until the patron chooses to provide residency information.

Our most recent change is the elimination of replacement costs. A few years ago, our library was all over local social media because someone was trying to help her friend raise enough money to replace the books she had lost a decade ago. However, the patron had checked out women's health information ten years before that was already five years old at the time of checkout, and the last thing I wanted was a replacement item covering women's health issues when that information was at least fifteen years old!

Grand County has a fee ordinance, and as a county department we are legally required to follow the fee schedule. The library board reviews and recommends changes to that fee schedule yearly. In 2018, they recommended that the fee for lost or damaged items be changed from "cost of item" to "replacement cost." If we are not going to replace the item, we do not charge the patron. If the lost or damaged item was already replaced, there is no reason to replace it again. If the determination is made to not replace the item, then there is no replacement cost. This is why it is so important we replace needed overdue materials in a timely manner. With our new mission, we recognize that materials have a short shelf life and people make mistakes. I am constantly asked about people "taking advantage," but we have not found this to be a problem. We do not have more materials going overdue than we did before, and hopefully those lost materials are somewhere in the community being used.

While it is difficult to see any good in COVID, the closure did result in a couple of positive changes to library service. First, we were already participating in a program called Kids Café, which is a partnership with the Utah Food Bank to provide nutritional snacks to children after school and during the summer. Because the Kids Café program addresses food insecurity within the community, we were allowed to distribute those meals within a few days of the Health Department closing the library. It did not take much to convince the Health Department that we should be able to start a curbside service for library materials as well. We implemented that within two weeks. Now the library is fully open again, but we continue offering curbside service for those who do not want to come into the library or who prefer the convenience of the service.

The second positive impact was the circulation of mobile devices. Prior to COVID, we had a limited number of Chromebooks and mobile hotspots available for checkout. We required the patron to agree to a wordy loan-agreement document that attempted to scare them with the cost of repairing or replacing a device. We had restrictions on who could check out a mobile device and for how long. With COVID, it became apparent immediately that people needed internet access and a large number relied on the library for that access. Using grants, we doubled, then doubled again, the number of circulating devices. We eliminated the unnecessary paperwork and removed the restrictions. The popularity of the mobile devices soared, and we are looking to double the number yet again. Interestingly, we have not experienced any higher loss rate, and the current process is much easier for both patrons and staff. We also kept the Wi-Fi network available 24/7 all throughout the pandemic, and we continually saw community members utilizing Wi-Fi from their vehicles or from the seating areas outside the library building.

So, what is next for the Grand County Public Library? Our current project is challenging the Dewey Decimal System. Most people in the library world now acknowledge that Melvil Dewey was a racist, misogynistic, cis, Christian, white man, but most do not attempt to question the system he created. Additionally, the US lives with the fact that our public libraries were racially segregated. We carry this history. If we are still operating under policies, procedures, rules, and standards from our past, we are operating under a racist umbrella. How can we justify doing what we have always done but not acknowledge that it is problematic? A few public libraries have switched to BISAC subject headings, but most have not. Why does it matter? Because, as I said before, just because it is not a problem for you personally does not mean it is not a problem . . . language matters. For example, in the Dewey Decimal System, "African American Culture" is classified separately from "American Culture." The LGBTQIA+ community is classified in an area dedicated to sex instead of as a group of people. Dewey's classification of religion is the 200s, but "Christianity" takes up the entire section except for 290, which is reserved for the remainder of all the world's religions. One of my biggest issues with the Dewey Decimal System is the way it classifies Indigenous, Black, immigrant, and women's rights history under "Social Sciences" instead of "History," which results in a white version of historical events.

I have three staff members working on changing our classification system: one is a full-time head of service, one is a full-time library assistant who does most of the cataloging, and the other is a part-time library clerk who does most of the material processing. They have been tasked with researching options and presenting me with their recommendations. I want input and ownership at all levels of staffing as we start what is likely to be a major project.

We are still working on identifying and eliminating institutional barriers. Often it is a matter of questioning why we do something the way we do. If the answer is because that is how we have always done it, it is time to reconsider. Most of our staff members are excited to do things differently, and I also rely heavily upon them to identify barriers that prevent them from serving the public. I have an open-door policy and allow staff to question any changes prior to implementation. My only rule is that they limit what-if questions—most what-if questions are scenarios that may or may not take place, and I prefer to address known issues, not imaginary concerns.

Most of our identified institutional barriers are procedural in nature; we have simply changed the procedures. There has been little resistance from the community, especially library users. I also operate under the maxim that it is often easier to beg forgiveness than to ask permission. With a supportive staff and library board, I am empowered to try things differently and attempt to move our public library from a book warehouse to a true community center.

I think about the young man from my college days who simply wanted to graduate. I do not know what happened to him, but I suspect he is not donating money to the university. I also think about the young police officer who did not use library services for more than a decade because of how his stepmom was treated. He regularly visits now with his nephew, and I want his nephew's experiences at the Grand County Public Library to be better than his childhood experience.

Summary

- Public libraries often provide some library services to all community members, but full library services only to those who are willing and able to deal with the barriers we put in place.
- Privilege and thinking "That's always how we've done things" can prevent library staff, management, or administrators from recognizing and/or seeking to change inequitable service models.
- Fully embracing public library mission statements can have numerous benefits, including positive PR, better relationships and trust with all community sectors, and increased return on investment for taxpayers.
- The chapter describes how identifying and eliminating institutional barriers have been an ongoing process of continual improvement.

Questions for Reflection and Discussion

1. Think about a time that enforcing a policy resulted in bad customer service interaction in your library. What parts of the policy contributed to the difficult situation? Are those elements grounded in equity? How could the policy be adjusted to result in a positive customer service experience for both patrons and library staff?

    ____

    ____

    ____

2. What is your library's mission or vision statement? It likely includes some language about inclusivity, free access, service, learning, community, and so on. Consider some of your recent library experiences, projects, plans, or goals. Is your library consistently living up to its mission or vision for all users? If not, what are you willing to change to become the library your mission or vision describes?

    ____

    ____

    ____

3. When you and your fellow library staff work with and discuss library materials, do you think and talk about them as though they are yours (the library's and/or library staff's) or the community's? What might change in your library's approach to service if materials are always considered the property of users, as opposed to items that the library staff collect and protect?

    ____

    ____

    ____

4. If an individual who uses your library lost or damaged an item, would they still be able to fully access all library services (check-outs, computer use, etc.)? Based on your answer, compare and contrast the potential consequences experienced by the library versus the patron.

   ____

   ____

   ____

5. Can an individual living in their vehicle in your community obtain a library card? Why or why not? What if that person has a school-age child—can the youth have a library card? What does the library and/or community truly stand to gain or lose by providing or denying these cards?

   ____

   ____

   ____

Resources

Dowd, Ryan. 2018. *The Librarian's Guide to Homelessness: An Empathy-Driven Approach to Solving Problems, Preventing Conflict, and Serving Everyone.* Chicago: ALA Editions.

Homeless Training. n.d. http://www.homelesslibrary.com/.

Wacek, Dawn. n.d. "Free Is Key: Library Fines and Access." Filmed at TEDxUWLaCrosse. TED Talk, 14:15. https://www.ted.com/talks/dawn_wacek_free_is_key_library_fines_and_access.

REFERENCE

Pemberton, Steve. 2012. *A Chance in the World: An Orphan Boy, A Mysterious Past, and How He Found a Place Called Home.* Nashville: Thomas Nelson.

10

Small Changes Make an Impact

How Access and Metadata Services Teams Address Cultural Humility

MELANIE BOPP, TRICIA MACKENZIE, AND KIMBERLEY A. EDWARDS

WHILE MANY LIBRARIES SEPARATE FRONT-OF-HOUSE OPERATIONS FROM those in back-of-house, at George Mason University (GMU), Access Services and Metadata Services are both part of the operational arm of the Libraries, and both departments perform a vital basic function: get the materials to the user.

In recent years, the two departments have begun to address that function through a lens of cultural humility. A greater focus on DEI issues isn't terribly unusual—an increasing number of American universities have been spurred by racially motivated attacks and murders in the US to work toward antiracism—but there can frequently be a long wait for antiracism discussions to become actionable items. Rather than waiting for those changes to take place, the managers of GMU's Access Services and Metadata Services have chosen to institute direct change at the departmental level and to make cultural humility a core departmental value. These adjustments to policies and procedures allow those throughout the organization, both staff and students, to benefit from their immediate effects.

Background

GMU offers undergraduate, graduate, and PhD programs to more than thirty-seven thousand students and was identified in 2020 as the most diverse public university in Virginia by *U.S. News & World Report* (Cristodero 2020). The Libraries hold more than one million circulating items and make available more than two million e-resources. The Libraries are distributed across three campuses, with collection development, acquisitions, and cataloging work centralized in the Fenwick Library on the main Fairfax, Virginia, campus. The Libraries consist of three divisions: Access and Resource Management, Learning Research and Engagement, and Digital Strategies and Systems. Access and Resource Management (ARM), the operational division of the Libraries, includes the centralized Metadata Services department, as well as the Fenwick Library Access Services department.

Tricia Mackenzie and Melanie Bopp, the managers of the two departments, have had a long-standing interest in cultural humility and DEI work. The Database Integrity and Analysis department, managed by Kimberley Edwards, supports their work by providing data and enacting change to the library system based on the policies and procedures adopted in the departments. As managers, we realize that we bring our own lived experiences into the workplace—that we, our staff, and our work are largely impacted by the intersections of race, ethnicity, ableism, socioeconomic status, and religion, to name a few. As white women, we understand that it is especially important for us to continually check our biases and work to ensure the library reflects the diverse nature of GMU's user population.

This mindset, combined with our desire to have a more immediate impact on library users, spurred the adoption of our departmentally driven approach. We believe that cultural humility can and should play a role in all library interactions, from those between staff and library users, to those between supervisors and staff.

Users

ACCESS SERVICES

Small things can make a huge difference for library users. In academic libraries, where users come in at all sorts of stress levels and from all sorts of backgrounds, there is no one-size-fits-all mentality that can work at a public services desk. GMU has a diverse student population, from varying socioeconomic backgrounds, racial and ethnic groups, and religious beliefs, and each student deserves full library support.

In working to support those populations, Melanie has taken the firm approach that policies need to be treated as guidelines, not hard lines. Library policies are in place for many reasons, but at the desk they are frequently meant to protect the library. Overdue fines ensure books are returned on time, checkout limits are to make sure no one is hoarding library material, and procedures for claims returns and proxies are to ensure the user is responsible for the items borrowed. However, none of this accounts for what the user needs from library staff: understanding and assistance.

Access Services staff at George Mason strive to remember both of those things during all interactions. Some policies are unfortunately unbending, due to university or state guidelines, but there are so many ways to make life easier for library users: understanding that the student in front of you has never used your academic library before—maybe they are a first-generation college student, transfer student, or graduate student from a country with different regulations at their libraries—and needs more explanation and time to figure out what they are doing or where they are going; understanding that the student in front of you is currently not only stressed about their classes, but perhaps also about where they are going to sleep that night, or how they will pay for dinner or groceries.

The department's staff have general approval to bend some policies as needed, such as overriding fines to check out books, extending due dates or times of library materials (so long as there are no other users waiting for the item), or adjusting space reservations as needed, to name a few. When staff have both the permission and the expectation to treat library users as individuals with individual needs, we can customize our services and make our department one focused on service to others. We can practice empathy and try to find ways to say yes within a set of policies that tell us to say no.

In addition to policy considerations, Access Services tries to recognize and mitigate the hierarchical differences between staff and user. For example, the library has behavioral expectations that users are expected to follow (noise zoning, disruptive behavior definitions, etc.), but the response to 99% of violations is a conversation with staff, not a call to campus police. Staff are told that campus police are there as a resource if they or others are being threatened, but, especially after more recent incidents of racial profiling and violence, we do not want to put ourselves or our users in a potentially uncomfortable or dangerous position. There are other actions Access Services can take first, and which should always be attempted before calling the police, like addressing the problem directly, asking the user to leave, or bringing a second staff member as backup or a witness to the interaction. It is important to note that some institutions have police forces that practice community policing, which emphasizes problem-solving and developing relationships with their community; but, sadly, this is not practiced across all of academia.

Access Services also generally tries to operate under "show, don't tell" guidelines—showing users how to navigate the library catalog and website, bringing them over to a browsing computer to walk them through the steps of how to book a study room or request an ILL. Having a metaphorical hand to hold can make such a difference in a one-on-one interaction. This also allows staff to meet the students where they are—mentally, emotionally, and culturally.

METADATA SERVICES

With a lack of daily interactions with users, it can be easy for those in metadata departments to focus their attention solely on the materials to be described. This can lead to becoming immune to the impact that description decisions have on users (or even resource creators). It also allows for complacency with the problematic standards used to describe materials and to fall back on the saying "But this is how it has always been done." The core goal of all metadata work, however, is to ensure that resources are accessible. Actively practicing cultural humility, and its cycle of reflection and learning, helps metadata staff to not lose sight of that goal when describing resources.

In GMU's Metadata Services department, a more thoughtful approach to description began to evolve in the Summer of 2018. It was at this point that the Libraries began to collect resources for the Mason Zines and Minicomics Collection. Typically handcrafted by the author or artist, zines are generally not published by traditional publishers and instead are distributed by their creators or zine publishers. The lack of traditional publishing of zines allows creators to express their unedited feelings and personal experiences on any topic. This might include topics of sexual abuse, drug use, sexuality, immigration status, physical or mental health, along with more general topics like social and political history and popular culture.

The Libraries have long been a contributor to the Name Authority Cooperative Program (NACO). NACO records, or authority records, are created to standardize forms of names or terms to facilitate efficient searching in library catalogs. Historically, the training for that program teaches catalogers to record as much information about creators as is made available. This is emphasized by the rules of RDA, which provide the option to describe gender, birth and death dates, affiliations, associated places, addresses, and so on. In researching zine cataloging in order to develop new cataloging guidelines, however, Tricia encountered the idea that some personal information about authors and creators that is included in zine content was not and should not be included in authority records or resource description. This made her reflect on previous NACO practice across the Libraries. It was obvious that, unless given explicit consent, catalogers should be more respectful of and work to protect the privacy of creators.

In 2019, local NACO creators began reading sections of *Ethical Questions in Name Authority Control* (Sandberg 2019) as a group, and resulting discussions led to the development of a LC/NACO Name Authority Record Policy for Personal Names. The document states, "Metadata Services is committed to reparative cataloging practices, promoting inclusivity, and protecting the anonymity and private details of persons in the description of library materials" (GMU Libraries 2020). In this policy, gender, ethnic, and racial identities are excluded in both free text and controlled fields; birth year may only be added with the permission of the creator; deadnaming is prohibited; and pseudonyms are used only with permission. In addition, all authority record creators check themselves with the following questions: Is this biographically necessary? Does this information impinge on someone's privacy? And finally, are my biases reflected in this record?

After this, the Metadata Services department initiated several projects to more appropriately reflect the diversity of the Libraries' users and to tackle the historically white, patriarchal, heteronormative, and Christian-centered Library of Congress (LC) vocabularies and classification schedules that existed in legacy catalog data. The first major project was to replace the racist Library of Congress Classification (LCC) Cutter ".N" for "Negroes" on approximately two thousand items in Mason Libraries. The ".N" Cutter was historically used across LCC on older materials and had not been a priority in past catalog cleanup projects. As a group it was decided to replace ".N" with ".B" for "Black people," as it is a more inclusive description than ".A" for "African Americans." The metadata librarian developed a crosswalk from ".N" to ".B" Cutters and created a workflow to update call numbers in the catalog and on the physical items. Progress on this was slowed due to the pandemic, but it is hoped the project will be completed during the fall 2021 semester.

Metadata Services also began to develop a local vocabulary of alternative subject headings to more appropriately depict the Indigenous peoples represented in the Libraries' Diverse Picture Books Collection for Early Childhood

Education. For this project, our metadata specialist used her experience working with Indigenous peoples and the X̲wi7x̲wa Library at the University of British Columbia to include names used by the tribes themselves. An example of this is changing "Nipissing Indians," as it appears in Library of Congress Subject Headings (LCSH), to "Nipissing First Nation." Currently, these new headings appear alongside the original headings in the MARC record and in the Primo display, the local discovery layer.

Finally, to open the process to input from users, a form has been created so users can report any offensive description they discover in the catalog. The form is posted on the Libraries' antiracism LibGuide, and there are plans to have it added to the library's main page soon. It is hoped this form will enable users both to notify MS of harmful language and to be empowered to become partners in describing themselves.

At the consortia level, there was additional work done to improve catalog data. As a member of the Washington Research Librarian Consortium (WRLC), the Libraries share a catalog and bibliographic records with nine partner institutions. As such, it is important to be aware of how any reparative cataloging choices might impact others in the consortium. In some cases, it is possible to make changes at a local level that are visible only to GMU patrons through Primo, but in other areas it is necessary to collaborate more closely with our colleagues in the WRLC.

In this capacity, GMU, along with WRLC colleagues, made the decision to hide the offensive term "Illegal Aliens" and replace it with "Undocumented Immigrants" in the public display. Unfortunately, because of the complexities of GMU's local print and electronic collections and the way resources are displayed in Primo, in many instances both terms still appear in local MARC records and GMU's Primo display. Having both the offensive and more appropriate headings side by side in the public display is not ideal, but it is a first step in remediating these issues until LC officially updates the heading.

CHALLENGES

For Access Services, one of the first major hurdles for building a department of empathy was cultural—this sort of practice was not available to departmental staff previously, and exceptions to the rules had to be cleared by the head of the department. Staff were hesitant to take on that responsibility—what if they made the wrong decision? Melanie spent months after starting at Mason assuring staff that she would back up their decisions 100%—if she disagreed with something, she would let them know for the future, but their decisions could and should stand. Staff who work the desk need to feel and be experts on applying policy, and that includes when to bend the rules. Over time, staff witnessed Melanie backing up their decisions with library administrative staff and have adopted more independence in making these decisions. Communicating about those exceptions and decisions also helps drive policy change—if Melanie knows where users are coming into conflict with standing policies, that directs attention to potentially outdated or, worse, harmful policies. Access Services has also struggled to form the desired relationships with outside university groups, such as campus police or university life. Melanie would love to expand relationships with these groups to further the department's goals of helping students and providing access to a range of resources, not just those specific to research. Unfortunately, the quickly changing environment over the past year has made it difficult at best to form those connections.

Metadata Services has also approached the difficulties inherent in the work by emphasizing a greater degree of autonomy—in their case, focusing on departmental autonomy. With support from the division's assistant university librarian, and further emboldened by the antiracist agenda of the new university president, Metadata Services has largely approached the work of ethical cataloging with the "ask for forgiveness, not permission" approach. This fits within the larger ARM division goal of approaching DEI work through a viewpoint of cultural humility—seeing the work as ongoing and under continuous revision, rather than a series of special projects requiring approval from the highest level of the Libraries.

As stated above, one challenge that Metadata Services is still working through is the replacement of the term "Illegal Aliens" with "Undocumented Immigrants" in GMU's local catalog. It was easy to add the new term to bibliographic records across the consortium, as it was a task that was handled by the central WRLC office; but to hide the offensive term from display required each institution to add over a hundred lines of specific code to their individual instances of Primo. At GMU, the systems department is often overworked and unable to rapidly address finite projects such as this. Additionally, the approach of adding hundreds of lines of code to replace a small number of subject headings in the catalog is not a scalable or practical long-term solution.

Staff

ACCESS SERVICES

It is imperative that any person working at the library's information desk practice service with cultural humility. The clear initial step was to foster that culture within the department. Enabling staff members to make exception-related decisions in the moment was the first step to getting users what they need and empowering staff to consider that individual user need.

This staff empowerment was begun through training, closely followed by outlining the boundaries within which exceptions can be made. Exceptions for material due dates are flexible, but fines and fees at GMU are less so. Training for staff covers the policy and procedural aspects at the desk, as well as the general acknowledgment and acceptance of users' differences. While this training is all currently casual—department meetings, emails, and the like—there are plans to formalize this training and make it available to student workers. Student employees may not have any previous workplace experience with cultural humility or DEI practices, so this is a great opportunity to provide that initial training for them. It also provides an opportunity to positively impact the next generation of employees as student workers graduate into multiple disciplines and fields.

Student employees are also the perfect staff to reflect the makeup of the general student population. Student supervisors in Access Services have worked hard to hire students who reflect said makeup. The current roster of student workers includes a variety of cultural, racial, and ethnic backgrounds, socioeconomic statuses, and sexualities and gender identities. Melanie is proud of one of our students for letting us know that they are nonbinary and have a different name than on their paperwork, and that our student supervisors were both approachable for the student and made the change immediately. It may seem like a small thing to a supervisor, but it makes a huge difference for the student workers, and carries over into how users are treated and the responses they receive.

METADATA SERVICES

As was shown with Access Services, an important part of empowering library staff in the practice of cultural humility is creating a departmental culture in which it is emphasized. Work on reparative cataloging projects is extremely important and engaging work for many members of Metadata Services, and it is work they can feel good about doing for both users and colleagues. As a manager, Tricia is a firm believer in ethical leadership and prefers to approach management in a more egalitarian way. This means that she solicits feedback for workflow planning and decision-making. She also likes to try to get a consensus when developing new policies, such as the LC/NACO Name Authority Record Policy for Personal Names.

When the pandemic started, Tricia implemented weekly virtual coffee meetings as an opportunity to literally see one another and check in, and to restore a small bit of normalcy. In addition to the weekly check-ins, last summer the department also had Friday lunchtime team-building events where they would watch documentaries or other shows as a group and have online discussions in real time via Slack. Many of the documentaries selected by Metadata Services members related to racism and historical inequities in the US, and the exercise offered those in the department a chance to empathize and learn together in a more relaxed way. Those team-building events were put on hiatus during the academic year, but Tricia received a request to reinstate this team-building activity during the summer months.

CHALLENGES/FAILURES

Changing culture is difficult during even the best of times. Melanie's tenure at George Mason University began shortly before the COVID-19 outbreak, so much of the cultural shift took place via Zoom meetings, emails, and messaging. While library closures and staff separation made communication and team building difficult at best, it also brought staff closer together. They also became more likely to speak up and discuss issues, and more amenable to change. However, there are a lot of projects and plans that had to be put on hold due to the more pressing issues with the pandemic (several of which are shared below, with the department's future plans). As a manager, Melanie has not been as available as she would have liked—COVID-related meetings and task forces have taken time and effort that in other times would have been directed toward formal policies, procedures, and trainings for staff and student workers. But the truth is that there will always be other things going on, and the key component to cultural humility—starting by examining your own beliefs and practices—is important enough to prioritize and carve out time for, and to encourage other staff members to do so as well.

Even before the pandemic and the transition to telework due to COVID-19, Metadata Services members had experienced quite a lot of recent change due to the migration to Alma and a shared consortial catalog environment. Many staff worked exclusively onsite with physical materials and had never worked on data-management projects, and some had never used Microsoft Excel professionally. Getting used to working from home and using software like Webex and Zoom were also new experiences for many of the staff. Like many other cataloging departments around the country, when GMU closed, there was a scramble to think through workflows for those rainy-day data-management projects that had been on hold for several years. Tricia collaborated with the department organizing these projects to identify priorities and test the workflow and online training with staff members from Metadata Services. Once training was completed, Tricia worked with her staff to make sure they were comfortable with the projects, responded quickly to concerns about the projects and software from other staff members, and did some online follow-up training as needed. For Tricia, the primary focus was prioritizing the needs of her staff, as she believes that the morale and safety of staff should always be at the forefront of leaders' and managers' priorities, especially during times of crisis.

Further Work

ACCESS SERVICES

Access Services would like to perform a full-scale review of its policies from a DEI and cultural humility standpoint. Recently it was brought to Melanie's attention that one of the building-use policies prohibited things like bathing in the library; however, GMU has Muslim students who use the Libraries' bathrooms to bathe before prayers. While the original line was meant as a statement of "The library is a shared, public space," there are religious and cultural problems with that and other lines in library policies and procedures.

In looking at policy, Access Services has also begun exploring the option to eliminate most fees for student users, both overdue fines and replacement costs. This is in part to increase access for students from lower socioeconomic backgrounds, but it is also an attempt to level the playing field for the entire student body, without relying on the student to know they can ask for an exception to standing policy. At the 2019 Midwinter Meeting, the American Library Association passed the "Resolution on Monetary Library Fines as a Form of Social Inequity" (2019, 1), stating that fines "present an economic barrier to access of library materials and services." Access Services has already extended the grace period to the maximum possible time period permitted in the system before items are declared lost, but overdue fines are added to the lost and processing charges, making an already large fee larger and staying on the user account even once the item is returned. Eliminating fines, however, is more involved at a state institution—going fine free isn't as simple as just saying so—and library staff of all departments need to ensure that making these changes does not jeopardize our stewardship of state funds. In addition, there are additional politics involved within the WRLC that complicates these decisions. Changes at one institution can and will affect the others, often in ways the home institution hasn't considered.

Long term, Access Services hopes to have department staff as well as student workers reflect the diversity of the George Mason University community. These efforts have already started for student workers—for example, different options are being explored for advertising available student-worker positions with different groups and student organizations; but that is a much longer-term conversation when discussing full-time staff.

The department has also talked about ways to extend customer service expertise to other library staff members. Libraries are a service profession, and any library staff member may end up interacting with a library user, whether or not it is part of their routine job duties. This sharing of expertise would have the dual benefits of improving user experiences within the Libraries and empowering all library staff to use interactions with patrons to inform their own daily work.

METADATA SERVICES

Much of Metadata Services' upcoming work will be collaborative in nature, both locally and with the WRLC. At GMU, the Metadata Services department and the Special Collections Research Center have joined forces with the Task Force for Ethical and Anti-oppressive Metadata (TEAM) to tackle reparative resource description across various silos and collections. TEAM also hopes to develop guiding principles for resource description for the Libraries. In addition, Metadata Services is in the initial stages of a larger-scale review of problematic subject headings and has already identified more classifications to be updated. They are also hoping to work with subject specialists, faculty, and other users when developing local subject headings.

At the WRLC level, a group was recently formed to develop policies and projects related to reparative cataloging in the shared catalog. The group will be evaluating alternative controlled vocabularies for use in records, identifying actions that can be taken collectively to address offensive language in the catalog, and developing policies for when one institution wants to adopt changes that the others do not wish to adopt.

Conclusion

There is no one-size-fits-all approach to the management of a department—whether that be managing the work of the department or the people who work within it. Everyone has their own lived experience, and that is largely impacted by the intersections of their identities. We carry each piece of who we are everyday in every environment we move through. Respecting this is vital to the health and continued development of any department, as well as to our user populations. By reflecting on our own experiences and points of view, we can then better understand those around us, with the end goal of fully and inclusively supporting our users and our university.

For Access Services and Metadata Services departments, much of the daily work is completed in the background of regular library activities. Yet that same work has the capacity to have a profoundly positive impact on all those who come into contact with it, and though the two departments operate in very different spheres, they work to provide the same end result: improving services and being responsive to user needs.

Summary

- Staff members of any department in the library, regardless of its focus, can implement cultural humility into their daily work in order to make a direct impact on the institution.
- The use of cultural humility helps staff maintain focus on user needs, especially when looking at library policies and procedures.
- Empowering staff to make decisions and participate in departmental decisions encourages new ideas from different backgrounds and points of view.

Questions for Reflection and Discussion

1. What staff training or policies would help make cultural humility a focus for your department?

2. What existing access services policies might be acting as a barrier to your users? Some things to consider: circulation, reserves, physical spaces, and behavioral policies.

3. What existing metadata services policies and procedures might be acting as a barrier to users and creators of content? Some things to consider: racist and offensive descriptions and classifications in your catalog, existing policies on the inclusion of personal information in authority records, and whether to include terms from alternative vocabularies that may improve user access.

4. What departments and/or communities outside the library do you need to foster relationships with in order to best serve your users from a cultural humility standpoint?

5. How does practicing cultural humility as a department differ from an individual practicing cultural humility? How does that translate into action?

____

____

____

____

Resources

Adler, M., and L. M. Harper. 2018. "Race and Ethnicity in Classification Systems: Teaching Knowledge Organization from a Social Justice Perspective." *Library Trends* 67, no. 1: 52–73. https://doi.org/10.1353/lib.2018.0025.

Association of College and Research Libraries. 2021. "ACRL Access Services IG: Equity, Diversity, Inclusion, and Anti-racism in Access Services." YouTube video, posted February 25, 1:12:50. https://youtu.be/JruTIY_U9mM.

Association of College and Research Libraries. 2021. "ACRL Access Services Interest Group: Dude, Where's My Yes?" YouTube video, posted March 4, 1:02:18. https://youtu.be/JuQxIUUfdYI.

Sandberg, Jane. 2019. *Ethical Questions in Name Authority Control*. Sacramento: Library Juice.

US Department of Justice, Office of Community Oriented Policing Services. 2014. *Community Policing Defined*. https://cops.usdoj.gov/RIC/Publications/cops-p157-pub.pdf.

WebJunction. 2021. "Eliminating Library Fines: Improving Community Access, Equity and Usage," July 22. https://www.webjunction.org/events/webjunction/eliminating-library-fines.html.

REFERENCES

American Library Association. 2019. "Resolution on Monetary Library Fines as a Form of Social Inequity." https://www.ala.org/aboutala/sites/ala.org.aboutala/files/content/governance/council/council_documents/2019_ms_council _docs/ALA%20CD%2038%20RESOLUTION%20ON%20MONETARY%20 LIBRARY%20FINES%20AS%20A%20FORM%20OF%20SOCIAL%20JUSTICE% 20Revised%201_27_0.pdf.

Cristodero, D. 2020. "Diversity Tops Mason's Big Gains in U.S. News Rankings." George Mason University. September 14. https://www2.gmu.edu/news/ 2020-09/diversity-tops-masons-big-gains-us-news-rankings.

George Mason University (GMU) Libraries. 2020. *LC/NACO Name Authority Record Policy for Personal Names Metadata Services.*

Sandberg, Jane. 2019. *Ethical Questions in Name Authority Control.* Sacramento: Library Juice.

11

Cultural Humility and Servant Leadership

MARK EMMONS

I AM A *THIRD-CULTURE KID* (TCK), HAVING SPENT MOST OF MY CHILDHOOD in six foreign countries as the son of a diplomat. A TCK is a "person who has spent a significant part of his or her developmental years outside the parents' culture. The third-culture kid builds relationships to all of the cultures, while not having full ownership in any" (Pollock 2009, 13). When I first encountered this concept much later in life, it struck a chord.

Upon my return to the United States for my senior year in high school, I did not really fit in. I felt different, even foreign. People would make assumptions about who I was based on my appearance as a white male with a California accent inherited from my parents. They saw minor differences in my clothing or how I wore my hair or my taste in music or how I danced—and teased me. But they did not see differences in my beliefs and values and assumed that I shared their views about the world. The most glaring example was beliefs about race. When I went to college, I was shocked by the casual racism uttered by white dormmates, who felt safe expressing their views to me. Unfortunately, they were right in one sense: I didn't share their views about race, but because I desperately wanted to fit in, I said nothing. I lacked the courage to confront.

Those assumptions about my values, on race and on other matters, had little basis in reality then, and that remains true today. One reason for the disconnect between how I appear and who I am is that TCKs like me tend to embrace diversity and do not necessarily feel an affinity for members of our own cultural group (Useem and Downie 1976; Pollock 2009). I think this is because I grew up in constant contact with values and social and cultural norms different from those of folks who grew up exclusively in the United States. I adopted some of the values and norms from cultures outside the United States. I learned languages other than English. Though I was privileged, especially because I was the son of a diplomat, I was still seen as the "other." As a result, I learned how to immerse myself in an unknown context and to observe before engaging. I learned how not to stand out, to hold back part of myself. I learned how to shift between cultural contexts. I learned to accept people for who they are. I developed a strong egalitarian philosophy.

While my TCK upbringing has been mostly beneficial, there has been at least one area where it has not served me as well. When I first returned to the United States, I saw Americans as being more alike than different, almost as a national culture. The differences across countries were far more visible to me than the differences between cultures within the United States. This included views that diminished the perceived differences between different racial groups, which was particularly problematic in light of my egalitarian views—the United States is definitely not equitable. And I did not always recognize my own privilege.

Perhaps most critical to my developing identity, and especially to my emerging ideas about leadership, growing up as a TCK viewed as the other built a strong desire to help people. Ruth Hill Useem's (1976) original research uncovered a common desire among TCKs to help, and it was one of several reasons the conceptualization of being a TCK reverberated with me. Even though a subsequent guide on how to respond to the experience of growing up a TCK (Pollock 2009) and a systematic review of TCK literature (Tan, Wang, and Cottrell 2021) did not confirm that the desire to help and serve others is a fundamental characteristic of TCKs, it remains one of the most salient features to me. To this day, I feel a strong desire to serve others. Being a TCK has greatly influenced my life, including my views on intercultural communication, cultural competence, and leadership. For leadership, that desire to serve fits naturally with servant leadership.

When the editors of this book introduced me to the idea of cultural humility, it resonated deeply. Because of my upbringing, I had always been suspicious of the idea of cultural competence, which I had understood to mean that it is possible to fully understand people with different cultural backgrounds. When I took an undergraduate course in intercultural communication, I turned my attention to cultures I did not grow up with, and this reinforced for me the difficulty of absorbing a culture not one's own. Instead, cultural humility supposes that it is possible to understand oneself and to use that understanding in interpersonal relationships to be open to another person's cultural identity. Cultural humility also seems a better approach to issues of diversity, equity, inclusion, and belonging.

In their article introducing cultural humility in libraries, Hurley, Kostelecky, and Townsend (2019, 553) write: "One question we have left unexplored here is how libraries can develop cultural humility in their leadership or among their staff." My intent is to explore the relationship between cultural humility and servant leadership, to make a case that cultural humility is a natural frame for servant leaders, and to consider how leaders might develop cultural humility.

Servant Leadership

Robert Greenleaf (1991, 27) coined the term *servant leadership* in the 1970s: "The servant-leader *is* servant first. . . . It begins with the natural feeling that one wants to serve, to serve *first*." He continues: "The best test is: do those served grow as persons: do they, *while being served*, become healthier, wiser, freer, more autonomous, more likely themselves to become servants? *And*, what is the effect on the least privileged in society; will they benefit, or, at least, not be further deprived?" (emphasis in the original).

The overall concept of servant leadership aligns well with the definition of cultural humility expressed by Hurley, Kostelecky, and Townsend (2019, 549): "Cultural humility involves the ability to maintain an interpersonal stance that is other oriented in relation to aspects of cultural identity that are most important to the other person, the ability to recognize the context in which interactions occur, and a commitment to redress power imbalances and other structural issues to benefit all parties."

Servant leadership is other oriented, concerned with the well-being of followers.* Leadership scholars have built upon Greenleaf's original ideas. Larry Spears, the first director of the Greenleaf Center for Servant Leadership,

* *Follower* is a standard term used in the leadership literature but is contested; it is mostly honored but sometimes disparaged. Joseph Rost (2008) argues for the use of *collaborator* instead of follower. Because the idea of a collaborator aligns better with cultural humility than does the word *follower*, I will follow his lead and use it in this chapter.

developed a list of ten characteristics common to servant leaders (Spears 2004). The characteristics intertwine with each other and together point to the central focus on the follower with attributes that include empathy, awareness, listening, healing, and a commitment to the growth of people. Dirk van Dierendonck (2011) conducted a thorough review and synthesis of the literature to develop a model of servant leadership. Within his larger model, he identifies six characteristics fundamental to servant leaders: empowering and developing people, humility, authenticity, interpersonal acceptance, providing direction, and stewardship. It is notable that he places the motivational concept of empowering and developing people first, as he characterizes servant leadership as primarily a development model.

Empowering employees allows them the freedom to perform. Accepting and having trust in employees engender trust in the leader and the organization. The expertise and knowledge and ideas employees bring means that the organization succeeds in its mission, performs well, and meets its goals.

The servant leader's role is to foster a shared purpose and direction and to provide support and resources. The servant leader's concern becomes the well-being and growth of employees. The outcome of the relationships built in an organization with authentic servant leaders is an organization that faces challenges and opportunities together and is more likely to reach the greatest potential working in concert.

Servant leadership might seem an ideal model, but it can have its drawbacks. First and foremost, it requires an authentic alignment with personal values. If a leader is self-centered or is not self-aware, then it will be difficult to be a true servant leader. Humility can help (a full discussion comes later in this chapter). Second, servant leadership is not well understood, and it can be challenging to communicate. Popular notions of leadership deny that leaders might also be servants. As a result, some employees may perceive servant leaders as weak or ineffective. Third, it is time consuming to build the relationships that are the foundation of servant leadership. Timeliness and urgency do not work well early in a servant leader's tenure. Fourth, even if servant leadership works, the servant leader's formal authority may be diminished—though this can be a good thing if relationships have been enhanced.

In addition, servant leadership can be difficult to implement. If a servant leader loses sight of a shared purpose and goals and does only what employees want instead of what the organization needs, then employees will lack motivation. If a servant leader does not hold employees accountable, then employees may reduce performance. If a servant leader assumes they know best and steps in to fix a problem instead of leaving it to the employees, it will reduce trust and motivation. If employees do not have the big picture, they may make poor decisions. If employees do not have the confidence, they may not step up. Finally, servant leadership is predicated on the idea that employees have positive motivations and intentions. If they do not, then servant leadership could be the wrong leadership style.

HUMILITY

Humility is a key characteristic of servant leaders, but it did not appear explicitly in the original work by Greenleaf (1991) or Spears (2004). Van Dierendonck (2011) included humility in his model because it emerged as an essential dimension in a number of later servant leadership models and instruments. Humility again emerged as a key dimension of servant leadership in a Delphi study (Focht and Ponton 2015) and a later systematic review that also involved van Dierendonck (Eva et al. 2019).

Servant leadership definitions of humility are consistent with the concept of humility embedded in cultural humility, as servant leadership emphasizes self-knowledge, personal responsibility, teachability, and a commitment to others. Patterson (2003), Dennis and Bocarnea (2005), and van Dierendonck (2011; van Dierendonck and Patterson 2015) cite the work of Sandage and Wiens (2001), which defines humility as the ability of leaders to put their own interests, talents, and achievements in perspective and who are not self-focused but rather focused on others. Thompson and colleagues (2008, 378) offer a similar definition:

> It refers to having a reasonable view of oneself—and an accurate understanding and acceptance of one's strengths and development opportunities. Humility means representing contributions accurately, accepting praise graciously, and showing sincere appreciation to others. We find that leaders who show humility are appropriately proud of their accomplishments and have self-confidence; but they are not arrogant. They fundamentally do not see themselves as better than others.

Focht and Ponton (2015, 50) write that "servant leaders do not promote themselves, they promote others . . . putting others first. They are truly humble, not humble as an act. Servant leaders understand it is not about them—things happen through others; exemplary servant leaders know they cannot do it alone." Owens, Johnson, and Mitchell (2013, 1518) derived a definition based on observable behavior of *expressed humility*: "an interpersonal characteristic that emerges in social contexts that connotes (a) a manifested willingness to view oneself accurately, (b) a displayed appreciation of others' strengths and contributions, and (c) teachability."

Humility is not a virtue that has been widely valued in leadership. In the popular mind, servant leadership confronts negative connotations, just as does humility. Whereas humility is often associated with meekness and low self-esteem, servant leadership is often associated with weakness and servitude. A servant leader may be seen as too nice, as someone who places a collaborator's wants above the organization's needs. As a result, a servant leader may be seen as being soft and passive, of being a doormat and a pushover. When servant leadership is done poorly, as described earlier, there is some truth to these negative views. When done well, nothing could be further from the truth. When done well, servant leadership helps organizations while improving the well-being of collaborators (Brewer 2010; Eva et al. 2019; Parris and Peachey 2013). While it is beyond the scope of this chapter to share all the ways that servant leaders might succeed, I believe that humility—and cultural humility in particular—is one frame that is essential.

HUMILITY AND PERFORMANCE

Humble leaders improve organizational performance. One reason for this is that leaders who exhibit humility foster trust in their collaborators (Collins 2001; Yang, Zhang, and Chen 2019), and having trust in a leader has been demonstrated to be a mediating factor for performance (Sharkie 2009). In his abstract, van Dierendonck (2011, 1228) summarizes the outcome portion of his model, claiming that "a high-quality dyadic relationship, trust, and fairness are expected to be the most important mediating processes to encourage self-actualization, positive job attitudes, performance, and a stronger organizational focus on sustainability and corporate social responsibility." Argandona (2015, 68) explores why humility in managers engenders trust:

> This may manifest in many ways: allowing (and asking) others to freely give their opinion, listening to them, not scorning them, not adopting threatening demeanors toward anyone who disagrees with her or who could overshadow her, sharing successes and accepting responsibility (while still demanding accountability from others) for her mistakes and failures, not seeking the limelight, apologizing and rectifying when she is wrong and expressing

> gratitude, appreciation and warmth, not emphasizing on outward forms of self-assessment, as the appearance and popularity, not giving praise or criticism of an exaggerated or inaccurate manner, or not setting excessive comparisons between people, especially if this leads to competitive attitudes.

Humble leaders enhance performance in a number of ways. They give credit where it is due and acknowledge that success comes from the efforts of collaborators (Caldwell, Ichiho, and Anderson 2017; Collins 2001). In fact, followers—Kelley deliberately uses the term in his article "In Praise of Followers"—are more important than leaders in getting the job done (Kelley 1988, 1992). They enhance teamwork by discovering and fostering collaborator capabilities, giving them responsibility and freedom to decide, and being open to their ideas (Owens, Johnson, and Mitchell 2013). They provide clear direction and focus because they know their own capabilities and values and the organizational mission (Caldwell, Ichiho, and Anderson 2017). Each of these performance measures aligns with the portrayal of humble leaders as other oriented and prioritizing the needs of collaborators.

POWER AND AUTHORITY

The second part of the Hurley, Kostelecky, and Townsend (2019) definition of cultural humility is "the ability to recognize the context in which interactions occur." A leader's tasks are too many to enumerate, so I will not attempt to cover them here; but I will note that all involve a relationship between a leader and a collaborator, as derived from Rost's (1991, 2008) literature review. This raises the reality of a power imbalance.

Hurley, Kostelecky, and Townsend (2022, 29) point out that

> a practice of cultural humility is essential at all levels of the library. But the nature of hierarchical organizations is such that the attitudes and behaviors of directors, deans, and other high-level leaders have an outsize impact on organizations and organizational culture. Leaders who practice cultural humility can transform an organization.

Power, at its most basic, is the capacity to influence. A leader with positional authority by definition holds power in an organization, but that power is granted purely by title or rank. Positional power bestows the ability to reward or to coerce, but I do not consider it to be legitimate power in and of itself. Instead, legitimate power derives from expertise or relationships. Leaders and collaborators will at times conflate leadership with positional authority. For the servant leader, power is based on relationships with collaborators and is a means to better serve collaborators and the organization.

Greenleaf (1991, 115) addresses the issue of power and authority, noting that leaders cannot give power away irretrievably and still be leaders. Greenleaf sees servant leadership as a path for leaders to share their power and to foster legitimate authority. I agree. However, from my perspective, Greenleaf's view of leadership veers dangerously close to noblesse oblige, or the idea that powerful people need to be benevolent to the less privileged. On the surface, noblesse oblige recognizes that powerful people attained their positions through privilege and should therefore be generous. However, noblesse oblige can lead to attitudes of superiority that disregard unearned privilege and can reinforce marginalization. The danger is especially acute for leaders whose power derives solely from positional authority and who are not egalitarian. For this reason, I prefer the later definitions of servant leadership that incorporate humility.

CULTURAL IDENTITY

Most troublesome for an exploration of cultural humility and leadership, servant leadership rarely addresses issues of cultural identity. Greenleaf and Spears do not consider the cultural identity of leaders or collaborators at all, nor do the leadership scholars who have developed the most cited subsequent servant leadership models. There are several cross-cultural studies that apply the GLOBE (global leadership and organizational behavior effectiveness) cultural attributes to servant-leadership dimensions. These studies found that such dimensions were valued across all cultures, but that some aspects of leadership were valued more than others, depending on the culture (Hale and Fields 2007; Mittal and Dorfman 2012; Pekerti and Sendjaya 2010; Winston and Ryan 2008). However, there are no similar studies around cultural identities within the United States or within other countries. This is a major problem because it is not clear how servant leadership might relate positively or negatively to issues of diversity, equity, inclusion, and belonging, especially as they connect to issues of power and privilege. As Hurley, Kostelecky, and Townsend (2019, 550) point out, "The intersection of the inherent power imbalances with cultural factors can exacerbate the negative aspects of those power imbalances." While their focus was primarily on the relationship between librarians and patrons, they acknowledge that "power imbalances among library employees can be trickier" (ibid.). This is particularly true of the relationship between library leaders and library staff.

The third part of the Hurley, Kostelecky, and Townsend definition of cultural humility includes "a commitment to redress power imbalances and other structural issues to benefit all parties." This aligns with Greenleaf's (1991, 27) final question in his conceptualization of servant leadership: "What is the effect on the least privileged in society; will they benefit, or, at least, not be further deprived?" I share Greenleaf's opinion that servant leadership should benefit the least privileged in society, but I do not think that their not being further deprived goes far enough. I agree with Hurley, Kostelecky, and Townsend that nurturing cultural humility is a means to redress power imbalances within an organization—in this case, for the benefit of the librarians and the library. In fact, I feel that redressing power imbalances is the main reason servant leaders should embrace cultural humility as a natural frame for their day-to-day work as leaders.

Nurturing Cultural Humility

So how can servant leaders nurture cultural humility within themselves? Hurley, Kostelecky, and Townsend (2019) argue that cultural humility is an ongoing practice. Their view aligns with developmental approaches to servant leadership. Argandona (2015, 69) explains that humility is a virtue and that "human virtues, being operative habits, are acquired by the voluntary and deliberate repetition of acts, with honest motivation and effort." While "it is unlikely that self-centered, dogmatic, narcissistic people can be trained to be other-centered, sensitive, empathetic, socially sensitive servant leaders" (Eva et al. 2019, 129), I would argue that most other people can indeed learn to be humble leaders: "What library leadership can do, however, is develop cultural humility in themselves" (Hurley, Kostelecky, and Townsend 2022, 27). In order to develop the habit of humility, leaders have to want it, understand it, and practice it. Wanting to be humble can be difficult, as humility runs counter to many other human motivations. As a leader, you might be motivated to protect your ego. You might want to impress or to be right or to look good in front of your colleagues. You might want to seek attention or be given credit. You might care deeply what others think of you and want to be liked. You might have privileges you take for granted. This is why the servant leader characteristics of self-knowledge, personal responsibility, and teachability matter. Understanding your own motivations along with your strengths and your weaknesses makes it possible to reflect on your relationships with your collaborators and to be clear about your own reactions. After an interaction, taking a pause to reflect and gain an authentic understanding of your own motivations and limitations means that you can change your reaction to respond with humility. The key to change is teachability, an understanding that humility is not innate or fixed, that you can change and improve. Humility is not a goal, but an everyday habit and demeanor.

A CAUTIONARY TALE

I do believe that cultural humility harmonizes well with servant leadership. However, as I mentioned earlier, servant leadership can be associated with servitude. Servitude, in turn, is associated with servility and subjugation. This idea is particularly fraught for marginalized peoples who have been historically subjugated and may lead to a reluctance to embrace a servant leadership philosophy. The workplace power dynamics related to race, gender, and class might make it difficult to disentangle the negative connotations of the word *servant*. There is very little in the literature on this idea, but there is a case study that provides an intersectional critique problematizing servant leadership.

Helena Liu (2019) shares the story of Jeff, an Asian cis-male heterosexual manager in a large Australian IT company. Jeff is a servant leader who exhibits "trust and honesty as he empowers his subordinates and support them to grow and succeed" along with "humility," "emotional healing" and a "selfless commitment to the greater good of the community" (1104). However, Liu concludes that his employees did not see him as a servant leader, but as a servant. Liu argues that this was because of "interlocking power dynamics around his race, gender, sexuality, age and class" that were "underpinned by the abiding stereotype of Asian identities as the model minority," along with racialized Asian stereotypes of passivity and of males that are feminized (1105). She concludes that "sociopolitical meanings of race, gender, sexuality, age and class inform the extent to which people can be accepted or rejected as a 'servant leader'" (1108). The lesson is clear and unsurprising: that conceptions of servant leadership are not neutral and are influenced by dynamics of race, gender, and class.

So what are the lessons from this cautionary tale? Does this mean that servant leadership cannot work for BIPOC leaders? That BIPOC leaders should adopt different models of leadership? Jeff's case is illustrative. Liu does not argue that Jeff was a poor leader, instead that he was *perceived* by several of his employees as a servant rather than a servant leader. She argues that Jeff did not fit the "the abiding white masculinist ideals of leadership as about an individualized assertiveness or aggression denied to male Asian bodies" (Liu 2019, 1106). Based on her description of Jeff and his leadership, it seems to me that he was in fact a good and effective servant leader, that the problem was with the misperception by his employees. This returns to the idea that servant leadership is not well understood and is challenging to communicate, meaning some employees may perceive servant leaders as weak or ineffective. The goal, then, is not to change the leadership, but to change the perception through increased communication about servant leadership and what makes it work. I will argue that servant leadership is a good model for leaders, including BIPOC leaders, and that despite the popular negative connotations tying *servant* to *servitude*, the fundamental advantages of servant leadership far outweigh popular misconceptions because they mean that the library belongs to the collaborators and the community it serves. I believe that cultural humility, when combined with the components of servant leadership, is a framework that can help servant leaders address these concerns.

The idea of servant leadership can be misconstrued and avoided by aspiring leaders due to the popular misconceptions of servant as servitude. In fact, I find it interesting that the notions of servant, humility, and follower are all commonly disparaged in popular culture. I find it interesting because these three notions are honored within their respective fields for embodying the very characteristics that make them powerful and successful behaviors. My personal belief is that, rather than reject these terms, leaders and aspiring leaders need instead to legitimize and embrace them because of their very real power to transform.

HOW DOES CULTURAL HUMILITY WORK WITH SERVANT LEADERSHIP?

If leadership focuses on the relationship between leaders and collaborators in pursuit of common interests and goals, then servant leadership distinguishes itself from other models of leadership by the nature of that relationship. In particular, servant leadership is characterized by the idea of serving through empowering and developing collaborators. I believe that the danger of framing leadership as paternalistic noblesse oblige can be surmounted by using cultural humility as a frame. The key element is to reorient concern for self toward concern for others, to put collaborators first. By viewing themselves and their collaborators clearly, by accepting themselves and appreciating their collaborators, and by understanding that work gets done through collaborators, leaders can apply a clear cultural humility lens to the social context and redress power imbalances.

I have tried my best to embody servant leadership in my role as a leader, with varying degrees of success. As I shared in the introduction, my ideas regarding leadership were influenced by my youth as a third-culture kid. In particular, the idea of a leader's role to serve others resonated with me. These ideas were crystalized and defined much later in life as I pursued a doctorate in educational leadership and advanced from informal leadership roles into formal leadership positions. As a leader (and a TCK), I strive to be other oriented, placing the needs of the community first and treating my followers as collaborators trying to accomplish shared goals. Practically, this means getting to know collaborators on both a work and a personal level and to be known myself—I remain better at getting to know others than at being known, as I still tend to hold a part of myself back. I most often take a procedural approach, trusting the process to get us where we want to go. I tend to consider both the collaborator and the organization within a learning frame, treating gaps in knowledge and skills as developmental needs.

I would like to think that my servant leadership approach tends to diminish power differentials. I believe that I have succeeded in this at the interpersonal level, where I consider employees to be collaborators. However, I do not believe I have succeeded in breaking down power differentials at the structural institutional level. This might be adequate if I were to accept Greenleaf's goal that the least privileged "at least, not be further deprived." It is not enough, though, when my goal is to benefit the least privileged. Now that I am older and less driven by a need to fit in and more by social justice, I feel more comfortable confronting racism when I see it—but that is not enough to break down systemic inequities. As Hurley, Kostelecky, and Townsend (2022, 31) conclude in their chapter on leadership:

> Powerful individuals within an organization are positioned to make an impact. Often they choose to support and maintain the status quo that brought them to positions of power. However, leaders can choose to take actions that

> challenge existing power structures. Even reactive action is better than indifference, even when that action simply involves supporting an agenda that less-powerful individuals and groups have worked to build.

I have only recently been formally applying a cultural humility lens to my work as a leader, so my thoughts are in a formative stage, but supporting agendas of the less powerful collaborators and taking actions that challenge the power structure seem like a promising path forward.

Conclusion

My intent was to explore the relationship between cultural humility and servant leadership, to make a case that cultural humility is a natural frame for servant leaders, and to consider how leaders might develop cultural humility. Cultural humility and servant leadership align well, with both featuring humility as a core characteristic. They share similar definitions of humility as an ability and willingness to see oneself accurately, an orientation and appreciation and commitment to others, and an openness to learning. Because they share definitions, cultural humility serves as a natural frame for servant leaders for two main reasons: (1) it obliges leaders to maintain an interpersonal stance that is other oriented in relation to aspects of cultural identity and (2) it seeks to redress power differentials, at least at the interpersonal level. Servant leaders can develop cultural humility by making it a habit, which means they have to want it, understand it, and practice it.

My background as a TCK and experiences as a leader and a collaborator lead me to believe that cultural humility can serve as a very useful lens and tool for servant leaders. I think this is because cultural humility indeed provides a sound approach to the problem that Hurley, Kostelecky, and Townsend (2019, 549) are trying to address that "my norms aren't the only norms, and unfamiliar norms aren't necessarily wrong." Their focus was on the librarian-patron interaction, which is usually transactional and transitory. My focus was on the leader-collaborator interaction, which is usually relational and long term. This means that there is also ample opportunity for leaders to develop cultural competence, at least to some extent. However, even a long-term relationship will take you only so far in truly understanding the intricacies of a culture different from your own.

Hurley, Kostelecky, and Townsend (2019, 550) emphasize the idea that "cultural humility requires us to be open to interactions having a cultural dimension, without anticipating what exactly it will be." My upbringing as a TCK means I am comfortable with unfamiliar people in an unknown context, at least most of the time. Despite this, I still have a lot of work remaining to develop my own cultural humility. I have mostly let go of my need to be right or to fit in or to impress, but I tend to take my privilege for granted. Even more than forty years after returning to the United States, I still observe before engaging and hold back part of myself to all but my closest family and friends, so I particularly need to work on sharing more of myself as demanded of many models of servant leadership and some definitions of humility. I plan to continue working on my cultural humility.

Ultimately, the lesson I learned from growing up as a TCK is to get to know the individual. Hurley, Kostelecky, and Townsend (2019, 551) call attention to the "danger that we lose sight of the fact that we are not interacting with a culture, but with an individual who has multiple identities." I agree with them wholeheartedly. An individual is shaped by their culture and their multiple identities and their experiences to become a unique person. Because there is a relationship between the leader and collaborator, we can get to know and accept each other for who we are, as individual human beings with inherent worth. A servant leader who uses the lens of cultural humility embraces that worth.

Summary

- Servant leadership is a leadership philosophy that is other oriented and prioritizes the needs of followers. Servant leaders see followers as collaborators and partners toward a common purpose.
- Humility is a key characteristic of servant leaders who see themselves and collaborators accurately and who place the needs of collaborators first.
- Leaders can learn to be humble.
- Humble leaders improve organizational performance.
- Leaders who practice cultural humility can redress power imbalances.
- Cultural humility can serve as a very useful lens and practice for servant leaders.

Questions for Reflection and Discussion

1. In addition to humility, van Dierendonck (2011) lists five other characteristics fundamental to servant leaders: empowering and developing people, authenticity, interpersonal acceptance, providing direction, and stewardship. How might these characteristics complement and enhance cultural humility?

2. How might a servant leader cultivate cultural humility? It is one thing to want to be humble and to understand what humility is; it is quite another to practice humility. What specific steps could leaders take to:
    a. Develop the habit of learning from collaborators?

    b. Take the collaborator's lead as to which of their cultural identities are relevant?

c. Overcome issues of ego such as:
   - Accepting feedback?
   - Acknowledging that they might be wrong or that they have shortcomings?
   - Being open to different values, beliefs, and opinions?
   - Changing ideas in the face of new information?
   - Overcoming defensiveness?
   - Understanding a collaborator who disagrees?

____

____

____

____

____

3. How might a servant leader overcome the negative connotations of the word *servant*? Of the word *humility*? Of the word *follower*?

____

____

____

____

Resources

Argandona, A. 2015. "Humility in Management." *Journal of Business Ethics* 132, no. 1: 63–71. https://doi.org/10.1007/s10551-014-2311-8.

Kelley, R. E. 1988. "In Praise of Followers." *Harvard Business Review* 66, no. 6: 142–48.

van Dierendonck, D. 2011. "Servant Leadership: A Review and Synthesis." *Journal of Management* 37, no. 4: 1228–61. https://doi.org/10.1177/0149206310380462.

REFERENCES

Argandona, A. 2015. "Humility in Management." *Journal of Business Ethics* 132, no. 1: 63–71. https://doi.org/10.1007/s10551-014-2311-8.

Brewer, C. 2010. "Servant Leadership: A Review of Literature." *Online Journal for Workforce Education and Development* 4, no. 2: 1–8.

Caldwell, C., R. Ichiho, and V. Anderson. 2017. "Understanding Level 5 Leaders: The Ethical Perspectives of Leadership Humility." *Journal of Management Development* 36, no. 5: 724–32. https://doi.org/10.1108/jmd-09-2016-0184.

Collins, J. 2001. "Level 5 Leadership: The Triumph of Humility and Fierce Resolve." *Harvard Business Review* 79, no. 1: 66–76.

Dennis, R. S., and M. Bocarnea. 2005. "Development of the Servant Leadership Assessment Instrument." *Leadership & Organization Development Journal* 26, no. 8: 600–15. https://doi.org/10.1108/01437730510633692.

Eva, N., M. Robin, S. Sendjaya, D. van Dierendonck, and R. C. Liden. 2019. "Servant Leadership: A Systematic Review and Call for Future Research." *Leadership Quarterly* 30, no. 1: 111–32. https://doi.org/10.1016/j.leaqua.2018.07.004.

Focht, A., and M. Ponton. 2015. "Identifying Primary Characteristics of Servant Leadership: A Delphi Study." *International Journal of Leadership Studies* 9, no. 1: 44–61.

Greenleaf, R. K. 1991. *Servant Leadership: A Journey into the Nature of Legitimate Power and Greatness*. Paulist Press.

Hale, J. R., and D. L. Fields. 2007. "Exploring Servant Leadership across Cultures: A Study of Followers in Ghana and the USA." *Leadership* 3, no. 4: 397–417. https://doi.org/10.1177/1742715007082964.

Hurley, D. A., S. R. Kostelecky, and L. Townsend. 2019. "Cultural Humility in Libraries." *Reference Services Review* 47, no. 4: 544–55. https://doi.org/10.1108/rsr-06-2019-0042.

———. 2022. *Cultural Humility*. Chicago: ALA Editions.

Kelley, R. E. 1988. "In Praise of Followers." *Harvard Business Review* 66, no. 6: 142–48.

———. 1992. *The Power of Followership: How to Create Leaders People Want to Follow, and Followers Who Lead Themselves*. New York: Doubleday/Currency.

Liu, H. 2019. "Just the Servant: An Intersectional Critique of Servant Leadership." *Journal of Business Ethics* 156, no. 4: 1099–112. https://doi.org/10.1007/s10551-017-3633-0.

Mittal, R., and P. W. Dorfman. 2012. "Servant Leadership across Cultures." *Journal of World Business* 47, no. 4: 555–70. https://doi.org/10.1016/j.jwb.2012.01.009.

Owens, B. P., M. D. Johnson, and T. R. Mitchell. 2013. "Expressed Humility in Organizations: Implications for Performance, Teams, and Leadership." *Organization Science* 24, no. 5: 1517–38. https://doi.org/10.1287/orsc.1120.0795.

Parris, D. L., and J. W. Peachey. 2013. "A Systematic Literature Review of Servant Leadership Theory in Organizational Contexts." *Journal of Business Ethics* 113, no. 3: 377–93. https://doi.org/10.1007/s10551-012-1322-6.

Patterson, K. A. 2003. "Servant Leadership: A Theoretical Model." PhD diss., Regent University, Virginia Beach, Virginia.

Pekerti, A. A., and S. Sendjaya. 2010. "Exploring Servant Leadership across Cultures: Comparative Study in Australia and Indonesia." *International Journal of Human Resource Management* 21, no. 5: 754–80. https://doi.org/10.1080/09585191003658920.

Pollock, D. C. 2009. *Third Culture Kids: Growing Up among Worlds.* Boston: Nicholas Brealey.

Rost, J. C. 1991. *Leadership for the Twenty-First Century.* Westport, CT: Praeger.

———. 2008. *Followership: An Outmoded Concept. In The Art of Followership: How Great Followers Create Great Leaders and Organizations,* ed. R. E. Riggio, I. Chaleff, and J. Lipman-Blumen, 53–64. San Francisco: Jossey-Bass/Wiley.

Sandage, S. J., and T. W. Wiens. 2001. "Contextualizing Models of Humility and Forgiveness: A Reply to Gassin." *Journal of Psychology & Theology* 29, no. 3: 201–11. https://doi.org/10.1177/009164710102900302.

Sharkie, R. 2009. "Trust in Leadership Is Vital for Employee Performance." *Management Research News* 32, no. 5: 491–98. https://doi.org/10.1108/01409170910952985.

Spears, L. C. 2004. "Practicing Servant-Leadership." *Leader to Leader* 34:7–11. https://doi.org/10.1002/ltl.94.

Tan, E. C., K. T. Wang, and A. B. Cottrell. 2021. "A Systematic Review of Third Culture Kids Empirical Research." *International Journal of Intercultural Relations* 82:81–98. https://doi.org/10.1016/j.ijintrel.2021.03.002.

Thompson, A. D., M. Grahek, R. E. Phillips, and C. L. Fay. 2008. "The Search for Worthy Leadership." *Consulting Psychology Journal: Practice and Research* 60, no. 4: 366–82. https://doi.org/10.1037/1065-9293.60.4.366.

Useem, R. H., and R. D. Downie. 1976. "Third-Culture Kids." *Today's Education* 65, no. 3: 103–5.

van Dierendonck, D. 2011. "Servant Leadership: A Review and Synthesis." *Journal of Management* 37, no. 4: 1228–61. https://doi.org/10.1177/0149206310380462.

van Dierendonck, D., and K. Patterson. 2015. "Compassionate Love as a Cornerstone of Servant Leadership: An Integration of Previous Theorizing and Research." *Journal of Business Ethics* 128, no. 1: 119–31. https://doi.org/10.1007/s10551-014-2085-z.

Winston, B. E., and B. Ryan. 2008. "Servant Leadership as a Humane Orientation: Using the GLOBE Study Construct of Humane Orientation to Show That Servant Leadership Is More Global Than Western." *International Journal of Leadership Studies* 3, no. 2: 212–22.

Yang, J., W. Zhang, and X. Chen. 2019. "Why Do Leaders Express Humility and How Does This Matter: A Rational Choice Perspective." *Frontiers in Psychology* 10, article 1925. https://doi.org/10.3389/fpsyg.2019.01925.

PART IV

HOPEFUL VISIONS

12

Knowing (un)Knowings

Cultural Humility, the Other(s), and Theories of Change

NICHOLAE CLINE AND JORGE R. LÓPEZ-MCKNIGHT

An Opening

We open with gratitude for the invitation to join this conversation, for and to the editors staging the conversation in this specific way—a way (which is here) that, we sense, is reaching toward us, and at the same time is a way of knowing, in itself, that is right alongside a way of being in relation. Such a reaching and knowing, such a relation, grounds this conversation in generosity and presence.

And it is our luck to express some thoughts here in this space, together, which, for us, is a way of breathing that has come to be here as writing, an expression that is listening and learning, unfolding; and, riding with Stefano Harney and Fred Moten (2013), is also to study (together)—thinking carefully and intentionally, playfully, joyfully meaning-making together, as we hold this ceremonial space, for us and you to grow and practice and study. We bring ourselves into being in this way, dreaming our own becoming, reaching out to another.

In this way, in this movement and exploration, we are seeking and reaching for new ways of understanding and loving ourselves, and one another, ways of being with and for that we have not, or have not always, and which are here and elsewhere coming to be. This is part of a larger, ongoing project, a variation on a theme, which is to say it is a way of articulating our shared dream for ourselves and our communities.

Introduction: Toward

The history and present of cultural humility, as a framework and set of practices, are known to us (Kostelecky, Townsend, and Hurley 2023). Cultural humility is also being written and developed across fields and workplaces as we begin to engage with its commitments. But as we consider and reflect on the possibilities of this approach for and within librarianship, a deeper understanding—through curiosity, inquiry, and critique—is needed. We need this, and we share this (be)longing with many others.

And so we begin, as ever, with questions: What is cultural humility dreaming of? And what are its visions? What is it demanding and refusing? Where is it pointing? And who is it in the direction of?

In these few pages, we devote ourselves to exploring these questions together, and with you, toward considering what cultural humility is, is doing, and might be within our field (and beyond). We hope to provide a sketch of the terrain that cultural humility maps out and helps us navigate, while also gesturing toward a horizon of possibility we might still be imagining.

Through Critique: A Note on Process

How can we hold and offer a loving, humble critique? Our field not only projects itself as "nice," but critique, as a practice and as an idea, itself (in the academic/professional discourse) is delivered and instantiated in ways that take up all the air in the room, is competitive, exhaustive (and exhausting), destructive, and—perhaps even worse—lacking critical, careful engagement. This is what gets circulated and marked as critique; a critique that tells and turns on itself.

We are here with this critique, in some ways to refuse it, which is to say that we are not against it but hoping to move beyond it, together, relationally, knowing very well that our imaginaries must be brighter and deeper, more alive than our critiques. We offer critique as a generative, generous, and creative act, and share it together as ceremony.

As we know, critique (which was never ours to begin with) can be absorbed and bend toward the institutional power of libraries—a circulative power of destruction, extraction, and accumulation—in order for it to become the best version of its imagined formation, which is another way to say that critique is often not performing the function it thinks it is performing; rather, even critique can be absorbed into oppressive and exploitative logics that serve and undergird structures of social domination. And yet, still, here we are with critique even as it possibly acts to (re)legitimize the power of the library, complicit in undermining the very efforts it is trying to strengthen.

But we know that, as Denise Ferreira da Silva (2018, 25) says, "we need to move beyond critique," which Smith (2020, 32) interprets as "the way that critical writing occupies a certain space, a stuck place at odds with itself." Nevertheless, that space is necessary to make room for a particular location of refuge (however briefly), for genuine, close exchange and deep study, for a refusal that pushes us right up to the edge of the limits of critique, which is a horizon, which can be our exit (toward, if not out of). An exit that leads to imagining and building together, which is the beyond.

Of course, as the poet Roger Reeves (2021, 43) suggests, "critique should always be an act and announcement of love . . . a pointing toward possibility salvaged from our intentions and actions." In that direction, though from a different approach, Keguro Macharia (2015, 71) shares that "love demands critique; love is a duty to critique." This love is necessary for cultural humility or for what cultural humility seeks to do and become, but it's a love as well for the editors of the collection who we know and care for, and for perhaps a soon-to-be love for the other contributors in the collection, and maybe you, the reader. A love for radical connection, an always already solidarity-in-waiting, and for living and working differently, together and not. Layered on that love, which is a possibility and condition, we hold and carry what Eve Tuck and K. Wayne Yang (2018, 8) offer regarding critique: "We mean to do it without eating each other. We mean to do it as a way of life."

It is in this way that we offer this critique, which is also an exploration, which is also love.

Cultural Competency, (We Sense) a Haunting

Embracing the concerns offered by the editors in their initial formulation of cultural humility (Hurley, Kostelecky, and Townsend 2019), we, too, see observable sharp differences that distinguish it away from cultural competency. And, further, we worry that cultural humility will take the shape, form, and direction of cultural competency, in that it will decorate résumés and CVs, conference programs and themes, find its location (only) in the scholarly discourse by way of articles, chapters, books, keynotes, and perhaps, then, arrive as professionally/institutionally sanctioned diversity (sub)standards, dis/organizing us just enough to not push beyond.

But our concerns also turn differently, as it seems we have arrived in this same, familiar place, at a different time, with the unchanging conditions of a racial/colonial project of social domination and violence that is trying to imagine itself in the future. Such a project thrives on violence and domination happening not just now and in the past but in the future. A project that will siphon the energies from any destabilizing effort to its own(ership) institutionalized and professional existence, extracting the transformative elements, neutralizing its demands, and coopting the practice, while leaving the fundamentally oppressive institution structurally intact. Such a project would exploit any effort against it. It must.

And our concerns keep turning, returning to cultural humility to ask: What is it inheriting from cultural competency? Not only in the sense of its practices, approaches, and frames—which is worth interrogating and considering too—but in the line of what has been, and continues to be, cultural competency's professional and institutional presence and course.

What is occurring to us is that perhaps this inheritance is also a haunting; that is to say that cultural competency is, and will, haunt cultural humility. That not only does cultural competency—its contours, function, horizon, and operation—cast a long shadow on the direction and form of cultural humility, but it actually haunts it, similar to how diversity is haunting equity and inclusion, which now seems to be haunting antiracism. A haunting that chases to control, entangles to close in (and close off), not allowing it to be in and of itself.

Yet not all, or even parts of, hauntings create difficulty or restrict, as they can be unfixed and shifting; they can be generative and comforting, invigorating how we are moved, how we move, how we are moved through; what we carry forward with us, consciously and, often, not. (n. cline, personal communication, February 5, 2018).

Cultural Humility

Through this haunting, through the work done to illuminate cultural humility and its relevance to libraries, and in trying to pin down its elementary particles and definitions, we wonder. And as we wonder and wander through the possibilities this approach opens up, we have felt called to deeply engage with, deconstruct, and play with these ideas not only to better understand them, but also to consider what it might mean to put them into practice in our contexts and communities.

Our encounters with others do not occur in a vacuum, whether at the reference desk, in meetings, during conflict, or as we move through our everyday lives. Cultural humility recognizes and attends to this. And yet, we must trouble humility, though not necessarily its principles or core elements presented here by the editors, but rather its very location and connection to institutions—in this case, the library and the profession. This is to say: we refuse the very idea that a practice or approach like (cultural) humility could be or become institutionalized or standardized, that humility—a central and necessary quality and capacity for being in the world with others—could be marked by a bounded, normative professional definition and categories. Holding and playing with writers and thinkers in the field(s) of critical ethnic studies, this refusal is not simply a saying no (though it is that too). But something more: a beginning toward, a move away, which is a letting-go, a position of generativity where imaginaries open up.

It's encouraging that practicing cultural humility demands attention to uneven and unjust power relations and structures (Hurley, Kostelecky, and Townsend 2019), as the profession and institution have had (and continue to have) difficulty conceptualizing and interrogating matters of oppressive social/political/professional/institutional power, much less acting on these in concrete, material ways. Considering this reality—which is a nightmare for most—a necessary foregrounding and sustained articulation of specific structures or systems of social domination, and their particularities, is critical, as power dynamics are operating and circulating within and through larger and connected institutions, systems, and structures. Yet, these systems and structures of social domination also must be understood not just historically and contemporaneously, but also set in location, in space, and temporally. And for all of this to arrive—which is not an end—we must consider a (cultural) humility with more understanding of who, and where, we are and desire to be, so that we can be with and for each other, whether that is in the library, or at the reference desk, or on the corner.

Along with this movement, with this arrival—which means it is already here—we should consider the critique of the profession's reliance on cultural competence and interpersonal, psychological understandings and approaches as dominant liberal antiracist action—which evades structural and institutional analysis (Hudson 2017)—to check in on cultural humility, to see if it is in on that line, following that path, committed to a type of reform that only further deforms, to an inclusion that only is a further exclusion, which might actually be a conclusion. We hope not. And it is too early to tell, though there is an absence in cultural humility, an unnaming, an unmarking that directs questions and possibilities—why does it not name or mark itself as a form of justice or resistance? Or as part of a critical praxis? What are the stakes in not naming these commitments, in not positioning cultural humility as a practice of (and toward) justice?

This absence is not to suggest a deficit, but rather an opening toward possibilities. Holding those questions in tension with the critique above, we see and feel—really hear—cultural humility in a connected register to what Shawn(ta) Smith-Cruz (2018a, 277) guides us to consider with their visions of Audre Lorde reference librarianship, where an attentive and deep "deconstruction of the imposed body and layers of societal implications" is needed to create an enfleshed practice (and relationship) that is along the course of justice. This practice and traveling construct and move us to what Smith-Cruz (2018b, 289) calls an "in-between space" during/at the reference encounter that forms the conditions for a series of three connected parts, "acknowledgement of differences, mutual stretching, and, then sharing our resources on our own terms" to be realized; and it is here in this space in between, where we share and meet and survive together, which in the Black feminist radical tradition is perhaps what we exactly need to be seeking. How might cultural humility vibrate and sing with and for this imagining justice practice?

In this register, and in harmony with and as just one example of many other ongoing and resonant efforts, DisCrit (disability critical race theory) Resistance resonates with humility and attends to lines of race and disability, while not collapsing other specific, intersecting social locations, and their interactions with white supremacy. In this particular theorization, and as a form of resistance to damaging and inhumane teaching and learning spaces, humility is anchored in and a precondition for the type of transformative resistance that is demanded from the educator. Further, for DisCrit Resistance—for which an ongoing commitment, energy, and knowing are required—humility is positioned as both relational and learning and toward a remaking of formal spaces of education (Annamma and Morrison 2018). Humility here marks a relation, a struggle, a solidarity, which is a possibility for what could be otherwise.

And so: What is happening, and what can be done? What if we can project a different horizon? A beyond and outside the horizon that these projects are anticipating?

Theory of Change

We call in for a different vocabulary, for a different but connected understanding and framing of cultural humility. One that does not obscure, does not disguise what it is that it actually is. In that, cultural humility is not just an approach or a practice—or perhaps a new/old way of sociality—to improve a service or exchange, but what it is is also a theory of change. Such a phrase (theory of change) might open up lines to consider the outline of the project, its course and movements as it tries to realize its own purpose, while it informs the understanding of what the issue is and what is at stake.

This phrase *theory of change* represents a small shift, yet an important one for, and to, us, as we think and feel our way through critical frameworks, radical thought, and poetic theories. We follow Eve Tuck and K. Wayne Yang's understanding of theory of change to mean a "belief or perspective about how a situation can be adjusted, corrected or improved" (2013a, 13), and/or, said a bit differently, "assumptions about how social change happens, is prompted, or is influenced" (2013b, 125). Directly, it is an idea of how change might happen.

And here, in the profession, when it comes to how racial change is realized, these are (some of the) dominant "diversity" theories of change: American Library Association Spectrum Scholars; Association of College and Research Libraries (ACRL) Diversity Alliance; Association of Research Libraries Kaleidoscope Program; ALA/ARL's "Cultural Proficiencies for Racial Equity Framework"; and ACRL's "Diversity Standards on Cultural Competency for Academic Libraries." With, and through, these theories of change is how the profession believes it will arrive at institutionalized (racial) transformation. These ideas, which are also actions, of change unmake space, forming containment and bounded normative, legible, orderly, and linear meanings of progress and evolvement, while foreclosing imaginaries and movement of actual radical change and futures, at the same time reproducing technologies (scarcity, individuation, assimilation, competition, meritocracy, respectability, accumulation) of the state.

To be sure, the above institutionalized/professional organizational theories of change, in many cases, not only shift the material conditions of the people involved but also constitute kinship and offer relief, and by and large are considered successful within their own limits. But even outside—that can be inside—the overarching framework in LIS that is responsible for racial transformation while responding to a dominant, defined problem is equity, diversity, and inclusion (EDI) (though, recently, antiracism, justice, and accessibility have been grafted on).

This EDI framework is positioned as the central way we think about, perceive, then act on racialized matters and realities in LIS as a whole. In this centrality and recognition, EDI as a theory of change is committed to improving (gradually) the structure that is already in place, not radically challenging the very core logics, terms, and conditions offered and set by the structure itself. Given its engagement and entanglement with the structure (that it is designed to improve), this framework can actually further exclude, subjugate, and oppress. This is considered progress, sometimes dangerously offered as (structural) transformation, even though, from our understanding, that is not the aim or goal, not what the framework is set out to do—fundamentally transform LIS. And what if we finally—with finality—acknowledge and admit that about this theory of change? That not only can it not work to transform LIS, but also that LIS cannot be transformed . . . what then?

What Must Be Done

So perhaps these theories of change don't actually change anything at all. Or maybe theories of change are actually not change. Perhaps we expect too much (and misrecognize) change (and ideas) from the theories of change that have been handed down to us.

But what might all this mean for cultural humility? How might cultural humility move—or not move—to disrupt, resist, unsettle what these progressive, dominant theories of change project? Is it im/possible to refuse EDI framing and logics all together and live outside (and against, pulling in opposing directions of) the normative social imaginaries of liberal reformist, multicultural ideas of change? Can cultural humility circulate in, around, through these theories of change while also cutting underneath and, perhaps, antagonizing them?

For us, humility is an attribute, a practice, and a necessarily embodied way of thinking of subjectivity and relationality that positions the self in relation to an other (or others) in particular ways and in a particular place and time. As individuals, it describes a capacity to see, and be seen, outside our own perspectives and attachments to ourselves as individual, atomized, and stable entities, as well as gesturing toward a willingness to do so, a grounded (the word *humility* itself flowing from the Latin *humilitas*, meaning, among other derivations, "grounded" or "from the earth"; from "humus" or "earth" [Harper, n.d.]) willingness to share in a necessarily ongoing, dynamic, and collective process of living in, understanding, (un)knowing, and making a world together (being together, in other words, in other worlds).

Given this, cultural humility holds (or can hold) necessary space for, and closely approaches, questions of knowing what one can and cannot, must not know—which itself is a way of knowing—from the other. To orient through humility in this way destabilizes and refuses the logic and desire of coloniality's authority—its demand and right to know. This orientation, which is a disorientation for some, is antagonistic to the core mission, conceptual pillars, and purpose of the profession and (some) libraries that are rooted in accumulation, access, and universality.

If we are to take seriously the responsibilities to honor unknowing and the incommensurability of experience, acknowledging our entanglements and collectivities, and centering otherness that humility—and thus cultural humility as an (dis)orientation (as praxis)—commits us to, we can begin to see how we are called toward a new and different horizon. If cultural humility is a theory of change that truly allows, facilitates, supports, enacts change, if it is a form or part of a larger project of and toward justice, then what it asks of us—and perhaps of justice itself—what it opens up, what must be done is beyond (isn't even in the same world as) the EDI paradigm and cannot be contained by/within librarianship as a field (and our work within it).

And yet, there are implications for our field (the ground upon which we move, resist, and hope) and our work. What would it mean to position humility (cultural and otherwise) at the center or as a fundamental principle of what we do and how we create and sustain relationships in our professional (as well as personal) lives? What other capacities and values might we need to cultivate in order to create change, and move toward justice, in our work? To be humble in our relationships to and interactions with others (human and otherwise) might require curiosity, care, and compassion as well.

Humility is an orientation and a practice; it is a capacity that we cultivate (and that must be aligned and working with other values as well); but it might also be more than that (might want to be more than that). It not only may be something we do ourselves, whether for or toward others; it also may be something we do with others, and perhaps necessarily so. In this way, we must do more than simply stepping back from ourselves and our assumptions in an interaction (of any kind, but certainly in our service work), more than recognizing our differences (what parts of ourselves we bring, as well as those brought by others), and more than being aware of the structural forces and factors that suffuse and structure these encounters.

Which is to say we must do, but there is more to be done. This more than is here and around, a more than that is still, dynamic, and kinetic. It moves us, and we move with it. This more than of something new to be born. This is a practice and project of imagination, a process of collectivity, a reaching within and toward.

Outro: The Dialectics of Humility

In what has become study—as in thinking, building, and being together—can you hear the discord that's in the break? Or the visceral and cerebral feeling in motion that is a rhythm in ceremony? All in this—but not only for this—occasion to consider cultural humility, what its insides are and its commitments; what is happening and occurring with and to it.

In stepping to the side, in remembering, maybe we're wrong (let us be wrong), maybe we disagree, maybe you disagree. Maybe we don't know; maybe we'll learn from one another anyhow. But through these hopeful, joyful failures, disagreements, questions, and uncertainties, we know that learning and knowing (as well as not knowing)—which is to say, humility—are still happening.

Through the writing of this, we have explored, learned, and tried to articulate the contours of (a) humility that contains within it the possibility of being with, for, and toward others of all kinds, of (a) humility that cannot be contained by professional boundaries, political borders, and structuring binaries. In this place, in our fumbling toward humility as a theory of change, as a practice, as a dream of justice, we have come to see that it is about relationality, community, and world-making; it is about the relations we have, the communities and collectivities in which are enmeshed (and of which we are), and the worlds we are trying to make and sustain at the same time, and often together. It is a movement (on the ground and in our dreaming) toward; a way of moving with and for.

And this same time is not even necessarily on time or a shared time, even if we are in this (world) together, as we can support and build without a single, universal, shared vision of humility, with different dreams and goals of justice that are not chasing after, about, or seeking to replace or reform EDI and/or antiracism. Such a humility—one that is alive in the spaces with(in) people and nonpeople that we care about and love—could never be in service to an institution or profession, even as we consider whether we are asking too much of our institutions, too much of humility. We suppose it might even be an impossible ask of humility, to ask it to make something be over, to create change, to push and hold us forward. And yet we're not afraid or unwilling to. We are here, with humility, before the possibilities.

Summary

- Cultural humility is haunted by its lineage with cultural competency, and this offers room for constructive, loving critique, reflection, and expansion. Understanding these linkages helps us not only see what it is and is capable of, but also provides a foundation for imagining beyond how cultural humility is presently known to us (toward what it can be with and for us).
- Cultural humility recognizes the complexities and possibilities of our relationships with others, gesturing toward different, deeper ways of being with one another, while also attending to the uneven and unjust systems and structures that shape our interactions within institutions.
- Humility, as an attribute and practice, is a way of thinking of subjectivity and relationality that positions the self within a constellation of connections, as always already oriented toward and entangled with others of all kinds, and thus responsible and responsive to them. Humility is something we are (and do) with others.
- While there are implications for our field and our work, if cultural humility is a theory of change that truly facilitates and enacts change, then it cannot be contained within librarianship; that is, it gestures beyond our work as library and information workers. In this envisioning, it is a form or part of a larger project of and toward justice.

Questions for Reflection and Discussion

1. What would it mean to position humility (cultural and otherwise) at the center or as a fundamental principle of what we do and how we create and sustain relationships in our professional (as well as personal) lives?

____

____

____

2. What other capacities and values might we need to cultivate in order to create change, and move toward justice, in our work?

____

____

____

3. What is cultural humility dreaming of?

____

____

____

Resources

Harney, Stefano, Fred Moten, Sandra Ruiz, and Hypatia Vourloumis. 2021. "Resonances: A Conversation on Formless Formation." *E-flux* 121 (October). https://www.e-flux.com/journal/121/423318/resonances-a-conversation-on-formless-formation/.

Metres, P. 2021. "Poetry as Untelling: A Conversation with M. NourbeSe Philip." *World Literature Today*, June. https://www.worldliteraturetoday.org/blog/interviews/poetry-untelling-conversation-m-nourbese-philip-philip-metres.

Spotify playlist

We lovingly hope readers engage the texts we have gathered in the reference list, particularly the ones that move in resonances and attunements. And we especially want to hold up the words and ideas of Shawn(ta) Smith-Cruz.

REFERENCES

Annamma, Subini, and Deb Morrison. 2018. "DisCrit Classroom Ecology: Using Praxis to Dismantle Dysfunctional Education Ecologies." *Teaching and Teacher Education* 73 (July 2018):70–80. https://doi.org/10.1016/j.tate.2018.03.008.

Ferreira da Silva, D. 2018. "Hacking the Subject: Black Feminism and Refusal beyond the Limits of Critique." *PhiloSOPHIA* 8, no. 1: 19–41. https://doi.org/10.1353/phi.2018.0001.

Harney, S., and F. Moten. 2013. *The Undercommons: Fugitive Planning & Black Study*. Minor Compositions. https://www.minorcompositions.info/wp-content/uploads/2013/04/undercommons-web.pdf.

Harper, D. n.d. "Humility (n.)." Online Etymology Dictionary. Retrieved August 17, 2022. https://www.etymonline.com/word/humility.

Hudson, D. J. 2017. "On 'Diversity' as Anti-racism in Library and Information Studies: A Critique." *Journal of Critical Library and Information Studies* 1, no. 1: 1–26. https://doi.org/10.24242/jclis.v1i1.6.

Hurley, D. A., S. R. Kostelecky, and L. Townsend. 2019. "Cultural Humility in Libraries." *Reference Services Review* 47, no. 4: 544–55. https://doi.org/10.1108/RSR-06-2019-0042.

Kostelecky, S. R., L. Townsend, and D. A. Hurley. 2023. "Introduction." In *Hopeful Visions, Practical Actions: Cultural Humility in Library Work*, edited by S. R. Kostelecky, L. Townsend, and D. A. Hurley. Chicago: ALA Editions.

Macharia, K. 2015. "Love." *Critical Ethnic Studies* 1, no. 1: 68–75. https://doi.org/10.5749/jcritethnstud.1.1.0068.

Reeves, R. 2021. "Minor Characters, Major Silences, or Against the Compulsion to Talk." *Black Scholar* 51, no. 1: 43–50. https://doi.org/10.1080/00064246.2020.1855092.

Smith, D. 2020. "Iterable Ciphers for Insurrection." *Communications in Information Literacy* 14, no. 1: 27–45. https://doi.org/10.15760/comminfolit.2020.14.1.3.

Smith-Cruz, S. 2018a. "A Blueprint on Self-Exploration to Justice: Introduction to 'Referencing Audre Lorde' & 'Lesbian Librarianship for All.'" In *Reference Librarianship and Justice*, edited by K. Adler, I. Beilin, and E. Tewell, 279–92. Sacramento: Library Juice Press.

———. 2018b. Referencing Audre Lorde. In K. Adler, I. Beilin, and E. Tewell, eds. *Reference Librarianship and Justice*, 277–78. Sacramento: Library Juice Press.

Tuck, E., and K. W. Yang. 2013a. "Introduction to Youth Resistance Research and Theories of Change." In *Youth Resistance Research and Theories of Change*, edited by E. Tuck and K. W. Yang, 13–36. New York: Routledge.

———. 2013b. "Thinking with Youth about Theories of Change." In *Youth Resistance Research and Theories of Change*, edited by E. Tuck and K. W. Yang, 125–38. New York: Routledge.

———. 2018. "Introduction: Born under the Rising Sign of Social Justice." In *Toward What Justice? Describing Diverse Dreams of Justice in Education*, edited by E. Tuck and K. W. Yang, 1–18. New York: Routledge.

13

Cultural Humility

A Journey to Radical Self-Love

NAGHEM SWADE AND DANIYOM "DANI" BEKELE

Humility does not happen by being submissive, shutting up and obeying, but it is about knowing how to listen, learn, respect, and above all help whenever possible.

—Unknown

Acknowledgments

As non-Native folks, the authors (we) of this chapter acknowledge, with respect, that the land on which we stand, live, and learn, is the traditional territory of the Ute, Cheyenne, and Arapaho peoples, as well as the forty-eight contemporary tribal nations that are historically tied to the lands that make up the state of Colorado. We honor elders' past, present, and future and those who have stewarded this land throughout generations. We recognize that government, academic, and cultural institutions, our nation, were founded on and continue to enact exclusions and erasures of Indigenous peoples. May this acknowledgment demonstrate a commitment to dismantling ongoing legacies of settler colonialism, oppression, and inequities, and to recognizing the hundreds of Indigenous nations who continue to resist, live, create, and uphold sacred relations across their lands. We intentionally honor and celebrate the Indigenous communities in Denver and express our gratitude for their ongoing contributions.

In addition to acknowledging the ongoing legacies of settler colonialism, the authors of this chapter are unapologetically calling out the racial and social injustices facing BIPOC communities in the US. We stand in solidarity with our Indigenous, Black, Latinx, and Asian American brothers and sisters. We stand with all marginalized communities. We understand that acknowledging our current reality is the first step to address and repair the harm that has occurred and continues today. Racial equity is not political but an issue of human rights.

Introduction

In the summer of 2019, the learning team at the Denver Public Library (DPL) asked the Cultural Inclusivity Services Department (formerly known as Services to Immigrants and Refugees) to create a training on cultural humility. The goal was for the cultural humility training to replace an existing training that focused on cultural competency. This simple task sparked a domino effect that forced active, uncomfortable, and honest conversations between everyone involved. Over the course of two years, the Cultural Inclusivity Services team members created a mandatory, self-paced e-learning that introduced the framework of cultural humility. This training was designed to assess individual and collective values, examine how unspoken power and privilege impacted daily relationships, and called for system-wide accountability. In addition to the e-learning, staff members were also encouraged to engage with one another to further unpack and understand cultural humility by attending facilitated quarterly workshops. The training design team quickly realized that before an authentic training could be created, the members had to go through an intense self-reflection process that required acknowledging harm and creating space for healing.

Although the discovery of cultural humility was a work-related accident, this framework quickly became a way of life—that aha moment where all the painful trials and experiences finally made sense. The ultimate goal of cultural humility is to build authentic and long-lasting relationships with oneself and others, which requires investing time, energy, and love into that person. This chapter is a self-reflection into our journey of radical self-love; for, to truly love someone, you must be brave and vulnerable in understanding your own journey through life. The next couple of pages contain snapshots into the lives of the two authors of this chapter, who are members of the Cultural Inclusivity Services (CI) team at DPL. We are not making general claims but sharing our personal stories in hopes of showing how we utilize cultural humility to highlight how individual, societal, and professional culture manifest in our everyday lives and interactions. We hope that lessons can be learned from our mistakes and experiences.

Moving from Self-Competency to Self-Humility

A person can, unintentionally, be the biggest perpetrator of toxic narratives that affect everyone around them. The first tool of cultural humility is committing to critical self-reflection and understanding that the work is never-ending; this is a lifelong journey. It is crucial to understand that everyone has a unique perspective shaped by personal culture in order to begin the self-reflection journey. When the CI team started researching cultural humility, we began by sharing our own stories with one another. Stories about our childhoods, stories about school, stories about growing up as Black people in America or growing up as Brown immigrants in the US, and stories about all the microaggressions we experienced at work. Throughout our storytelling, a common thread appeared. All of us were shaped by our personal experiences. Home, school, friends, the neighborhood that we lived in—all these spaces and the people who occupied them took part in shaping who we would become.

Our storytelling also shed light on how our personal culture was partially responsible for the stories we tell about other people. Those stories that were etched into the strands of our childhood would unconsciously flare up in our everyday interactions with others. Team members of the training agreed that to begin the healing process and move to an authentic relationship-building, or rebuilding, a deep dive into one's personal culture was needed to identify toxic narratives. Why do we act the way we do? Why are we comfortable with one group of people over another group? What unconscious stories were we telling ourselves and others, and how are those stories manifested in our actions? Once those narratives are identified, conscious and constant unlearning and relearning can be established.

Dani

When I moved to the US at age sixteen, I assumed that it would be the end of all my worries. I had finally made it back home to the land of the free. Even though I was born in New York and gained US citizenship by birth, my parents did not have the legal documents to raise me here. My memories of growing up in Addis Ababa, Ethiopia, bring me so much joy. The people, the music, the culture, the food, the history, and the love are all part of me and will always play a role in how I define myself. Even with all the great things about life in Addis Ababa, I also remember the unpredictable violence. The abrupt chaos would cause deep anxiety in me and leave me wondering if I would make it back home. The last abrupt chaos that took place in April 2001 saw the death of forty-one university students who were peacefully protesting at Addis Ababa University. This incident prompted my parents to come face to face with the reality that Addis Ababa might not be the ideal place for me to live.

After moving back to the US, life was not as I expected it to be. Unfortunately, all my hopes and dreams of finally living safely and independently did not last long. After I began attending high school, my failure to create meaningful friendships and the absence of my family left the door wide open for me to associate with individuals prone to drugs and violence. Before I knew it, I was back to witnessing violence and tension beyond my comprehension. Before I even had the chance to understand this new place that I was in, I was already in trouble with my school and law enforcement. The kids who I thought were my friends were participating in activities that ultimately brought harm to me.

Looking back at this period, the clash of my Ethiopian and American culture, mixed with the need to fit in with others, created a reality I did not know how to handle. In this state of limbo, my education suffered the most. The relationships I had with others ceased to exist. When I sought guidance, my teachers and counselors were quick to remind me that I was foolish to ignore my education, unlike other East African kids who were well known for achieving excellent grades. During this time, my Ethiopian family members were also eager to remind me that my absence from our local church and my parents' absence brought disarray into my life.

As I attempted to figure out and correct the issues I faced while I was still in high school, I discovered libraries. When I learned that public libraries were free and could provide me with access to computers in a sheltered environment, I decided to spend much of my time at the local library. During weekends, I would spend my entire day at my library and leave with a few books to read at home. All of a sudden, I realized that I had time to complete my schoolwork. I began considering what colleges to apply for, and most important, ceased spending time with the kids who were always causing issues.

These days, when I look back at my high school days in the US, I am reminded of other teens like me who come from all over the world, trying to find themselves. Trying to fit it. Trying to make friends. Trying not to get bullied. Trying not to get overwhelmed by everything around them. Working in a public library, I see myself in some of the children and teens. I am always reminded of the library staff who welcomed me, helped me buy snacks on the days I spent my entire day at the library, checked in on me, asked me about my schoolwork, and, above all, did not make me feel like a nuisance. This experience has shaped my current work and approach in libraries. It has also failed me at times simply because I assumed that every child I encountered needed my help, my guidance, and my saviorism. As I consider the successful interactions and the not-so-successful ones, I hope there will be moments where my experience will connect with readers who have had the same intent at heart but might have failed at execution. And that's okay.

Naghem

Born in Basra, Iraq, I came to the US when I was seven. My parents were, are, very traditional and raised me to value religion, culture, and tradition above all else. That was hard to do when I was one of the few Muslim girls at school. Kids and teachers alike mocked my hijab and my overall personality. In order to survive, I learned what was expected of me and I did it. It almost felt like I was two different people wearing different masks that reflected the space I was in. At home, I was نغم, and in public, I was Naghem. At home, I was expected to help my parents with everything and to do so without complaint. Interpreting during doctor appointments, translating paperwork, grocery shopping for a family of eight, upholding the family name, and dealing with all school-related activities for myself and my five siblings. One day, I got so tired of having to do everything that I complained to my father. "It's your responsibility," he told me, and I believed him. I never complained again. My mother would always remind me to dress modestly and never raise my voice. I became a living, breathing manifestation of all her rules. I became her "perfect" daughter. Since I was the oldest child, I enforced the rules with my siblings, which caused a lot of tension, misunderstanding, and resentment between us. Whenever we would argue, I would always ask them why they couldn't be good kids and just listen to what our parents were saying.

School was more or less the same thing, with me doing what was expected of me. My parents had raised me to love and respect my teachers and treat them as if they were my second parents. Some of my teachers didn't like me because I wore a hijab. One teacher actively encouraged and joined in when other students bullied me. I tried so hard to get all my teachers to like me. When they told me I was too loud, I grew quiet. When a teacher made fun of my lunch, I threw it away and went hungry for the rest of the day. I molded myself into the shape my teachers wanted me to be. My friends would always ask me why I didn't talk back to my teachers whenever they said or did something I didn't like. "I'm not a bad person—I can't be like you and talk back" was my response.

Each mask that I wore had a different set of rules and expectations for me to follow. I've always described myself as a hybrid of two worlds, forced to live on the edges but not really belonging to one space or another. I mastered this shifting of masks so easily that I didn't notice how lost I had become. I was acting and behaving within the boundaries and restrictions of a box that was constructed without my input, and I was expecting others around me to follow the rules that I was following. If someone followed the rules, they were "good," and if they didn't follow the rules, they were "bad." I lost out on creating some potentially amazing relationships with others because of this "good vs. bad" mentality. That mentality stayed with me until adulthood. It wasn't until I consciously unshackled myself from those childhood narratives that I was able to begin healing and repairing my relationship with others and, more important, with myself.

Everyone is a product of their environment. In addition to family and friends, school and the media play an essential role in shaping our perception of culture and expectations. As this perception grows, personal culture begins to play an increased role in how a person treats others. When those interactions turn negative, it is essential to know why. Self-reflection should not be a singular event but rather a continuous process with intentional pauses that challenge a person to offer grace to themselves and others. This creates space for honest reflection, no matter how painful and uncomfortable that might be.

The sad reality is that everyone living in the US has been intentionally or inadvertently exposed to toxic narratives that promote the alienation of others who are different. This constant exposure is everywhere: via family, friends, school, and media, and even at the grocery store. If left unchecked, these narratives carry the ability to cause an immense amount of harm to an individual and everyone they encounter, their community, and ultimately, society itself. We believe that self-reflection in the form of intentional pauses can aid in personal growth and accountability.

Questions for Reflection and Discussion

1. What do you think of when you hear the word *culture*?

   ____

   ____

   ____

2. What other cultural groups/identities and practices did you encounter when you were younger: ethnic, race, class, sexual orientation, religion, and so on?

   ____

   ____

   ____

3. What messages were you given about people who were different from you: messages from family, from peers, from the media, and from others? What did you do to promote and perpetuate these messages?

   ____

   ____

   ____

4. How have your background experiences influenced your perceptions of other "cultures" that you encounter in your life?

   ____

   ____

   ____

I Get to Say Who I Am

An individual's personal culture is heavily influenced by everything around them, and they contribute to the overall societal culture by helping set demands and expectations. Societal norms are created, dominated, and maintained in the image of those with power and privilege. Anyone outside these "norms" will often find it hard to exist in contrast to the status quo. It might be hard to identify with others who do not share our cultural norms, or we might feel that our cultural norms are in a fabricated competition with someone else's cultural values. It's not a matter of whose culture is better or who is right or wrong, but rather letting others show up as their authentic selves without putting our expectations and biases on them.

There are a lot of unspoken cultural norms in the US. For the most part, these cultural norms reflect the standards and expectations of the ruling class. Traits like being white, practicing Christianity, earning a college degree, being cisgendered, being middle class, and speaking perfect English are some examples. While these norms may be someone's personal identity, they should not have a universal expectation behind them. Once we place expectations behind societal traits, they can be harmful, especially to marginalized groups and newcomers in the US. Often, immigrants and refugees are expected to assimilate into mainstream society. This assimilation process can force people to take on identities that are unauthentic to themselves. The message behind the assimilation expectation is that you are not welcome here unless you think, act, eat, and do as mainstream society expects you to. From the authors' personal experiences, if marginalized individuals, immigrants, and refugees do not assimilate into mainstream culture, they are deemed untrustworthy, unreliable, unintelligent, dangerous, and not "American."

Dani

Even though I was raised on a different continent, I have always identified as an American. Before returning to the US, my friends and family in Ethiopia always called me Ferenje ("foreigner" in Amharic). Even though I spoke Amharic fluently, proudly celebrated all the national holidays, and practiced the dominant Greek Orthodox religion, I always had a shadow that identified me as someone different from everyone else.

Moving to the US did not help solidify my identity either. Even if my racial profile symbolized that I was an African American, neither my accent, attire, mannerisms, or culture fit well within the African American racial construct. Although I recognized myself as an American, I was immediately identified as an African. The typical *Coming to America* references, the "do you need to go hunting for dinner tonight" comments, or the "aren't you too overweight to be from Africa" remarks were an everyday reminder telling me that I was a foreigner. When I sought comfort with the African/Ethiopian community in the US, I felt distant and disconnected from a community with tumultuous relationships and history in the US.

It was only after my foray into trying to fit in with the different cultures and communities and failing miserably that I realized the need to respect myself and understand my need to fit in with others that brought relief. I had assumed I could finally get accepted by others by fixing what others made fun of about me. From my accent to my attire, from the media I consumed to the social norms I embraced, I assumed I would be accepted by others by erasing the bits and pieces that made me different from others. I relegated my culture, my history, my true identity in the hopes of assimilation and being accepted. What's worse is that I took it upon myself to hold others who were, for the most part, newcomers to the US to the same exact standards I was held to, helping perpetuate the culture of alienating newcomers.

Retroactively understanding the evolution of my personal culture within the context of my identity helps illuminate the societal influences I experienced. Fully embracing this journey and understanding how my personal culture shifted based on the societal interactions I experienced show how I inadvertently continued to preserve and promote societal standards on others. In the same way I was chastised for not prioritizing my education, I disparaged teens that did not do well at school. The same way I was told to be a strong Black man, I made fun of Black men who showed any emotional weakness. In the same way my Ethiopian family decried vocational skills, I devalued individuals with trade skills. It was only after years of being part of this toxic interaction with the constant battle of attempting to assert my own identity that I realized how I was perpetuating the toxic narrative. The same way I yearned for others to understand who I was, I refused to accept others for who they were. Ultimately, coming face to face with the power I gave myself to define who I was, was the same power I had to pass to others to determine who they were. I got to say who I was. Now, they get to say who they are.

Naghem

The first day that I was called a terrorist was on 9/11/2001. I was twelve. For the longest time, I've always believed that to the American public I was one of two things—a terrorist or a smart, obedient, respectful immigrant; but never truly an American. That belief has had detrimental effects on me even to this day. Whenever I speak up at work, an internal voice is always causing doubt within: "Who are you to speak up?" Or the ever-present "Don't speak up or cause a scene—you will get fired." I'm always trying to prove to the world, and to myself, that I do belong and that what I have to say matters. Sometimes I am met with resistance, or even shock, if I behave in a way that contradicts a person's expectations of who they presume me to be. For example, when I first started working at DPL, a colleague of mine mentioned that they were surprised that I was so outspoken. When I questioned why, they told me that they have always believed Muslim women to be quiet and demure. I was the only Muslim woman they knew. If I speak up or critique something about Western society, people get defensive. Hearing comments like "If you don't like it here so much, why don't you go back to your country" or "We don't even want you here" are common. Still, I find myself trying to show the world that I am a "good" Muslim, that my humanity is valid. Living in a society that has demonized and alienated my very existence has empowered me to be an active catalyst for change. By identifying and working toward creating a society where all truly belong, I am able to write myself into society. Cultural humility has affirmed my experiences. I get to say who I am, and who I am matters and is good enough. Even though I say this and am actively unlearning, I still find myself unconsciously playing to the expectations of mainstream society and expecting others to behave within the parameters of those false narratives. It's a lifelong journey of intentional unlearning.

Shedding the Status Quo

The workplace is one stage where personal culture, societal culture, and professional culture interact and engage. Unfortunately for staff from different cultural and societal backgrounds, it should not be surprising that the qualities and traits deemed of high value in the workplace align with those in power. A few examples of these qualities include the attire worn at work, communicating with perfect English, having reliable transportation, always being on time, and vocally expressing your opinion without fear. Unfortunately, the standards by which we value these traits rely on subjective qualities that often depend on messaging we have received about others. Rectifying these subjective trait standards in the workplace requires accountability, especially for those holding leadership positions.

Dani

When my career in libraries began, I was enamored with the resources and access the library provided to immigrant and refugee populations. Since my primary role was to work with this specific demographic, I was happy to provide resources to community members who had life experiences similar to mine. Helping with job searches, practicing interview questions, studying for the US citizenship exam, practicing conversational English, learning how to use a computer, training how to create and manage a website—my work was always exciting, unpredictable, and very practical to the community that came to the library.

However, the services I helped provide always had a distinct and specific theme: the library was the place that had the answers, and it had the resources that every immigrant and refugee needed. Unfortunately, the library had assumed that every immigrant and refugee who came to the library needed to practice English, or needed to study and pass the US citizenship exam, or needed to learn how to use a computer. Although this need was there for some, it did not resonate with every immigrant and refugee.

When I look back at my past, the library was a place that gave me shelter. Library staff helped make me feel welcome, and, in some cases, staff members who had experienced the same tribulation as I had understood how I wanted to utilize the library. Had these staff members simply assumed I needed to practice English or study for the US citizenship exam, or had no idea how to use a computer, I'm not sure I would have had a positive relationship with libraries. Yet while working with immigrant and refugee populations that came to the library, my approach was the opposite of my experience.

As I began expanding my role in libraries, my overarching vision was still pigeonholed, and I still assumed that libraries' primary role was to aid immigrants and refugees in the assimilation process. My reference recommendations for immigrants and refugees centered on providing English reading resources for beginners. My children and teen programming ideas concentrated on simply helping immigrant and refugee children improve their reading skills. Every chance I got to provide resources to our community, I approached it with the mentality that the library was there to make things better because we knew better.

When I began conversing with community members who asked me where the books, movies, and programs in languages other than English were, I had no answers. I was unprepared to receive the reality that immigrants and refugees still cherished their language, culture, and traditions. Understanding that libraries can help celebrate the different cultures of their community through programs, collections, staffing, and displays was the epiphany I needed to reinvigorate my library journey. I no longer relied on predetermined expectations for my community, and I began approaching every interaction with a fresh state of mind. Every individual is different and needs to be treated as such. It was a relief to shift my mentality from someone who knew what others wanted to someone who can let others convey what they want.

Naghem

As one of a handful of Muslim women working at the Denver Public Library, I have experienced my fair share of racism, Islamophobia, and microaggressions at work. Navigating all of that with a severe case of imposter syndrome has left me emotionally and physically drained. A colleague once justified their microaggressions by gaslighting me into believing that my writing was bad. Another colleague spent over thirty minutes trying to convince me that my marriage to my partner was an arranged marriage and not one of free will. I kept asking myself that if my colleagues treat their counterparts like this, how are they treating customers who look like me? In an effort to show all the unspoken biases people have and how they are affecting services, programs, customers, and the overall work culture, I became vocal and started calling people in. As the cultural inclusivity services coordinator, I am responsible for creating services and programs aimed at immigrant and refugee populations. At first, my programs catered to receiving white community members. Educational programs showcasing the immigrant and refugee experience were done with the intention of trying to find common ground, but even that felt foreign. I kept asking myself why. What need was I trying to serve, and who was I serving? Unpacking this through a cultural humility lens, I can see how my personal culture of trying to convince people that I am good and I belong here was reflected in these programs. I was unconsciously trying to appease mainstream society by creating and implementing programs that catered to white fragility. By taking many frequent intentional pauses, I have been reframing my approach. The library programs and staff workshops that I am responsible for no longer cater to the status quo; rather, my programming is now done with the intent of aiding immigrant and refugee peoples in claiming library space and resources where folks from all walks of life can celebrate their individual and collective identities.

Closing with Humility

Cultural humility is internal accountability and constant unlearning. Even after writing this chapter, we went through a self-reflection journey and learned so much more about ourselves. The cultural humility training at DPL has had overwhelmingly positive feedback. By showing humility, vulnerability, and bravery, the Cultural Inclusivity Services team has been able to offer space for dialogue where staff can share and explore personal, societal, and professional culture. The training isn't perfect, nor is it designed to be—and people appreciate that. Our advice to you, the reader, is this: don't be afraid, as this isn't about getting it right all the time. Be open minded and start by acknowledging that your personal cultural values are not the only values that matter. This is not a competition of whose values are right or wrong. This is us honoring the validity and humanity in one another. Accept the discomfort that comes with identifying these moments without resorting to defensiveness.

As we close out this chapter, keep in mind these main points and questions to aid you in your journey:

- What is your personal culture? Take intentional pauses and self-reflect. This will help you decipher the messages you received in your past regarding others in your community. Understanding the source of these messages will help you understand the root of your perception of others, negative or positive.
- How are you perpetuating harmful narratives? Another benefit of self-reflection is that it supports individuals in understanding their true selves while challenging them to reframe harmful messages. Cultural humility asks that individuals define who they are and should also allow others to do the same.
- How are your personal culture and societal culture showing up in the workplace? Be honest with yourself and reflect on how you might have upheld harmful stereotypes and engaged in microaggressions.

Think of implicit bias as the stories you tell yourself about others. Microaggressions are the physical and verbal manifestations of those stories.

Resources

Robinson, D., C. Masters, and A. Ansari. 2021. "The 5 Rs of Cultural Humility: A Conceptual Model for Health Care Leaders." *American Journal of Medicine* 134, no. 2: 161–63. https://doi.org/10.1016/j.amjmed.2020.09.029.

Yeager, K. A., and S. Bauer-Wu. 2013. "Cultural Humility: Essential Foundation for Clinical Researchers." *Applied Nursing Research: ANR* 26, no. 4: 251–56. https://doi.org/10.1016/j.apnr.2013.06.008.

ABOUT THE EDITORS

SARAH R. KOSTELECKY (Zuni Pueblo) is the director of Digital Initiatives and Scholarly Communication (DISC) for the University of New Mexico (UNM) University Libraries. Her research focuses on outreach efforts to underrepresented communities, diversity in academic libraries and library collections, and Native American language resources. Previously at UNM, Sarah served as the Education Librarian and Access Services Librarian in the Indigenous Nations Library Program (INLP). She earned both her MA in information resources and library science and BA in sociology from the University of Arizona. Prior to working at UNM Libraries, Sarah was the library director at the Institute of American Indian Arts (IAIA) in Santa Fe, New Mexico, the premier educational institution for contemporary Native American arts and cultures. Along with David A. Hurley and Paulita Aguilar, she coedited "Sharing Knowledge and Smashing Stereotypes: Representing Native American, First Nation, and Indigenous Realities in Library Collections," a special double issue of the journal *Collection Management*. Sarah has enjoyed working in a variety of libraries, including university, public, tribal college, and museum.

LORI TOWNSEND (Shoshone-Paiute) is the learning services coordinator and a social sciences librarian for the University of New Mexico University Libraries. Her research interests include genre theory and information literacy, source evaluation, and cultural humility. Lori holds a BA in history from the University of New Mexico and an MLIS from San Jose State University. She is coauthor, along with Amy R. Hofer and Silvia Lin Hanick, of the book *Transforming Information Literacy Instruction: Threshold Concepts in Theory and Practice* (Libraries Unlimited, 2018); she and Silvia Lin Hanick are series editors for the just-launched Libraries Unlimited Series on Teaching Information Literacy Today.

DAVID A. HURLEY is the discovery and web librarian for the University of New Mexico University Libraries. He writes and presents on search, reference services, and information literacy in addition to cultural humility. He was previously the director of the Diné College Libraries on the Navajo Nation, chief of the Library Development Bureau at the New Mexico State Library, and branch and digital services manager for the public library of Albuquerque and Bernalillo County. David, Sarah, and Lori wrote *Cultural Humility*, an ALA Editions Special Report published in 2022.

ABOUT THE CONTRIBUTORS

DANIYOM "DANI" BEKELE is an Ethio-American senior librarian with seven years of experience working for the Denver Public Library (DPL). Dani was born in the US and raised in Addis Ababa, Ethiopia; his work and passion have always been advocating for increased immigrant and refugee services in libraries. Dani is also a part of a few committees that promote culturally inclusive programs within DPL, implement long-term library strategies with a DEI perspective, and address the disproportionate lack of access to library services for teens. Dani provides Amharic translational services for DPL, expanding access to one of Denver's largest immigrant and refugee demographics.

MELANIE BOPP is the head of Access Services at George Mason University, having moved recently from Northeastern University, where she worked as an access services librarian. In both positions, she has handled a variety of customer service and information provision challenges, working to create that link between user and information. Melanie received her MLIS from Louisiana State University in 2011. Her primary interests in fifteen years of access services have been on customer service and the student-worker experience.

AMANDA CLICK is the head of research and instruction at the US Naval Academy in Annapolis, Maryland. Previously, she was the business librarian at American University in Washington, DC, and the coordinator of instruction at the American University in Cairo. In 2016, she completed her PhD in the School of Information and Library Science at the University of North Carolina at Chapel Hill. She earned her MLIS at the University of North

Carolina at Greensboro. Her research interests include open access, information literacy, evidence-based practice, and cultural adaptation.

NICHOLAE CLINE and **JORGE R. LÓPEZ-MCKNIGHT** are loving collaborators in an ongoing series of projects, encounters, and imaginings toward dreaming up and exploring the possibilities of liberation within, and beyond, the present. nicholae (they/them) is a librarian for media studies, gender studies, and philosophy at Indiana University Bloomington, while Jorge (he/him) is a community college library worker in Austin, Texas.

KIMBERLEY A. EDWARDS is the head of database integrity and analysis at George Mason University Libraries. Prior to her current role, she worked in the circulation and technical services departments of several college and government libraries. She has presented on collection management and analysis tools and techniques at a range of national and international conferences. She received her MLIS from the University of Kentucky.

MARK EMMONS (MLS, EdD) is the associate dean and a professor in the College of University Libraries & Learning Sciences at the University of New Mexico. Dr. Emmons has over thirty years of professional experience as an academic librarian, spending the past ten years in administrative and leadership roles. He is an active member in the Association of College & Research Libraries.

XAN GOODMAN is an associate professor and health sciences librarian at the University of Nevada, Las Vegas, where she supports the School of Public Health, School of Dental Medicine, School of Nursing, and School of Integrated Health Sciences. Xan teaches workshops on cultural humility and is the author of a three-pillar model of cultural humility for libraries. Xan is also an ALA Spectrum Scholar.

TWANNA HODGE is pursuing her PhD in information studies at the University of Maryland, College Park. Her previous position was the diversity, equity, and inclusion librarian at the University of Florida. She graduated from the University of Washington with her MLIS in 2015. She wrote "Integrating Cultural Humility into Public Services Librarianship," published in *International Information & Library Review*. She is a 2013 ALA Spectrum Scholar, a 2018 ALA Emerging Leader, and a 2022 ALA Spectrum Doctoral Fellow.

MEGGAN HOULIHAN is the head of Student Success at Colorado State University and was previously the coordinator of Instruction and Outreach at New York University Abu Dhabi. Meggan has published and presented on international librarianship.

JARROD IRWIN is the behavioral and health sciences librarian at Eastern Michigan University (EMU), working as the liaison for EMU's psychology department and programs in the School of Health Promotion and Human Performance. He previously served as the consumer health coordinator for the National Network of Libraries of Medicine, Southeastern/Atlantic Region, at the University of Maryland, Baltimore. There, his instructional work focused on equipping library staff, medical professionals, and community organizations to partner with the people they serve in promoting health literacy and informed decision-making about health and wellness.

KELSEY KEYES (white) is an associate professor and librarian for instruction and research services at Boise State University. She holds an MLIS and an MA in literature from the University of Illinois at Urbana-Champaign. She served on Rise: A Feminist Book Project for Ages 0–18, including terms as cochair, from 2017 to 2020. Her research is focused on supporting parenting students at the academic library, and she is currently writing a book on this topic (expected publication 2023, with ACRL).

SILVIA LIN HANICK (she/her) is a Taiwanese American professor, chief librarian, and chairperson of the library department at LaGuardia Community College (CUNY). She holds an MLIS from the University of Illinois at Urbana-Champaign and an MA in literature from the University of New Mexico. She served on Rise: A Feminist Book Project for Ages 0–18, including terms as cochair, from 2019 to 2022.

TRICIA MACKENZIE is the head of Metadata Services at George Mason University Libraries. She received her MLS with a specialization in Digital Libraries from Indiana University and has an MA in history from Southern Illinois University Edwardsville. Prior to her current role, she was the metadata librarian at George Mason University Libraries. She has presented at regional, national, and international conferences on topics relating to cataloging and metadata creation and quality control, authority control, and data management.

DINA MEKY is the global campus outreach and online learning librarian at Northeastern University Library. Previously, she was the reference and instruction librarian at Berkeley College Libraries in New Jersey, and she has worked for Syracuse University Libraries and the American University in Cairo. She is a 2013–2014 ALA Spectrum Scholar. She earned her MLIS at Syracuse University and her MEd from Northeastern University in e-learning and instructional design. Dina's research interests include distance learning, diversity in librarianship, outreach and advocacy in information literacy, and digital pedagogy.

LILIANA MONTOYA, PhD, is currently finishing her master of information studies degree at the University of Ottawa. Her research interests include metadata creation and data management, as well as cultural inclusion in libraries, and information literacy.

LEISA MOORHOUSE is Ngāpuhi tribe, from Aotearoa/New Zealand. Until recently she taught in the Social Work Programme at the University of Waikato, Tauranga, where she extensively incorporated mātauranga Māori (traditional Māori knowledge and wisdom). Leisa manages a private practice in professional supervision and contract work, including the role of external moderator for some Te Wānanga o Aotearoa (Māori tertiary education provider) programs. She developed and sells a card-based resource set grounded in whakataukī (Māori proverbs) designed to assist people to utilize traditional Māori wisdom and values in life and work (see www.hepunarauemi.co.nz). It was through the sale of the whakataukī cards that Leisa met Dr. Loriene Roy, who invited her to co-contribute on their chapter.

MICHAEL MUNGIN, MLIS, is a research and instruction librarian serving the University of Washington Bothell and Cascadia College since 2017. His professional interests center on equity, inclusion, and representation in libraries and media. Outside of libraries, his passions are tennis and cinema, though he is still always looking for sneaky ways to incorporate them into his practice. He would like to thank his partner, Brian, for their support and patience while completing this chapter.

SARAH POLKINGHORNE, PhD, works as a librarian at the University of Alberta in Edmonton, Canada. She has taught in the library and information studies programs at the University of Alberta and the University of Ottawa. In her research, Sarah is interested in information practices and systems that have been overlooked or underexamined. She primarily works from an interpretivist perspective, using qualitative methods to analyze people's experiences and to illuminate their connections to larger social structures.

DR. LORIENE ROY is Anishinabe (Minnesota Chippewa Tribe). She taught public libraries, reference, and information literacy at the University of Texas (UT) at Austin and Indigenous librarianship at the University of Hawai'i at Mānoa. She serves on the Library of Congress Literacy Awards Advisory Board. She was president of the American Indian Library Association (AILA) and the American Library Association. She received numerous honors, including the AILA Distinguished Service Award; the UH–Mānoa Sarah Vann Award; and the Leadership Award from the Association of Tribal Archives, Libraries, and Museums, and is part of the UT–Austin Distinguished Service Academy. She has given more than seven hundred presentations and written more than two hundred publications.

RHIANNON SORRELL (Diné) is an assistant professor and the instruction and digital services librarian at Diné College in Tsaile, Arizona, on the Navajo Nation. Born to Kinłichíí'nii (Red House People) and Ta'neezahnii (Tangle People) Clans, Rhiannon has an interdisciplinary background in English and information literacy instruction, creative nonfiction, and special collections and archival services. She is a member of the 2018 cohort of ALA's Emerging Leaders and a member of Rare Books School's second cohort of the Andrew W. Mellon Fellowship for Diversity, Inclusion & Cultural Heritage. Rhiannon is a partner and Diné coordinator for the NEH-funded project "Tribesourcing Southwest Film: Digital Repatriation."

NAGHEM SWADE, born and raised in Basra, Iraq, is an eternal advocate for radical social change. She serves as the cultural inclusivity services coordinator for the Denver Public Library. Her responsibilities include creating and implementing diverse and culturally inclusive library programming to BIPOC communities as well as leading teams in creating and implementing staff workshops that address cultural competence, cultural humility, bias, microaggressions, power, privilege, and other key areas. Naghem sits on the Equity, Diversity and Inclusion Advisory Council, whose purpose is to advise the library on equity, diversity, and inclusion goals, strategies, plans, policies, and projects.

CARRIE VALDES has been the director of the Grand County Public Library in Moab, Utah, since 2007, and she has worked for that library for almost twenty-one years. She has an MLS from the University of North Texas and a bachelor's in human resources from Utah State University. She has lived in Utah all her life (except for a brief stint in Mexico) and is passionate about reducing institutional barriers to library access for all community members.

INDEX

D

E

F

H

M

P

R

Ingram Content Group UK Ltd.
Milton Keynes UK
UKHW021853090723
424785UK00009B/61